Debating
Psychic Experience

Debating
Psychic Experience

Human Potential or Human Illusion?

Stanley Krippner and Harris L. Friedman,
Editors

Foreword by Ruth Richards

 PRAEGER

AN IMPRINT OF ABC-CLIO, LLC
Santa Barbara, California • Denver, Colorado • Oxford, England

Copyright 2010 by Stanley Krippner and Harris L. Friedman

Library of Congress Cataloging-in-Publication Data

Debating psychic experience : human potential or human illusion? / Stanley Krippner and Harris L. Friedman, editors ; foreword by Ruth Richards.
     p. cm.
   Includes bibliographical references and index.
   ISBN 978–0–313–39261–0 (hard copy : alk. paper) — ISBN 978–0–313–39262–7 (ebook)
1. Parapsychology. I. Krippner, Stanley, 1932- II. Friedman, Harris L.
BF1031.D343   2010
130—dc22   2010020253

ISBN: 978–0–313–39261–0
EISBN: 978–0–313–39262–7

14 13 12 11 10   1 2 3 4 5

This book is also available on the World Wide Web as an eBook.
Visit www.abc-clio.com for details.

Praeger
An Imprint of ABC-CLIO, LLC

ABC-CLIO, LLC
130 Cremona Drive, P.O. Box 1911
Santa Barbara, California 93116-1911

This book is printed on acid-free paper (∞)

Manufactured in the United States of America

This book is dedicated to the memory of Robert L. Morris, Ph.D. (1942–2004), the first Koestler Professor of Parapsychology, University of Edinburgh, who served a term as president of the psychology section of the British Association for the Advancement of Science, and whose devotion to rigorous scholarship won him the admiration of both advocates and counteradvocates of the psi hypothesis.

Contents

Foreword: Pondering Exceptional Human Possibilities

Ruth Richards

> This is in the end the only kind of courage that is required of us: the courage to face the strangest, most unusual, most inexplicable experiences that can meet us. The fact that people have in this sense been cowardly has done infinite harm to life; the experiences that are called "apparitions," the whole so-called "spirit world," death, all these Things that are so closely related to us, have through our daily defensiveness been so entirely pushed out of life that the senses with which we might have been able to grasp them have atrophied. To say nothing of God. (Rilke, 1986, pp. 88–89)

It is an honor to write this Foreword, to commend those creative investigators and scholars who have been willing to look, to explore, and to take risks. These individuals have not believed blindly—in fact they have done anything but. What, after all, is the harm of looking scientifically at a compelling topic, say, at purported psi phenomena—or processes of energy or information transfer "currently unexplained in terms of known physical or biological mechanisms" (Bem & Honorton, 1994, p. 4)? Unobjectionable indeed is the way this book proceeds: with careful consideration of all sides of the question—and with adequate information so that we, in our own creative and open-minded wisdom, can judge for ourselves, and make up our own minds.

Is not this how science is supposed to work? Let's generate a hypothesis and test it rigorously. What's the problem with doing this? None, one might think.

What after all do we tell our graduate students? Or tell, for that matter, our young children? Find a question. Take a look. Science, after all, is supposed to do this. Make a prediction and see what happens. Good research can support, or reject a hypothesis, statistically speaking, and help us see if there is something there to pursue (or not). Yet this logical and sensible orientation we promote in Research Methods 101 does not tell the whole tale; it does not account for human bias, fear, and our all too human unconscious commitment to certain beliefs. This includes, I learned some years ago, the so-called "taboo topics" (Richards, 1994). Do not tamper with these. We scientists may approach them at our own risk.

I first read about taboo topics in a book edited by Norman Farberow (1963) with a foreword by Gordon Allport. Back in the 1960s, what were the topics we might customarily swerve away from? Death, the list went, along with sex, suicide, homosexuality, parapsychology, graphology, religion, hypnosis, and politics—the last involving international relations and, remarkably, questions of "peace." Fortunately, today, most of these areas have become much more open to inquiry.

But what about parapsychology? Is it still taboo? According to Farberow (1963), "taboo" has two meanings—"sacred" on the one hand, or alternatively "dangerous" or "forbidden." Of course, it may mean both at once. Yet taboos "all serve the same goal," he continued, "preservation of the status quo" (p. 2). Indeed they can be so powerful that they evoke major defensive counter-maneuvers. "People 'pass away'; they do not die. Extrasensory perception is just too far beyond credibility, so why bother investigating?" (Farberow, 1963, p. 6).

How surprised I was then, one February morning in Boston, in 1993, to read a major headline about parapsychology on the front page of the *Boston Globe* (Chandler, 1993). And furthermore, it was positive! Or at least, this front page feature was asking us to be very open-minded skeptics. The American Association for the Advancement of Science (AAAS) had been meeting in Boston, and one presentation, published later by Bem and Honorton (1994) in the prestigious *Psychological Bulletin*, had people buzzing. Their meta-analyses of two major ESP ganzfeld databases had supported anomalous information transfer in the highly controlled ganzfeld conditions even including electrical and acoustical isolation and computer generation of stimulus orders not known even to the investigator. That is, inexplicably, information had made it from one room to another, from a random computer generator, to an isolated individual acting as receiver, across multiple studies. And everywhere, it seemed, the methodological "i's" had been dotted and the "t's" crossed.

So compelling was this AAAS paper that Harvard University's Psychology Chair, Robert Rosenthal, was quoted in the *Boston Globe* as saying, "The statistical evidence [in the study] is quite clear ... that there is a phenomenon there that does require explaining" (as cited in Chandler, 1993, p. 8). The final published article was entitled, *Does Psi Exist?: Replicable Evidence for an Anomalous Process of Information Transfer* (Bem & Honorton, 1994).

The point is not to argue whether or not "psi exists." For the present discussion, it does not matter. It is, rather, about whether we have freedom of inquiry in our scientific endeavor. It is about whether there is fairness and objectivity in what researchers study—including what gets funded—and then in what becomes of the results. It is also about the difficulty, socially and scientifically speaking, of asking certain questions and then keeping that conversation visible. In the previous example, when a taboo finding finally did reach the light, quite publicly and unavoidably, it even became headline news.

Significantly, the ruckus faded in time. For example, a major book, *Varieties of Anomalous Experience: Examining the Scientific Evidence* (Cardeña, Lynn, & Krippner, 2000) (the title is taken from William James' groundbreaking book *Varieties of Religious Experience*), was published in 2000 by the American Psychological Association. One of its three editors includes Stanley Krippner, the co-editor of this volume. The book is a model of scientific presentation and critical thinking, published by one of the most respected mainstream presses in psychology. Surely, things were shifting somewhat. Yet we know from many sources how the selection and presentation of scientific knowledge is far from being an objective process in general, never mind in parapsychology (Myers, 1990; Richards, 2007). If one looks, for example, at the *Psychological Bulletin* (rather than a specialized journal in anomalous phenomena), how many articles on parapsychology will be found, compared to, say, reports on mainstream topics of perceptual or cognitive functioning? The area still seems relatively taboo.

Some may rightfully say there are special problems in these investigations. For instance, certain phenomena may strike irregularly, like a bolt of lightning. Take an alleged precognition, for instance; how can this event be called up at will (Combs, 2010)? And if it cannot be elicited in controlled experiments, then how, some say, can it be studied? Nonetheless, multiple replications can be cited for many anomalous phenomena (e.g., Radin, 1997). Combs (2010) has suggested that parapsychologists may be held to a vastly higher standard of evidence than are researchers in other areas.

Indeed, what if these researchers *are* playing by the rules? What if the findings *are* valid? The topics are of momentous importance, potentially enlarging on the laws of nature, potentially altering our worldview. Do we really want this to happen? How far could such resistance take us? How does an all-too-common investment in the status quo relate to the question of scientific freedom, for us, for the public, for researchers in all areas? And how can a citizen even begin to evaluate the evidence for any controversial topic if a doubting editor or other "gatekeeper" has already marginalized or eliminated it? We cannot judge a phenomenon when the data are invisible.

Would it be different, one might ask, would the unconscious resistance be less, if potential benefits to us and our daily lives were more evident? For instance, if there were clear benefits for our health or longevity? Consider, for instance, research supporting new and powerful ways of healing (Achterberg et al., 2005; Krippner & Achterberg, 2000), or work that suggests that death (another taboo topic) may in some ways be less fearsome than suspected (Greyson, 2000). Or consider that we have transpersonal ways of relating and knowing that could expand our human possibilities and life meaning. Indeed considerable work has been done on transpersonal psychological assessment (Friedman, MacDonald, & Kumar, 2004; MacDonald, LeClair, Holland, Alter, & Friedman, 1995), and this opens further doors to research. With a clear view of benefit to our lives, would there be less fear, more enthusiasm? First, one needs to know that some promise exists, what has already been researched, how good the evidence is and what it means for us, and then what else needs to be explored. That is the way of the researcher.

It is important, in this regard, that risk-taking and bravery are central to personal creativity (Richards, 2007), never mind creativity in conducting research. Each of us who takes a creative chance, whether as *initiator* or *appreciator* of innovative work, is taking a brave and powerful step. As creative initiators, we are true upstarts, presenting the world with something that could change it—and perhaps change us! Rollo May (1975), aware of these enormous challenges, even wrote a book called *The Courage to Create*.

What keeps us comfortably in line, and stills our protests? There can be both internal and external resistance to novelty, and this can even take on major proportions. Some of the present readers have, possibly, at one time or another, had a difficult boss, a teacher or, earlier in life, a harried parent who resisted some essentially brilliant idea, without even giving it a fair hearing. Things can get even scarier in the greater world when groups of people self-organize *unconsciously* to repel unpopular scientific (or political) views—perhaps for reasons having nothing to do with science, logic, or fact (see Richards, 2007). For example, a graduate student, whose research supported a once entertained but later marginalized theory of cellular membrane transmission, was told by his superior that, in spite of his findings, "membrane pump theories were correct and [other perspectives] had been disproved" (Bloom, 2000, p. 188). Thus, should the student throw out his doctoral findings? What happened to open-minded inquiry?

It can take creativity to respond to the new, as well as create it, along with openness and flexibility to change one's life or worldview accordingly. A large demographic labeled as *cultural creatives* (Ray & Anderson, 2000) is now showing unusual potential for certain types of personal and social change in Western culture.

It is worth noting some stellar persons from the past who kept open minds where parapsychology was concerned, alongside other celebrated names who dismissed the area outright. The physicist Hermann von Helmholtz, for example, was a sworn disbeliever no matter what happened, not unlike the dismissive research supervisor mentioned before. According to Allport (1963), Helmholtz insisted that "absolutely no evidence, not even his own experience, could convince him of telepathy, 'since it is manifestly impossible'" (p. viii). By contrast, physicist Wolfgang Pauli (1955) and Carl Gustav Jung (1955) together published companion treatises (Jung & Pauli, 1955), bringing together support for anomalous phenomena including alleged synchronicity.

Furthermore, Arthur Koestler (1972) in *The Roots of Coincidence*, noted that, despite the hostility of mainstream psychology, "the giants had always taken telepathy and allied phenomena for granted—from Charcot and Richet through William James to Freud and Jung. Freud thought that telepathy entered into the relations between analyst and patient ... " (p. 13). Koestler also noted the eminence of past presidents of the British Society for Psychical Research. Included were three Nobel Laureates, ten Fellows of the Royal Society, one Prime Minister, and a diverse and celebrated group of philosophers and physicists.

What does such "expert validity" tell us? Nothing, really. We still need to view the evidence for ourselves. Yet this lineup of eminent figures does remind us that this is not just an area for charlatans and hucksters (who may indeed have given it a bad name). We, ourselves, perhaps more like the eminent figures above, are scientifically oriented and creative. Can we ourselves keep an open mind toward new phenomena, and not reject them outright just because they clash with our current worldview and beliefs?

This is just what the editors and contributors to the current book are asking us to do: to keep our minds open and our assessments fair. These contributors are to be celebrated for their bravery, for being willing to tread new ground, with honesty and with rigor. They follow in the footsteps of Nobel Laureate Marie Curie who told us, "Nothing in life is to be feared. It is to be understood" (as cited in Benarde, 1989, p. v).

Some of these contributors advocate acceptance of the evidence for anomalous phenomena. Some refute the same evidence. Yet all take the risk to address these phenomena. And all ask us to pay good attention. One might also add, they ask us to make the public discussion of these topics *less* taboo in our culture. We the readers can learn a lot from this book and, by doing so, can also help change the norms for cultural discourse.

Our creative response, in any case, is to show up with open minds and creative curiosity, matched fully by critical thinking: to give the new a chance. On the one hand, we do not want to be taken in by some faddish belief that has no basis, the wishful thinking of somebody's fantasy, which may nonetheless spawn dozens of popular books. Yet we do not want to miss "the big one" either, and be left standing on the corner saying "the world is flat," while right behind us, through a store window, a television set shows a satellite orbiting a spherical globe. May our assessments as readers then be neither inflated by wishful thinking nor limited by prejudice.

Let us recall that there has been enough interest in the topics of this book to have crossed centuries and continents and to have intrigued both charlatans and Fellows of the Royal Society. Now it is our turn. We should take a very good look at the evidence. Perhaps we will not be convinced. Fair enough. Yet let us also recall that many a scientific advance has come from dismissive beginnings—only to elicit a later embarrassed retraction. Whatever the verdict in this case, may the present readers be among those who get it right the first time.

REFERENCES

Achterberg, J., Cooke, K., Richards, T., Standish, L. J., Kozak, L., & Lake, J. (2005). Evidence for correlations between distant intentionality and brain functions in recipients: A functional magnetic resonance imagining analysis. *Journal of Alternative and Complementary Medicine, 11,* 965–971.

Allport, G. (1963). Foreword. In N. L. Faberow (Ed.), *Taboo topics* (pp. vii–xii). New York: Atherton Press.

Bem, D., & Honorton, C. (1994). Does *psi* exist? Replicable evidence for an anomalous process of information transfer. *Psychological Bulletin, 115*, 4–18.

Bloom, H. (2000). *Global brain: The evolution of mass mind from the Big Bang to the 21st Century.* New York: Wiley.

Benarde, M. A. (1989). *Our precarious habitat.* New York: Wiley.

Cardeña, E., Lynn, S. J., & Krippner, S. (Eds.). (2000). *Varieties of anomalous experience: Examining the scientific evidence.* Washington, DC: American Psychological Association.

Chandler, P. S. (1993, February 15) Study finds evidence of ESP phenomenon. *Boston Globe*, pp. 1, 8.

Combs, A. (2010). Foreword. In S. Krippner & H. Friedman (Eds.), *Mysterious minds: The neurobiology of physics, mediums, and other extraordinary people* (pp. ix–xi). Santa Barbara, CA: Praeger.

Farberow, N. L. (Ed.). (1963). Introduction. *Taboo topics* (pp. 1–7). New York: Atherton Press.

Friedman, H. L., MacDonald, D. A., & Kumar, K. (2004). Validation of the self-expansiveness level form with an Indian sample. [Special issue: The Horizon of Consciousness], *Journal of Indian Psychology, 22*, 44–66.

Greyson, B. (2000). Near-death experiences. In E. Cardeña, S. J. Lynn, & S. Krippner (Eds.), *Varieties of anomalous experience: Examining the scientific evidence* (pp. 315–352). Washington, DC: American Psychological Association.

Jung, C. G. (1955). *Synchronicity: An acausal connecting principle.* New York: Bollingen Foundation.

Jung, C. G., & Pauli, W. (1955). *The interpretation of nature and the psyche.* New York: Bollingen Foundation.

Koestler, A. (1972). *The roots of coincidence: An excursion into parapsychology.* New York: Vintage Books.

Krippner, S., & Achterberg, J. (2000). Anomalous healing experiences. In E. Cardeña, S. J. Lynn, & S. Krippner (Eds.), *Varieties of anomalous experience: Examining the scientific evidence* (pp. 353–395). Washington, DC: American Psychological Association.

MacDonald, D. A., LeClair, L., Holland, C. J., Alter, A., & Friedman, H. L. (1995). A survey of measures of transpersonal constructs. *Journal of Transpersonal Psychology, 27*, 171–235.

May, R. (1975). *The courage to create.* New York: Norton.

Myers, G. (1990). *Writing biology: Texts in the social construction of scientific knowledge.* Madison: University of Wisconsin Press.

Pauli, W. (1955). *The influence of archetypal ideas on the scientific theories of Kepler.* New York: Bollingen Foundation.

Radin, D. I. (1997). *The conscious universe: The scientific truth of psychic phenomena.* New York: HarperEdge.

Ray, P., & Anderson, S. R. (2000). *The cultural creatives: How 50 million people are changing the world.* New York: Three Rivers Press.

Richards, R. (1994). Psi Fi?: "Acceptable" and "unacceptable" research. *Creativity Research Journal, 7*, 87–90.

Richards, R. (Ed.). (2007). *Everyday creativity and new views of human nature.* Washington, DC: American Psychological Association.

Rilke, R. M. (1986). *Letter to a young poet* (S. Mitchell, Trans.). New York: Vintage.

Acknowledgments

The editors express their gratitude to the Floraglades Foundation, the Saybrook University Chair for the Study of Consciousness, Dr. Gert Reutter, the Leir Charitable Foundations, and the John Brockway Huntington Foundation for their support in the preparation of this book. They also thank Christian Gaden Jensen, who served as managing editor, Steve Hart, who served as coordinating editor, Cheryl Fracasso for additional editorial assistance, and Debbie Carvalko, our editor at Praeger/ABC-CLIO for her continued support. The editors are especially grateful to Dierdre Luzwick, the visionary Wisconsin artist, for allowing us to use several of her original drawings as illustrations.

"Cradlesong" (© Dierdre Luzwick. Used by permission.)

Introduction: An Invitation to a Debate

Stanley Krippner and Harris L. Friedman

Over the millennia, people in all known cultures have reported phenomena that are described in the English language as *psychic*, among other terms used. These alleged psychic phenomena appear to defy conventional notions of time and space, as when information supposedly has been received or transmitted in inexplicable ways or when influence purportedly has been exerted without the use of known agents such as muscles or machines. These reports serve as inspiration for those known as *parapsychologists* who attempt to study these experiences from the perspective of Western science. These investigators implicitly conclude that psychic phenomena warrant study, whether or not they may be ontologically "real" (rather than delusory or illusory), or they simply would not invest their time in conducting such studies. Although parapsychologists suspect there is something important about these phenomena, even if that suspicion turns out to be unwarranted, many of them go further by advocating that the extant research findings already have solidly demonstrated the existence of psychic phenomena, even though current scientific beliefs may be inadequate for fully explaining them. In other words, many parapsychologists attribute the inability to explain psychic phenomena as due to the limitations of the prevailing scientific understandings, not due to the veracity of the phenomena.

On the other hand, there are those who can be called counteradvocates who doubt the veracity of psychic phenomena. They tend to believe that virtually all of these reported phenomena can be explained away through what is already known

within such fields as psychology, psychiatry, medicine, biology, anthropology, physics, and related disciplines. Counteradvocates generally regard the widespread
popular belief in the validity of psychic phenomena as "a frustrating fact of life"
(Dennett, 2006, p. 304) and a sad commentary on the lack of critical thinking
and gullibility pervasive in modern society.

However, there has been a surge of interest in the ongoing debate between
advocates (or proponents) and counteradvocates (or critics) of parapsychology
exemplified by a series of recent books by authors not associated with parapsychological research, who have noted what they perceive as its unfair treatment
over the decades (e.g., Broderick, 2007; Carter, 2007; Lloyd Mayer, 2007; Powell,
2009). These writers, each with impressive resumes and advanced academic
degrees, have joined the ranks of the advocates for the importance of parapsychological research—and, as one writer phrased it, "It's time for parapsychology to
come in from the cold" (Broderick, 2007).

The counteradvocates, however, insist that there is nothing to be brought out
of the cold, a perspective developed by recent writers, such as J. C. Smith (2010),
carrying on debunking traditions. Examples of such debunking efforts include
Paul Kurtz's (1985) A Skeptic's Handbook of Parapsychology, which contains chapters written by several contributors to this book, and Victor Stenger's (1990)
Physics and Psychics, which uses the principles of contemporary physics in an
attempt to refute the possible existence of psychic phenomena.

What can one believe about parapsychology? The counteradvocates attempt
to debunk the field, claiming it is based on unwarranted assumptions that violate
the very laws of nature on which all knowledge rests, and that its findings are
unsubstantiated, claiming it has consistently failed scientific tests. Some of these
critics allude to incompetence or even make innuendos about intentional fraud
to explain away some of the more compelling findings. In contrast, the advocates
for the legitimacy of these findings persistently present evidence supportive of
the existence of psychic phenomena, much of which exceeds the standards of
acceptance set in comparable scientific fields such as mainstream psychology.
Some of these advocates also make innuendos about conspiracies to suppress
their work, regardless of the quality of any evidence they might present. Amidst
this rancor, including its various charges and countercharges of impropriety,
many people not directly involved in this controversy find parapsychology a fascinating topic but are frustrated with the many competing views. The way the
evidence actually points, supporting or not supporting psychic phenomena, cannot be easily determined in this cacophony.

But this is also true for so many other important human endeavors. Global climate change is an example of an area in which complex data are differentially
interpreted. Although almost the entire scientific community acknowledges that
climate change is really occurring (and at an alarming rate, see Houghton, 2004),
there is a vociferous minority who deny that climate change is real (e.g., Leroux,
2005). A third group agrees that climate change is occurring but doubts that
human activity is the crucial cause (e.g., Taylor, 1999). The unpredictability of
the weather, as well as various vested interests competing for different positions

on this controversy, leaves many people not directly involved as players within this controversy in utter confusion. Of course, this gets translated into few firm conclusions about climate change being unanimously accepted, resulting in a lack of coherent social policy to address what is potentially humankind's greatest challenge since evolving as a species. This failure to achieve a consensus is accompanied by discord, including conspiracy theories from both sides. Opponents of climate change argue that the proponents have somehow rigged the scientific data (e.g., Spencer, 2008), while the proponents of climate change argue that opponents are profiting from their opposition (e.g., Gore, 2009). Although the fate of many species, including humanity, may ultimately rest on how climate change is handled (or ignored), this example illustrates the difficulties of knowing in complex areas where interpretations can vary greatly, especially when accompanied by divisive accusations that are passionately fueled.

The prevailing controversies around psychic phenomena are in some ways comparable to disputes over many divisive issues, not just the role of human activity in possibly accelerating climate change. How we deal with such competing claims, where supposed experts vie against each other to convince the public one way or another, indicates toward a deeper issue, how we might fundamentally see our world and choose to live our lives. In the case of AIDS, for example, viral causation has been established to the satisfaction of mainstream science (e.g., Blattner, Gallo, & Temin, 1988), but some investigators hold that the HIV virus requires co-factors so a viral theory alone is inadequate (e.g., Root-Bernstein, 1993), while others reject the link between the HIV virus and AIDS completely (e.g., Duesberg, 1988). And the controversy over AIDS is obfuscated in some groups by a cloud of moral beliefs regarding this disease that raises the emotional level of almost any discussion.

To put this into a broader context, the evolution of modern thought can be seen as emerging from a constant struggle between sacred-religious and secular-scientific beliefs. One of the more recent aspects of this ongoing conflict involves controversies between beliefs in "randomly-driven" evolution (e.g., Dawkins, 1986; Shermer, 2002) as opposed to so-called "intelligent design" (e.g., Behe, 1998). Prevailing scientific opinions tend to reject the scientific viability of "intelligent design," but the number of Americans who accept the data for Darwinian evolutionary theory is exceeded by those who disbelieve (Harris Poll, 2005). Despite the near unanimity of the scientific community that evolution provides a sufficiently inclusive accounting for change over time within biological phenomena, the "randomness" descriptor has not been unequivocally established, according to advocates of "punctuated equilibrium" (e.g., Gould, 1980) and "dynamic systems" models of evolution (Laszlo, 1987). These do not ascribe to "intelligent design" speculations, but balk at the term "randomness" because it bypasses the role of organism/environment interaction (e.g., Pembry et al., 2006). Indeed, Darwin did not attach the word "random" to such words as "variation" and "natural selection," much less the widely used term "blind chance."

Laszlo (1987) has opted for a model in which "life continually explores novel combinations of structures and functions as existing species interlock their catalytic cycles in shared habitats and jointly converge in higher-level systems" (p. 82). In the meantime, some of the more extreme advocates of "chance variation" have modified their positions (e.g., Dawkins, 2009). But it remains unsettling for much of the scientific community to even consider the possibility of any forces providing a viable alternative to the assumption of randomness as the source of biological diversity, and so a hard-line position is often taken to defend a narrow view of randomly driven evolution, despite some of the limitations of such a view.

In these three examples, there are the "cranks" who disclaim the viral etiology of AIDS, who dismiss the notion that the world is getting warmer and who advocate an "intelligent design" origin of the universe. There are also the "mavericks" who accept the evidence for global warming, the viral linkage with HIV/AIDS syndrome, and Darwinian evolutionary theory, but refrain from accepting mainstream explanations for their specific causes or modes of action. As readers go through this book, they might ask themselves whether parapsychologists are "cranks" or "mavericks." If they are the latter, there is hope for rapprochement with established scientific principles, especially as these might broaden; if they are the former, the gulf between advocates and counteradvocates likely will only widen. In all fairness, we must note that some extreme counteradvocates are considered "cranks" by members of the parapsychological community.

Any belief in nonmaterial forces acting under principles other than randomness, let alone possibly moved by "supernatural" forces, such as the actions of gods and spirits, has essentially been banished from the secular scientific worldview, with few exceptions, the field of parapsychology being one of these. In essence, parapsychology is the secular-scientific study of what formerly would have been seen as the sacred, the so-called "miracles" that defy rational understanding. In this regard, to even entertain the possibility that such phenomena could exist is to allow a chink in the armor that has been used since the Enlightenment to wrest power away from religious authority. It is our belief, however, that the long struggle between the "sacred" and the "secular" may lend itself to a synthesis, something we will consider in our concluding comments. For now, it is important to set the stage for an exciting series of position statements, and retorts to each others' positions, from a group of renowned advocates and counteradvocates of parapsychology, by discussing briefly some of the basic issues and approaches in parapsychology.

Parapsychologists use the term *psi* (short for psychic) when referring to reported interactions between organisms and their environment (including other organisms) that appear to transcend the physical and biological demarcations of Western science. Examples include remote perception (often referred to as "extrasensory perception" or "psi gamma"), remote influence (often called "psychokinesis" or "psi kappa") and survival of bodily death (or "psi theta"). Remote perception is often subdivided into "clairvoyance," "telepathy," and "precognition," while remote influence (or perturbation) can be categorized as "influence on static objects" (such as purported metal-bending), "influence on distant objects" (such as attempts to influence random event generators or falling dice), and "influence of living objects" (as in anomalous healing experiences).

Parapsychology is the field of disciplined inquiry that studies psi experiences by arranging controlled experiments and systematic observations to determine if any of these experiences are more than just subjective in nature. Parapsychology began as an interdisciplinary field consisting of psychologists, psychiatrists, physicians, neuroscientists, anthropologists, historians, and members of several other disciplines. However, the field has reached a state where a common body of practices, especially concerning research methodologies, has evolved making it necessary for all serious parapsychologists to have mastered a considerable literature and skill set. As a result, what was once a multidisciplinary field has moved to being interdisciplinary and toward becoming what Minati and Collen (1997) have called a "transdisciplinary" area of inquiry, one in which separate disciplines are transcended and a common body of knowledge is assumed.

Parapsychologists hold varying opinions regarding the authenticity and veridicality of psychic experiences. Indeed, an investigator can be considered a parapsychologist even if he or she is not convinced that there are subjective psychic experiences that can be considered objective psychic events. In their chapter in *Varieties of Anomalous Experience: Examining the Scientific Evidence* (Cardeña, Lynn, & Krippner, 2000), Krippner and Achterberg (2000) differentiated "experiences" from "events," the former referring to subjective reports (e.g., of unusual healings and other inner experiences) and the latter referring to documented outcomes that can be observed by others, in other words the possible veridicality of an experience. Two people may report an experience in which they saw a bright light suddenly appearing in the evening sky. Photographic data may establish this experience as an event. Even if established as an event, however, one person may explain the bright light as a comet, while another may attribute its brightness to radiation from an unidentified flying object (UFO). Additional study may establish whether or not the comet explanation could be verified. If so, the comet trail becomes a known event. If not, the UFO explanation would become one of several alternative explanations, subject to further analysis and study. If no conventional explanation is forthcoming, and if no UFO debris is located, the experience could remain in limbo, perhaps indefinitely.

The situation with psychic experiences is somewhat analogous. Many psychic experiences, upon close examination, become classified as conventional events—instances of misperceptions, misattributions, false memories, perceptual illusions, convoluted cognitions, or even downright fraud. Other psychic experiences do not yield so easily, and those are the ones that many parapsychologists insist are actual events, verifiable instances of precognition, psychokinesis, and the like. In other words, they may represent a poorly understood phenomenon, such as a yet to be verified human capacity, rather than something simply illusory or delusory.

Most parapsychologists are members of the Parapsychological Association (PA), the Society for Scientific Exploration (SSE), the Society for Psychical Research (SPR) or all three. Many counteradvocates are members of the Committee for Skeptical Inquiry (CSI), a group of scholars and laypeople that maintains that "the scientific paradigm is their surest guide for sound thinking and living" (Anon., 2009, p.10). Needless to say, most professional parapsychologists would agree with this statement. In principle, someone could be a member of all three groups; one of the editors of this book (i.e., Krippner) is a member of the PA, the SSE, the SPR, and an associate member of the CSI. He is also a member of the Skeptics Society, whose Web site states that its mission is "to serve as an educational tool for those seeking clarification and viewpoints on those controversial ideas and claims." The other editor (i.e., Friedman) has no affiliation with any of these organizations.

This book is an invitation to a dialogue between those advocates who take the position that psychic experiences are often valid events that represent extraordinary human potentials, in contrast to those counteradvocates who hold that these experiences, although possibly worthy of study, are basically a human delusion or illusion. In either case, we believe that science has a great deal to learn from continued rigorous examination of these experiential reports and findings that may or may not rise to the level of being consensual events—and we hope that this book will make a contribution toward that end. Some readers may decide that parapsychology might not be ready to come out of the cold, but we hope that they will conclude that, at the very least, it deserves more than a comfort blanket.

The following section provides a brief introduction to the contents of the book.

Dean Radin, in "A Brief History of Science and Psychic Phenomena," describes how fascination with psychic phenomena is evident in all cultures, can be traced throughout history, and that it persists at all educational levels. These phenomena permeate the world of popular fiction and entertainment, but it is less well known that many aspects of modern scientific techniques (including blinded protocols, use of statistical analyses in the behavioral sciences, and development of the electroencephalograph) were stimulated by scientists' interests in studying psychic experiences. His chapter introduces the advocates' claim for the legitimacy of parapsychology, as well as a sample of its many findings.

In "Attributions About Impossible Things," James Alcock in contrast argues that, while parapsychological researchers continually strive to establish a scientific basis for parapsychological phenomena, their research efforts are plagued by a number of serious problems that keep them from achieving acceptance within mainstream science. Alcock claims that many researchers sidestep these problems through defensive attributions that try to explain away the lack of acceptance within science in terms of failings on the part of mainstream scientists, not on problems within parapsychology. Alcock maintains that it is deep-seated belief, rather than tangible scientific data, that motivates the continuing search for evidence of what he calls "impossible things."

In "Parapsychology's Achilles Heel: Persistent Inconsistency," Ray Hyman continues this counteradvocate theme by asserting that, although some parapsychologists argue that the evidence demonstrates the existence of paranormal phenomena, a growing number of parapsychologists admit that the evidence is inconsistent, elusive, and non-replicable. If they are correct, and the more than a century of parapsychological research demonstrates that they are according to Hyman, then parapsychology has failed to achieve its goal of becoming a science with a demonstrable phenomenon. Hyman emphasizes that, although many para-psychologists admit not having a repeatable effect in the field, they persist in claims that psi is real and, indeed, may even argue that resistance to scientific observation is an essential property of psi itself, which he concludes begs the question.

"Reflections of a (Relatively) Moderate Skeptic" continues this theme as a personal reflection upon the current state of parapsychology and also upon what sort of evidence might cause its author, Christopher C. French, to move from currently believing that psi probably does not exist to possibly believing that it probably does. Issues discussed in this chapter include the scientific status of parapsychology, difficulties in assessing meta-analyses, problems with replicability, and the need for parapsychologists to demonstrate some practical applications of psi.

In "How I Became a Psychic for a Day," Michael Shermer recounts his deceptively enacting the role of a psychic, astrologer, tarot card reader, and palm reader—and how easy it was to dupe people with his enactment. In the process he deconstructs how cold readings, warm readings, and hot readings are done, how psychics, astrologers, tarot card readers, and palm readers appear to talk to the dead, read people's minds, tell them about their past, and predict the future. Shermer's skeptical analysis reveals that many convincing phenomena can be duplicated through fraud by using a process of subtle psychological manipulation at the expense of those naïve enough to be duped. This is presented as the advocate's *coup de grace*, namely if these convincing phenomena can be so easily faked, it can also be argued that there can be little confidence placed in the whole range of psychic phenomena investigated.

Chris Carter, in "Persistent Denial: A Century of Denying the Evidence," argues the other side, that consistent, replicable evidence for the existence of psi has been amply provided—contrary to what the critics of parapsychology continue to insist. Carter maintains that, if this were any other field of inquiry, the controversy would have been settled by the data decades ago. However, he also points out that the data of parapsychology challenge deeply held worldviews, worldviews that are concerned not only with science, but also with religious and philosophical issues and, as such, the evidence arouses strong passions and, for many, a strong desire to dismiss it. Carter presents a strong case for the advocate position, including a direct challenge to the frequent claims that parapsychologists may be disingenuous by presenting an equally compelling case for why the counteradvocates also might be disingenuous.

In the second part of this book, the advocates and counteradvocates square off against each other, making comments on the previous chapters, noting their points of disagreement and, surprisingly, what they have in common. This section is followed by essays by Richard S. Wiseman, a counteradvocate and Stephan A. Schwartz, an advocate. We, the editors, then provide our perspectives on this debate, hoping that readers will have enjoyed working their way through the divergent positions taken by our chapter authors. Final salvos are fired by Damien Broderick, an advocate, and Elizabeth Loftus, a counteradvocate. A glossary of terms brings our book to a close. We hope that this anthology represents a worthwhile contribution to a long-standing controversy, even though our intention has been to illuminate, rather than resolve it.

REFERENCES

Anonymous. (2009, July/August). Ignite the adventure. *Skeptical Inquirer*, p. 10.

Behe, M. (1998). *Darwin's black box: The biochemical challenge to evolution*. New York: Touchstone Books.

Blattner, W., Gallo, R. C., & Temin, H. M. (1988). HIV causes AIDS. *Science, 241*, 515–516.

Broderick, D. (2007). *Outside the gates of science: Why it is time for parapsychology to come in from the cold*. New York: Thunder's Mouth Press.

Cardeña, E., Lynn. S. J., & Krippner, S. (Eds.). (2000). *Varieties of anomalous experience: Examining the scientific evidence*. Washington, DC: American Psychological Association.

Carter, C. (2007). *Parapsychology and the skeptics: A scientific argument for the existence of ESP*. New York: Sterling House Books.

Dawkins, R. (1986). *The blind watchmaker: Why the evidence of evolution reveals a universe without design*. New York: W. W. Norton.

Dawkins, R. (2009). *The greatest show on Earth: The evidence for evolution*. New York: Free Press.

Dennett, D. (2006). *Breaking the spell: Religion as a natural phenomenon*. London: Penguin.

Duesberg, P. H. (1988). HIV is not the cause of AIDS. *Science, 241*, 514–517.

Gore, A. (2009). *Our choice: A plan to solve the climate crisis*. Emmaus, PA: Rodale.

Gould, S. J. (1980). *The panda's thumb*. New York: W. W. Norton.

Harris Poll (2005). *Nearly two-thirds of U.S. adults believe human beings were created by God*. Retrieved February 14, 2010 from http://www.harrisinteractive.com/harris_poll/index.asp?PID=581

Houghton, J. (2004). *Global warming: The complete briefing* (3rd ed.). Boston: Cambridge University Press.

Krippner, S., & Achterberg, J. (2000). Anomalous healing experiences. In E. Cardeña, S. J. Lynn, & S. Krippner (Eds.), *Varieties of anomalous experience: Examining the scientific evidence* (pp. 353–395). Washington, DC: American Psychological Association.

Kurtz, P. (Ed.). (1985). *A skeptic's handbook of parapsychology*. Amherst, NY: Prometheus.

Laszlo, E. (1987). *Evolution: The grand synthesis*. Boston, MA: Shambhala.

Leroux, M. (2005). *Global warming: Myth or reality?* New York: Springer-Verlag.

Lloyd Mayer, E. (2007). *Extraordinary knowing: Scientific skepticism and the inexplicable power of the human mind*. New York: Bantam/Doubleday.

Minati, G., & Collen, A. (1997). *Introduction to systemics*. Walnut Creek, CA: Eagleye Books International.

Pembry, M., Bygren, L.O., Kaati, G. P., Edvinsson, S., Northstone, K., Sjostrom, M., & Golding, J. (2006). Sex-specific, sperm-mediated transgenerational responses in humans. *European Journal of Human Genetics, 14*, 159–166.

Powell, D. (2009). *The ESP enigma: The scientific case for psychic phenomena*. New York: Walker.

Root-Bernstein, R. (1993). *Rethinking AIDS: The tragic cost of premature consensus*. New York: Free Press.

Shermer, M. (2002). *Why Darwin matters: The case against intelligent design.* New York: Times Books.

Smith, J. C. (2010). *Pseudoscience and extraordinary claims of the paranormal: A critical thinker's toolkit.* New York: Wiley-Blackwell.

Spencer, R. (2008). *Climate confusion: How global warming hysteria leads to bad science, pandering politicians and misguided policies that hurt the poor.* New York: Encounter.

Stenger, V. J. (1990). *Physics and psychics: The search for a world beyond the senses.* Amherst, NY: Prometheus.

Taylor, K. (1999). New evidence shows that earth's climate can change dramatically in only a decade. *American Scientist, 87,* 320–327.

PART ONE

Presentations

"The Riddle" (© Dierdre Luzwick. Used by permission.)

CHAPTER 1

A Brief History of Science and Psychic Phenomena

Dean Radin

> If we have learned one thing from the history of invention and discovery, it is that, in the long run—and often in the short one—the most daring prophecies seem laughably conservative.
>
> Arthur C. Clarke (1951, p. 111)

The philosopher George Santayana (1905) once wrote that those who cannot remember the past are condemned to repeat it. That is an excellent piece of advice if one wishes to avoid making mistakes in life. But in science one is condemned for *not* repeating the past. That is, the gold standard for establishing scientific facts, and the single most important criterion for distinguishing science from religious faith, is repeatability. Claimed effects must be repeated by independent observers to be considered real.

In the case of psi phenomena, two classes of repeatability are of interest. The first are reports of human experience and the ways that people have tried to study them; the second are the results of experiments conducted under controlled conditions. The former provides face validity that something interesting has been going on for a long time; the latter provides confidence about how to interpret those observations. This chapter considers the first class—the history of scientific interest in psi phenomena.

Edited version of Chapter 4, "Origins" from ENTANGLED MINDS: Extrasensory Experiences in a Quantum Reality by Dean Radin. Copyright © 2008 by Dean Radin, Ph.D. Reprinted with permission of Pocket Books, a Division of Simon & Schuster, Inc. All rights reserved.

ANCIENT HISTORY

In the beginning, there were no cell phones or grocery stores and life was hard. Nature was capricious and unforgiving. People sought ways to cope with the uncertainties of life by praying or cajoling Nature spirits to be kind to them. Shamans in every culture became the first healers, magicians, spiritual functionaries, and intermediaries to the spirit worlds. Magical thinking reigned supreme and everyone believed in supernatural forces.

Magic has been defined as "the employment of ineffective techniques to allay anxiety when effective ones are not available" (Thomas, 1971, p. 800). While many old wives tales were futile superstitions, some of their therapies were effective and based on repeated observations passed down through the ages, presaging the origins of modern empiricism. Today we still take some of those methods for granted, especially refined herbal remedies like aspirin. The use of maggots and leeches, once associated with the worst horrors of medieval medicine, are also back in vogue because those ancient folk remedies can accomplish things that even today's medical miracles cannot surpass. The explosion of modern interest in alternative and complementary medicine suggests that in the rush to adopt synthetic drugs some effective traditional remedies may have been prematurely dismissed as superstitions. Some of those old wives were probably smarter than we know.

As magical concepts evolved, they tended to fall into two classes: natural and supernatural. The former pertained to properties inherent in objects themselves, the latter to acts of invisible forces and entities. The study of natural magic presaged science; supernatural magic would become subsumed within religious doctrine.

Millennia passed. Knowledge about the natural world advanced slowly.

All early civilizations were aware that sometimes, some people had extraordinary experiences in which information was apparently obtained about distant and future events. Many divination methods were developed to cultivate these experiences.

In 2000 BCE, Egyptians practiced dream incubation as a technique for evoking oracles. They slept in special temples in the hopes of inducing divinely inspired dreams (Tolaas & Ullman, 1979). A few hundred years later in China, oracles would toss tortoise shells into the fire and read the resulting cracks in the shells as omens about future events. The predictions and outcomes of these divinations were inscribed on the shells (Tao, 1996). Today, the 50,000 known Shang Dynasty "Oracle Bones" are among the earliest known parapsychological "experiments," and also the earliest forms of written language. They indicate not only that oracles were commonplace, but also that oracles could—and should—be put to the test by comparing predictions with outcomes.

In 650 BCE, one of the longest-lived businesses in history began—the Delphi Oracle at the Temple of Apollo in Greece, which lasted for some 700 years. The God Apollo was said to foretell the future through his priestess, the Pythia. She inhaled vapors rising up through cracks in the temple's floor to induce an altered state of consciousness, and then while in a trance she responded to the questions of visitors. An interpreter inscribed her resulting moans and mumblings (Roach, 2001).

It is difficult to know today how effective the Delphi Oracles might have been in forecasting the future, as few written records remain. Fortunately, Herodotus documented one interesting test case. He wrote that King Croesus of Lydia wished to consult an oracle, and he knew that most of the oracles of the day were fakes. So the King devised a test to find one with genuine skill. The Pythia of the Temple of Apollo was the only oracle who responded to his experiment with the correct answer. She said through her interpreters, in traditional hexameter verse:

> I can count the sands, and I can measure the ocean;
> I have ears for the silent, and know what the dumb man meaneth;
> Lo! on my sense there striketh the smell of a shell-covered tortoise,
> Boiling now on a fire, with the flesh of a lamb, in a cauldron—
> Brass is the vessel below, and brass the cover above it.[1]

In fact, King Croesus had taken a tortoise and a lamb, cut them into pieces, and boiled them together in a brazen cauldron covered with a lid, also made of brass. On the basis of the Delphi Oracle's accuracy, the King consulted her about what would happen if his army invaded Persia. She replied that this action would "destroy a great empire." King Croesus assumed this meant his invasion would crush Persia, but unfortunately he didn't verify that flattering interpretation. As history shows, his invasion did indeed destroy a great empire—his own (Ebon, 1978, p. 20). Moral of the story: When dealing with oracles, it's a good idea to check your assumptions.

In Greece, Democritus believed in dream telepathy and divination (Dodds, 1971), but Aristotle was less certain. He wrote:

As to divination which takes place in sleep, and is said to be based on dreams, we cannot lightly either dismiss it with contempt or give it implicit confidence. The fact that all persons, or many, suppose dreams to possess a special significance tends to inspire us with belief, based on the testimony of experience. . . . Yet the fact of our seeing no probable cause to account for such divination tends to inspire us with distrust. (Ebon, 1978, p. 21)

Cicero agreed. In a typically caustic comment, he wrote about Democritus: "I never knew anyone who talked nonsense with greater authority" (Woods, 1947).

Half a millennium later, in 1484, Pope Innocent VIII published a "bull" against Witches, followed by the notorious document, *Malleus Maleficarum* (The Witches' Hammer).[2] The Pope's pronouncement made witchcraft a capital crime and inspired a madness known as the "witch hunt," which unfortunately became a wildly popular sport throughout Europe. A hundred and twenty years later, King James I of England issued the Witchcraft Act: "An acte against conjuration witchcrafte and dealinge with evill and wicked Spirits."[3] Practicing witchcraft was now officially against the law as well as against Church doctrine.

Jumping ahead a thousand years, in 1627, Sir Francis Bacon published *Sylva Sylvarum: Or A Naturall Historie in Ten Centuries.*[4] Bacon was an author, barrister, and eventually Lord Chancellor of England. He is credited with developing the basis of empirical reasoning, one of the core concepts underlying what today we know as the "scientific method." In *Sylva Sylvarum*, Bacon proposed that the effect of mental intention (his actual term was the "force of imagination") could be tested on objects that "have the lightest and easiest motions. And therefore above all, upon the spirits of men," by which he meant the emotions. Bacon continued, "As for inanimate things, it is true that the motions of shuffling of cards, or casting of dice, are very light motions," presaging the use of cards and dice and other random physical systems in parapsychological experiments.

Bacon further proposed that in studies on the "binding of thoughts," or what we would now call telepathy, that "you are to note whether it hit for the most part though not always," anticipating the use of statistical techniques. Further, he noted that one might be more likely to succeed in such tests "if you . . . name one of twenty men, than . . . one of twenty cards," that is, tasks involving meaningful targets might be more effective than tasks involving the guessing of simple playing cards. Bacon's ideas were not only 300 years ahead of their time. They also show that interest in testing psi effects (parapsychological phenomena) was among the very first proposed uses of the new empirical science.

The scientific revolution in Europe began to accelerate. Ideas promoted by Bacon and other "natural philosophers" like Copernicus, Kepler, Galileo, Descartes, and Newton took hold, science proliferated, and the stranglehold that religious dogma had held on understanding the natural world began to loosen.

EIGHTEENTH CENTURY

Emanuel Swedenborg was a renowned metallurgist in the mid 18th-century. Among his many scientific accomplishments, Swedenborg displayed an astonishingly modern understanding of brain functioning. Two hundred years before the neurosciences became a scientific discipline, Swedenborg correctly described sensation, movement, and cognition as functions of the cerebral cortex, the function of the corpus callosum, the motor cortex, the neural pathways of each sense organ to the cortex, the functions of the frontal lobe and the corpus striatum, circulation of the cerebrospinal fluid, and interactions of the pituitary gland between the brain and the blood (Gross, 1997). Swedenborg was also an accomplished psychic. On the afternoon of June 19, 1759, he arrived in Göteborg, Sweden. At a dinner party that evening, he suddenly announced to his friends that he was having a vision of Stockholm burning, about 300 miles away. Later that evening he told them that the fire stopped three doors from his home. The next day, the mayor of Göteborg, who heard about Swedenborg's surprising pronouncement, discussed it with him. The following day, a messenger from Stockholm arrived and confirmed that Swedenborg's vision was correct (Lamm, 2000).[5]

A century later, the American colonies declared their independence from Great Britain. While George Washington was battling the British, Austrian physician Franz Anton Mesmer was advancing the concept of "animal magnetism." At the time, electricity and magnetism were evoking great interest as newly discovered, still-mysterious forces of nature. Mesmer proposed that animal magnetism was a biological force analogous to those physical forces (Alvarado, 2006). Mesmer's ideas are reflected today in the origins of hypnosis, psychoanalysis, and psychosomatic medicine.

The French aristocrat Armand Marie Jacques de Chastenet, known as the Marquis de Puységur, was one of Mesmer's early students. Puységur accidentally discovered the first method claimed to reliably evoke psi phenomena. He called his discovery "magnetic somnambulism," a type of "sleep-walking" trance we now call deep trance hypnosis. He found that some somnambulists showed the full range of purported psychic skills, including telepathy, clairvoyance, and precognition.

The explosion of popular interest in Mesmer and Puységur's methods outraged the physicians of the day, and in 1784 their indignation triggered an investigation by the French Academy of Sciences. The Academy was charged with evaluating the scientific status of mesmerism. A month later, a second commission was formed under the auspices of the French Royal Society of Medicine. It was asked to determine whether mesmerism was useful in treating illness, regardless of whether there was any scientific explanation for it. After numerous tests, both commissions concluded that there was no evidence for the "magnetic fluid" proposed by Mesmer, and that all of the observed effects could be attributed to imagination (what we now call the placebo effect). But the Royal Society's conclusion wasn't unanimous. A minority report declared that some healing effects could not be attributed solely to imagination (Crabtree, 1993).

NINETEENTH CENTURY

A half-century later, mesmerism was still raging unchecked throughout Europe, so the French Royal Society of Medicine felt compelled to launch a new investigation. This time the report was uniformly favorable not only to mesmerism but also to the somnambulistic psi phenomena reported by Puységur. The report ended with a recommendation that the Royal Society continue to investigate these phenomena. For the next five years those studies took place and the commissioners described many examples of psi phenomena that they had personally witnessed (Crabtree, 1993). This was one of the first major government-sponsored scientific investigations of psi effects that had an entirely positive outcome. It wasn't just the Royal Society that was impressed. Jean Eugene Robert-Houdin, the most famous stage magician of his day (from whom Ehrich Weiss, better known as "Houdini," would later adopt his stage name), "confessed that he was completely baffled" about a somnambulist named Alexis, who displayed the clairvoyant ability to read playing cards while blindfolded (Beloff, 1993, pp. 30–31).

Meanwhile, in the United States in 1848, as war with Mexico was winding down and conflict between the Northern and Southern states was heating up, two young sisters named Margaretta and Catherine Fox of Hydesville, New York, reported that they had established communications with spirits who were respond-ing to their questions with rapping sounds. Similar poltergeist ("noisy ghosts") out-breaks had been reported from antiquity, but this one caught the public fancy and the spiritualism craze quickly spread throughout the United States and Europe. Séances to contact the dead became a wildly popular parlor game. Con artists immediately took advantage of gullible public interest by offering performances staged as legitimate séances, and many of these so-called mediums were unmasked as frauds. A few remain genuine enigmas. A Scottish medium named Daniel Dunglas Home astounded European audiences by, among other things, levitating in plain view, with many witnesses present. He performed this and other feats not matched before—or since (Beloff, 1993, p. 45). Despite dozens of performances, Home was never caught cheating. His unusual performances remain a mystery.

The British scientist Sir William Crookes, President of the Chemical Society, the Institution of Electrical Engineers, the British Association for the Advance-ment of Science, and Vice-President of the Royal Society was so intrigued by Home's performances that he created special laboratory equipment to study him. Crookes was impressed with the results and considered Home to have genuine abilities.

In 1850, California became the 31st state of the United States. On October 22 of that year, German physicist Gustav Theodor Fechner had an inspiration that led to the origins of modern experimental psychology and psychophysiology. Fechner's insight was based on his belief that mind and matter arise from the same, non-material, spiritual source. In his attempt to refute materialism by dem-onstrating relationships between mind and matter, he placed the fledgling disci-pline of psychology on firm scientific grounds. Despite his many scientific achievements, his less celebrated colleagues considered his mystical inspirations the eccentricities of a mad genius (Boring, 1951; Sexton & Misiak, 1971).

A quarter century later, in 1876, the American Civil War had come and gone and the Heinz company began selling ketchup. That same year in England, the physicist Sir William Barrett from the Royal College of Science in Dublin, Ireland, presented his research on "thought transference" to the British Association for the Advancement of Science (Playfair, 2003, p. 24). Six years later, Barrett helped found the London-based Society for Psychical Research (SPR), the first scientific organization established for the study of psi phenomena. In his inaugural report to the SPR's Committee on Thought-Reading, Barrett complained about the prejudice against these topics within the scientific community:

> The present state of scientific opinion throughout the world is not only hostile to any belief in the possibility of transmitting a single mental con-cept, except through the ordinary channels of sensation, but, generally speaking, it is hostile even to any inquiry upon the matter. Every leading physiologist and psychologist down to the present time has relegated what,

for want of a better term, has been called "thought-reading" to the limbo of exploded fallacies.

Despite much skepticism among the scientists of the day, many prominent members of British, European, and American science, scholarship, and politics became members of the SPR. They included the physicist Sir Oliver Lodge, best known for his contributions to the development of wireless telegraphy, and another physicist Baron Rayleigh, who was married to Evelyn Balfour, sister of Arthur James Balfour, the Prime Minister of Britain. Rayleigh was later awarded the Nobel Prize for his discovery of the inert gas argon. American members of the SPR included the astronomer Samuel P. Langley, Director of the Smithsonian Institution; psychologist William James of Harvard University; the astronomer Simon Newcomb, President of the American Association for the Advancement of Science; and Edward C. Pickering, Director of the Harvard Observatory (McConnell, 1976).

A few years after the formation of the SPR, the French physiologist Charles Richet published an article describing his experiments on telepathy using playing cards. He introduced "a method which is extremely rarely in usage in the sciences, the method of probabilities" (Hacking, 1988, p. 438). This was the first scientific use of statistical inference for studying telepathy in the general population. Richet concluded that there did exist, "In certain persons at certain times, a faculty of cognition which has no relation to our normal means of knowledge" (Warcollier, 2001, p. xii). Richet would later win the Nobel Prize for his research on anaphylaxis, and at one point he served as President of the SPR.

In light of Richet's claims about telepathy, the eminent British economist F. Y. Edgeworth was asked by members of the SPR to provide his opinion of Richet's use of statistical inference. Edgeworth published two papers in the *Proceedings of the SPR*, which have been described as "fine papers, beautiful enough almost to justify the entire subject of parapsychology" (Hacking, 1988, p. 440). Edgeworth, a staunch skeptic about psi effects, confirmed that Richet's card guessing experiments were not due to chance, as they resulted in odds against chance of 25,000 to 1. He concluded that Richet's claims:

May fairly be regarded as physical certainty, but is silent as to the nature of that agency—whether it is more likely to be vulgar illusion or extraordinary law. That is a question to be decided, not by formulae and figures, but by general philosophy and common sense. (p. 441)

At the close of the 19th century, the British physicist J. J. (Joseph John) Thomson discovered the electron, for which he was awarded the Nobel Prize in 1906. Two years later, in an address to the British Association for the Advancement of Science, Thompson speculated that electromagnetic fields were carriers of information between people, and hence they provided a physical mechanism for telepathy. Sir J. J. Thomson served as a member of the Governing Council of the SPR for 34 years.

About the same time, the Austrian psychiatrist Sigmund Freud (1972) wrote his first paper on "the occult." His second paper was published in 1904 and a third in 1919. His initial attitude was entirely negative, associating the occult solely with superstition. Later his attitude changed to caution and intellectual curiosity. By 1921 he wrote, "It no longer seems possible to brush aside the study of so-called occult facts" (p. xix).

TWENTIETH CENTURY

At the dawn of the 20th century, the German physicist Max Planck postulated that energy was radiated in tiny, discrete units, which he called quanta. The quantum era was born. Two years later, Nabisco's *Animal Crackers* went on sale, and the Swiss psychiatrist Carl Jung wrote his doctoral thesis on a psychological study of a medium. The following year, 1903, Frederic Myers of the SPR published one of the first scholarly volumes investigating the possible survival of consciousness, entitled *Human Personality and Its Survival of Bodily Death*.

In 1905, the delicious iced treat known as the Popsicle was born, and in Switzerland, an unknown 26-year-old patent clerk named Albert Einstein published three papers that would change the face of physics for the next century, and might someday help to explain psi phenomena.

In 1911, Thomas Welton Stanford, the brother of the founder of Stanford University, donated £20,000 to Stanford for a fund to be used "exclusively and wholly for the investigation and advancement of the knowledge of psychic phenomena and the occult sciences." When Thomas Stanford died twenty years later, his will left an additional $526,000 (worth about $10 million in 2005 U.S. dollars) to this fund. The first Thomas Welton Stanford Psychical Research Fellow was a man named John Edgar Coover; he held the chair from 1912 to 1937. His research on telepathy was one the first examples of a randomized, blinded, controlled study, a technique that has since become the gold standard design in the psychological and medical sciences. Coover (1917) reported statistically significant evidence for telepathy in his experiments, although he dismissed his own results as coincidence.

In England, Sir J. J. Thomson at Cambridge University hired Francis Aston as an assistant. Aston had read a 1908 book, *Occult Chemistry*, by British Theosophists Annie Besant and Charles Leadbeater (1951/1908). In that book, Besant and Leadbeater described their clairvoyant vision of the internal structure of atoms, including a new form of the element neon, which they call "meta-neon." They claimed that meta-neon had an atomic weight of 22. In 1912, Aston discovered a substance at that atomic weight while analyzing neon gas. He dubbed it meta-neon in a paper presented to the annual meeting of the British Association for the Advancement of Science. Aston's discovery was later labeled an "isotope," a key discovery about atomic structure (which ultimately led to development of the atom bomb), for which he received the 1922 Nobel Prize (Hughes, 2003).

Around this time, much of the Northern Hemisphere was plunging into the First World War. In the midst of all the anxiety, in 1917 the psychologist

Leonard Troland at Harvard University obtained successful results with one of the first automated ESP testing machines (Mauskopf & McVaugh, 1980, p. 56). A few years later, as the war was winding down, the Institut Metapsychique International was founded in Paris, France. Its first President was the Nobel Laureate physiologist Charles Richet. A few years later, the French researcher René Warcollier (1921) described some of the first highly successful picture-drawing psi experiments in a book entitled *La Télépathie*.

Between the end of the First World War and the U.S. stock market crash of 1929, the British statistician Sir R. A. (Ronald Aylmer) Fisher solved problems in statistical inference for use in card guessing tests by psi researchers (Hacking, 1988, p. 450), and the German physicists Werner Heisenberg, Max Born, and Pascual Jordan developed matrix mechanics, an early form of quantum theory. Jordan, like his Nobel Prize winning colleague Wolfgang Pauli, was fascinated by psi phenomena. Jordan (1951) would later write in the *Journal of Parapsychology*,

> The existence of psi phenomena, often reported by former authors, has been established with all the exactness of modern science by Dr. Rhine and his collaborators, and nobody can any longer deny the necessity for taking the problem seriously and discussing it thoroughly in relation to its connections with other known facts. (p. 280)

Sigmund Freud had also become increasingly interested in psi. In writing to a friend, he explained why his earlier public stance on telepathy had been so reserved, and why he had changed his mind:

> As you remember I already expressed a favorable bias toward telepathy during our trip to the Harz. But there was no need to do so publicly; my conviction was not very strong, and the diplomatic aspect of preventing psychoanalysis from drawing too close to occultism very easily retained the upper hand. . . . In the meantime, however, my personal experience through tests, which I undertook with Ferenczi and my daughter, have attained such convincing power over me that diplomatic considerations had to be relinquished.

Just before the stock market crash of 1929, the biologist Joseph Banks Rhine started a psi research program at Duke University, sponsored by the chair of the psychology department, William McDougall, who had founded the august *British Journal of Psychology*. Rhine's so-called "parapsychology" research continued at Duke until 1965 (Hövelmann, 1987). A few years before he left the university, in 1962, Rhine established the Foundation for Research on the Nature of Man (FRNM) with the assistance of his benefactor Chester Carlson, founder of the Xerox Corporation. The FRNM ran for 40 years, from 1962 to 2002, when it was renamed the Rhine Research Center.

Just before the beginning of the Second World War, the social activist and author Upton Sinclair (2001) published a popular book entitled *Mental Radio*.

In it he described a series of successful picture-drawing telepathy tests with his wife, Mary Craig Sinclair. A few years later, Rhine's (1934) book, *Extra-Sensory Perception* was published, evoking an enormous response in both academic circles and among the general public. Around the same time, the *Journal of Parapsychology* began publication, a peer-reviewed journal founded by J. B. Rhine and his colleagues.

During the Second World War, J. B. Rhine and his colleagues (Pratt, Rhine, Smith, Stuart, & Greenwood, 1940) published the book, *Extrasensory Perception after Sixty Years*. It analyzed in detail all known ESP card-guessing experiments conducted over the sixty years from 1880 through 1939. In England, British psychologist Whately Carrington (1940) conducted picture-drawing experiments with large groups of people. His goal was to develop a repeatable free-response clairvoyance experiment. The results were highly significant, supporting the psi hypothesis.

After the war, in 1950, British mathematician Alan Turing, a seminal figure in the foundations of modern computer science and the man who broke the code of the German Enigma cryptograph machine, wrote about the evidence for psi:

> I assume that the reader is familiar with the idea of extrasensory perception, and the meaning of the four items of it, viz., telepathy, clairvoyance, precognition and psychokinesis. These disturbing phenomena seem to deny all our usual scientific ideas. How we should like to discredit them! Unfortunately the statistical evidence, at least for telepathy, is overwhelming. It is very difficult to rearrange one's ideas so as to fit these new facts in. Once one has accepted them it does not seem a very big step to believe in ghosts and bogies. The idea that our bodies move simply according to the known laws of physics, together with some others not yet discovered but somewhat similar, would be one of the first to go. . . . Many scientific theories seem to remain workable in practice, in spite of clashing with ESP; that in fact one can get along very nicely if one forgets about it. This is rather cold comfort, and one fears that *thinking* is just the kind of phenomenon where ESP may be especially relevant. (Turing, 1950, p. 453, emphasis added)

In 1953, Dow Chemical introduced the ever-popular Saran Wrap, and Sir John Eccles introduced the concept of mind-matter interaction (resembling psi) in his model of mind-brain interaction (Erhenwald, 1977; Wolman, 1977). Despite the radical nature of his ideas, Eccles was awarded the Nobel Prize a decade later. About the same time, J. B. Rhine received a grant from the United States Office of Naval Research to investigate ESP in animals.

In 1957, the same year that General Foods introduced Tang, an orange-flavored instant breakfast beverage, the Parapsychological Association, an international organization of scientists and scholars, was founded, and the Czech physician Štepán Figar (1958) developed a method for testing unconscious telepathic connections in pairs of isolated people.

In 1963, the one billionth McDonald's hamburger was served by founder Ray Kroc on Art Linkletter's popular television show,[6] and the Russian physiologist

Leonid Vasiliev (2002/1963) published the book, *Experiments in Mental Suggestion*. Vasiliev had pioneered Russia's exploration of "remote hypnosis" in the 1920s and 1930s, replicating the somnambulistic phenomena discovered more than a century before by the Marquis de Puységur. Vasiliev demonstrated that somnambulists could be induced to fall into deep trance states when given hypnotic suggestions from a distance, in some cases thousands of miles away.

In 1964, the Beatles tune "I Want to Hold Your Hand" became the #1 pop song in the United States, and psychiatrist Montague Ullman launched a series of dream telepathy studies at the Maimonides Medical Center in Brooklyn, New York. That same year in Europe, Irish physicist John Bell mathematically demonstrated that quantum theory requires "spooky action at a distance," or the existence of nonlocal connections analogous to what Einstein described as "telepathy" between elementary particles.

The following year, the journal *Science* published an article entitled "Extrasensory electroencephalographic induction between identical twins." It reported striking—one might say "spooky"—correspondences in the electroencephalographs (EEGs) of distance-separated pairs of identical twins. Unbeknownst to practically everyone at the time, the study was funded by the U.S. Central Intelligence Agency.

In 1969, the Apollo 11 astronaut Neil Armstrong became the first person to step on the moon, and Helmut Schmidt, a German-American physicist at Boeing Scientific Laboratories, published a paper about an automated psychokinesis experiment using an electronic "coinflipper" circuit called a random number generator (RNG). This would become a model for one of the most frequently replicated psi experiments over the next several decades. The Parapsychological Association was elected an affiliate of the American Association for the Advancement of Science in 1969, marking the first mainstream science acknowledgement of psi research as a legitimate scientific effort.

In 1972, the first successful video game (Pong) was released, and physicists Harold Puthoff and Russell Targ began a program of classified research on psi phenomena for the U.S. government. The following year, Apollo 14 astronaut Captain Edgar Mitchell, the sixth man to walk on the moon, founded the Institute of Noetic Sciences. Mitchell (1971) had conducted a successful ESP card experiment from the Apollo 14 space capsule.

In 1979, there was a meltdown at the Three Mile Island nuclear power plant near Harrisburg, Pennsylvania, and Charles Honorton founded the Psychophysical Research Laboratories in Princeton, New Jersey, with the support of James McDonnell of McDonnell-Douglas aircraft. Robert Jahn, the Dean of the School of Engineering and Applied Science at Princeton University, established a second psi research laboratory in Princeton. The Princeton Engineering Anomalies Research (PEAR) program would become of one the world's principal psi research groups for decades. A few years later, French physicist Alain Aspect and his colleagues at the Institut d'Optique in Orsay, France, published the first widely accepted experimental evidence that "spooky action at a distance" was an experimental fact.

In 1981, members of the U.S. Congress asked the Congressional Research Service to assess the scientific evidence for psi. The review was prompted by concerns that if psi effects were genuine, the United States would have to assume that foreign governments would exploit it. Over the next 15 years, the U.S. Army Research Institute, the National Research Council, the Office of Technology Assessment, and the American Institutes for Research prepared similar reports at the request of the Central Intelligence Agency. While disagreeing over details, all five reviews agreed that some of the experimental evidence for psi warranted continued study.

In 1985, Coca Cola's soft drink campaign for "New Coke" was a spectacular failure, and Yale University psychologist Irvin Child (1985) published a favorable article on "ESP in Dreams" in the flagship journal of the American Psychological Association, *American Psychologist*. In England, author Arthur Koestler and his wife Cynthia had bequeathed funds to establish an endowed Chair of Parapsychology at a British University. The Chair was adopted by the University of Edinburgh, and the first holder of the Chair was the American psychologist Robert Morris, who held the post from December 1985 until his death in August 2004. Morris had also served as President of the Psychology Section of the British Association for the Advancement of Science. By 2008, the nearly 50 students who had earned their PhDs under his aegis had helped to establish psi research as a legitimate topic of academic study in the United Kingdom.

In 1989, Sony Labs researcher Yoichiro Sako approached one of Sony's two founding fathers, Masaru Ibuka, about establishing a psi lab within Sony. Ibuka agreed, and the "ESPER" lab began operations. Some years later Ibuka died, and the lab closed. When asked about the ESPER lab's research, Sony Labs spokesman Masanobu Sakaguchi reportedly said: "We found out experimentally that yes, ESP exists, but that any practical application of this knowledge is not likely in the foreseeable future" (*South China Morning Post*, 1998).

In 1994, interest in the World Wide Web began to explode and the Bial Foundation in Portugal began offering research grants in parapsychology. This Foundation would become one of the world's major sponsors of psi research. The following year, the existence of the U.S. government's 24-year secret program of psi research and applications, code-named STARGATE at the time, was publicly confirmed and then promptly cancelled. Around this time, a new psi research program was supported by the Japanese government, and headed by Mikio Yamamoto. It began operations at the National Institute of Radiological Sciences, part of Japan's Science and Technology Agency. That program closed in 2005, when Yamamoto retired.

In 1998, as the world's economy began to expand at an unprecedented rate due, in part, to the rise of the Internet, the first U.S. patent for a psi-operated electronic switch was granted (number 5830064). The patent was based on the research of the Princeton Engineering Anomalies Research Laboratory. That same year a psi research program began at Interval Research Corporation, a consumer electronics research lab in Silicon Valley.[7] Two years later, University of Amsterdam psychologist Dick Bierman began another psi research program at StarLab, an industrial research lab in Belgium.[8]

TWENTY-FIRST CENTURY

At the turn of the 21st century, a trickle of new patent applications for psi-related applications began to appear. A patent was issued in 2005 for a precognition application, entitled "electrophysiological intuition indicator" (worldwide patent WO 2005/015157 A2). Two years later, a patent was issued for a "device and method for responding to influences of the mind" (worldwide patent WO 2007/014031 A1).

Projecting the future is fraught with uncertainty, but a few trends seem to be taking shape as of this writing (2009). Entrepreneurs have been paying attention to psi research and are becoming interested in capturing intellectual property in this domain, so provisional patents for psi-related effects are being filed more frequently. Increasingly plausible theoretical justifications for some psi effects, and possible applications, may emerge that are based on advancements in understanding macroscopic quantum entanglement, especially as more quantum processes in living systems are detected (as is already the case in 2009, for example, in photosynthesis).

Before 2015, we may see a few psi applications in common use for enhancing intuition, and psi-based methods may be used to improve the efficiency of some electronic, biochemical and biological processes. It is also conceivable that the Western world will be shocked one day when long-simmering rumors about psi applications in China are officially unveiled and found to be true. Unburdened by Western science's centuries of scientific disquiet about these phenomena, we may learn that significant resources had been poured into investigating the relationship between *qi* (or *chi*)—the concept of "life energy" at the root of traditional Chinese medicine for millennia—and the Western concept of psi.

The same may be true of Russia. After decades of rumors, in 2009 it was confirmed that for many years the Russians had funded top-secret, multi-million dollar psi research programs, mostly focused on military and intelligence applications. Much of what they learned is still unknown in the West.

By the mid-21st century I speculate that the scientific landscape will have advanced so far beyond our current (2009) understanding that further historical speculations would be indistinguishable from fantasy. So this is a good place to end this chapter.

NOTES

1. Internet Ancient History Sourcebook. URL: http://www.fordham.edu/halsall/ancient/herodotus-creususandsolon.html, accessed December 12, 2004.

2. Papal bull (1484), *Summus desiderantes*, retrieved from http://www.fordham.edu/halsall/source/witches1.html; the book (1487), *Malleus Maleficarum*, retrieved from http://www.sacred-texts.com/pag/mm/

3. The *Witchcraft Act of 1604* retrieved from http://www.corvardus.f9.co.uk/religion/wicca/witch1736.htm

4. Retrieved from http://echo.mpiwg-berlin.mpg.de/ECHOdocuView/ECHOzogiLib?mode=imagepath&url=/mpiwg/online/permanent/library/WX8HY2V2/pageimg

5. Also see http://www.swedenborgdigitallibrary.org/, as of January 2005, for many references on Swedenborg's life and thoughts.

6. See http://www.foodreference.com/html/html/yearonlytimeline.html, accessed as of March 17, 2005.

7. For a history of Interval, see http://www.wired.com/wired/archive/7.12/interval.html (accessed March 2005).

8. For a history of StarLab, see http://www.space-time.info/starlab/StarlabArchive.html (accessed March 2005).

REFERENCES

Alvarado, C. S. (2006). Human radiations: Concepts of force in mesmerism, spiritualism and psychical research. *Journal of the Society for Psychical Research, 70*, 138–162.

Beloff, J. (1993). *Parapsychology—A concise history*. London: Athlone Press.

Besant, A., & Leadbetter, C. (1951). *Occult chemistry; investigations by clairvoyant magnification into the structure of the atoms of the periodic table and of some compounds*. Madras, India: Theosophical Publishing. (Original work published 1908)

Boring, E. G. (1951). *History, psychology, and science: Selected papers*. New York: John Wiley and Sons.

Carington, W. (1940). Experiments on the paranormal cognition of drawings. *Proceedings of the Society for Psychical Research, 46*, 34–151.

Child, I. L. (1985). Psychology and anomalous observations: The question of ESP in dreams. *American Psychologist, 40* (11), 1219–1230.

Clarke, A. C. (1951). *The exploration of space*. London: Temple Press.

Coover, J. E. (1917). *Experiments in psychical research at Stanford University*. Palo Alto, CA: Stanford University Press.

Crabtree, A. (1993). *From Mesmer to Freud: Magnetic sleep and the roots of psychological healing*. New Haven, CT: Yale University Press.

Dodds, F. R. (1971). Supernormal phenomena in classical antiquity. *Proceedings of the Society for Psychical Research, 55*, 189–237.

Ebon, M. (1978). History of parapsychology. In M. Ebon (Ed.), *The Signet handbook of parapsychology* (p. 20). New York: New American Library/Penguin.

Ehrenwald, J. (1977). Psi phenomena and brain research. In B. B. Wolman (Ed.), *Handbook of parapsychology* (pp. 716–729). New York: Van Nostrand Reinhold.

Figar, S. (1958). The application of plethysmography to the objective study of so-called extrasensory perception. *Journal of the Society for Psychical Research, 40*, 162–172.

Freud, S. (1972). Psychoanalysis and telepathy. In R. Van Over (Ed.), *Psychology and extrasensory perception* (pp. 109–126). New York: New American Library.

Gross, C. G. (1997). Emanuel Swedenborg: A neuroscientist before his time. *The Neuroscientist, 3*(2), 142–147.

Hacking, I. (1988). Telepathy: Origins of randomization in experimental design. *Isis, 79* (3), 427–451.

Hövelmann, G. H. (1987). Max Dessoir and the origin of the word "parapsychology." *Journal of the Society for Psychical Research, 54*, 61–63.

Hughes, J. (2003, September). Occultism and the atom: The curious story of isotopes. *Physics World*, pp. 31–35.

Jordan, P. (1951). Reflections on parapsychology, psychoanalysis, and atomic physics. *Journal of Parapsychology, 15*, 278–281.

Lamm, M. (2000). *Emanuel Swedenborg: The development of his thought.* West Chester, PA: Swedenborg Foundation.

Mauskopf, S. H., & McVaugh, M. R. (1980). *The elusive science: Origins of experimental psychical research.* Baltimore: Johns Hopkins University Press.

McConnell, R. A. (1976). Parapsychology and physicists. *Journal of Parapsychology, 40,* 145–150.

Mitchell, E. (1971). An ESP test from Apollo 14. *Journal of Parapsychology, 35,* 94–111.

Myers, F. W. H. (1903). *Human personality and its survival of bodily death.* London: Longsman, Green.

Playfair, G. (2003). *Twin telepathy: The psychic connection.* New York: Vega.

Pratt, J. G., Rhine, J. B., Smith, B. M., Stuart, C. E., & Greenwood, J. A. (1940). *Extrasensory perception after sixty years.* Boston: Bruce Humphries.

Radin, D. (2006). *Entangled minds.* New York: Simon & Schuster.

Rhine, J. B. (1934). *Extra-sensory perception.* Boston: Bruce Humphries.

Roach, J. (2001, August 14). Delphic oracle's lips may have been loosened by gas vapors. *National Geographic* (online). Retrieved from http://news.nationalgeographic.com/news/2001/08/0814_delphioracle.html

Santayana, J. A. N. Ruiz de (1905). *The life of reason; or the phases of human progress.* New York: C. Scribner's Sons.

Sexton, V. S., & Misiak, H. (Eds.). (1971). *Historical perspectives in psychology: Readings.* Belmont, CA: Brooks/Cole.

Sinclair, U. (2001). *Mental radio.* Charlottesville, VA: Hampton Roads.

South China Morning Post. (1998, July 7). Retrieved from http://www.forteantimes.com/articles/115_sonypsi.shtml

Tao, W. (1996). Colour terms in Shang oracle bone inscriptions. *Bulletin of the School of Oriental and African Studies, 59* (1), 63–101.

Thomas, K. (1971). *Religion and the decline of magic.* London: Weidenfeld & Nicolson.

Tolaas, J., & Ullman, M. (1979). Extrasensory communication and dreams. In B. B. Wolman (Ed), *Handbook of dreams: Research, theories and applications* (pp. 168–202). New York: Van Nostrand Reinhold.

Turing, A. M. (1950). Computing machinery and intelligence. *Mind, 59,* 433–460.

Vasiliev, L. (2002). *Experiments in mental suggestion.* Charlottesville, VA: Hampton Roads. (Original work published 1963)

Warcollier, R. (1921). *La télépathie, recherches expérimentales.* Paris: F. Alcan.

Warcollier, R. (2001). *Mind to mind.* Charlottesville, VA: Hampton Roads. (Original work published 1948)

Wolman, B. B. (1977). Mind and body: A contribution to a theory of parapsychological phenomena. In B. B. Wolman (Ed.), *Handbook of parapsychology* (pp. 861–879). New York: Van Nostrand Reinhold.

Woods, R. L. (Ed.). (1947). *The world of dreams, an anthology.* New York: Random House.

"Children of Light" (© Dierdre Luzwick. Used by permission.)

CHAPTER 2

Attributions about Impossible Things

James E. Alcock

Alice laughed: "There's no use trying," she said; "one can't believe impossible things."
"I daresay you haven't had much practice," said the Queen. "When I was younger, I always did it for half an hour a day. Why, sometimes I've believed as many as six impossible things before breakfast."

Lewis Carroll

Parapsychologists believe in "impossible" things. By definition, their subject matter involves phenomena that cannot possibly occur if modern materialistic science has things right. And the first goal of parapsychology is to demonstrate that these supposedly impossible things—purported paranormal abilities such as extrasensory perception, psychokinesis and the like—are indeed real and not impossible after all. If they are demonstrated to be correct, the laws of physics as we know them will have been shown to be terribly wrong in some very important respects.

Has the case for the reality of the paranormal been made? There is a spectrum of confidence amongst parapsychologists in this regard: Some believe that conclusive evidence has already been produced, while others are less certain, and still others opine that a solid scientific case has not been made at all, but remain hopeful that this can be achieved one day. On the other hand, much to the chagrin of parapsychologists, the mainstream scientific community continues to reject or simply ignore their claims and their evidence.

Attributions play a vital role in how we make sense of a very complicated world. We constantly seek the causes of significant events, and we often feel uneasy, and sometimes even very distressed, if we cannot find a likely cause for a significant event. Imagine that if, while making breakfast, a rather energetic toaster pops the toast a few inches into the air. Nothing paranormal there. But suppose the toast does not fall down again, and instead remains suspended in the air a few inches above the toaster. Not many people would be able to simply chalk this up to being a "strange anomaly" and go on about their normal day. Nor is it likely that anyone would conclude that the "law of gravity" was suspended for a moment, here, in one's own kitchen. Instead, most would be astonished, even troubled, and would seek out an explanation: Wave one's hands above the toast to see if someone rigged up a thread to hold the toast in the air and look around to see if one is being filmed by a candid camera for the amusement of others. It would no doubt be a relief if young nephew Billy emerged from a closet and explained how he had played a trick.

So it is with the strange events of a mental nature that almost everyone encounters from time to time, and the subject matter of parapsychology relates directly to a range of such experiences: One thinks for the first time in a long while about a distant relative, who then telephones a short while later; a dream of an airplane crash is followed the next day by a newspaper reports of just such a tragedy; the gambler wishes for "snake eyes" and after rolling the dice, sure enough, they come up; one grieves over the recent death of a loved one, whose presence is then felt nearby. Such experiences are very striking, even though they can be produced by our brains without anything paranormal being involved (Alcock, 1981), most people faced with such experiences are not only unaware of possible normal explanations, but are in any case too emotionally moved by the event to consider any "normal" explanation to be reasonable. It may be relatively easy for the scientist who doubts or denies the existence of paranormal phenomena to accept as sheer coincidence the fact that his or her dream about a car accident was followed the next day by news that a friend had been injured in a vehicle pile-up. However, for most people, the "coincidence" would be too great, and it would call out for a more arcane explanation—"extra-sensory perception" perhaps? Thus, in the absence of a "reasonable" normal explanation, the strange experience is attributed to the paranormal. Once having made the extrasensory perception attribution, the experience will now likely serve, in a circular manner, as evidence that extrasensory perception really occurs.

Important attributions are also made in the course of formal parapsychological pursuits. First of all, there are the attributions about parapsychological data themselves. When a statistically significant effect is noted in a guessing task, to what is the extra-chance result attributed? So long as the experimental procedure seems appropriately well-controlled, the parapsychological advocate is likely to attribute it to extrasensory perception (or perhaps even psychokinesis), while the counter-advocate is more likely to make an attribution in terms of undiscovered experimenter error, procedural flaws or even fraud. In fact, both sorts of attributions involve an interpretive leap from the data themselves, a leap guided by prior belief.

Attributions are also made regarding the continuing rejection of parapsychology and its data by most scientists. While the scientists are likely to attribute this state of affairs both to the absence of persuasive data and to the incompatibility of parapsychological claims with modern scientific theory, parapsychologists on the other hand typically attribute it to dogmatism rooted in the belief that paranormal phenomena are impossible because their existence would violate the laws of physics. Britain's Society for Psychical Research expresses this position clearly:

> Opposition to psychical research is often against its implications and not the quality of the evidence. The evidence of psychical research, if accepted, challenges the fundamental assumptions about how the world works generally accepted by the scientific community. (Society for Psychical Research, 2009)

Parapsychologists also have made other attributions regarding the failure of parapsychology to gain admission into mainstream science. For example, it has been suggested that scientists react negatively because of the anxiety that they would experience were the phenomena actually real (e.g., Eisenbud, 1946; Irwin, 1989; LeShan, 1966; Wren-Lewis, 1974), and it has been further suggested that this negativity may be due to an unconscious fear of their *own* psychic powers (Tart, 1982, 1984). Yet others have attributed continuing skepticism both to worries about competition for scarce research funds (Carter, 2006), and, in the case of psychologists, to anxiety about the "unwanted implications" that scientific acceptance of paranormal phenomena would have for their own science (Parker, 2003).

While such attributions about scientists' motives may appear reasonable to the parapsychologist, they fall far wide of the mark in terms of what is really going on. These misattributions unfortunately serve to insulate the parapsychological researcher from an understanding of why parapsychology has such difficulty being heard in the hallways of science, and they preclude due consideration to valid critiques that might promote better research. Of course, parapsychologists who strive to be careful scientists find tiresome and insulting the flip and unsupported comments of some critics, who automatically attribute their experimental data to sloppiness or fraud. However, it needs to be understood that careful critics who make every effort to digest the very extensive parapsychological literature also find it tiresome and insulting to have their methodological criticisms framed as reflections of dogmatic bias or ignorance or underlying anxiety. Such attributions on either side of the dispute about the paranormal serves no one well.

It is simply wrong to claim that parapsychology's entry into the hallways of science is barred by scientific bigotry. Indeed, there have been a number of scientists over the years who have taken an interest in parapsychological matters, to the extent that they have conducted their own research (Alcock, 1987) but then later abandoned it when their data showed no evidence of paranormality (e.g., Jeffers, 2003). Parapsychologists who strive to be good scientists must consider the very real possibility that their scientific critics may be correct, at least some of the time. That does not mean that they should abandon parapsychological research, but it does mean that they should take seriously the methodological critiques provided by knowledgeable critics, for only in that way can their procedures be improved, and the opportunity to provide robust evidence of the paranormal, if it exists, be realized. It would also be wise to take seriously the *possibility* that there are no paranormal phenomena after all.

If it is not ignorance or anxiety or dogmatism, why does mainstream science continue to ignore or reject parapsychology? There are a number of reasons and they relate to some serious and somewhat overlapping problems that plague parapsychological research, as I have previously discussed (Alcock, 1986, 1987, 1990, 2003, 2010).

AMBIGUOUS DEFINITION OF SUBJECT MATTER

The subject matter of parapsychology is rather difficult to narrow down, and there is no clear consensus amongst parapsychologists as to which phenomena fall within its proper realm. Some researchers would limit the range of subject matter to putative phenomena such as telepathy, clairvoyance, remote viewing, psychokinesis, psychic healing, and precognition (as listed on the web page of the *Parapsychology Association*—www.parapsych.org), but others would want to include a host of other supposed phenomena including channelling, post-mortem survival, dowsing, poltergeists, ghosts, and the like (as is listed on the web page of the *American Society for Psychical Research*—www.aspr.com). The web page of Britain's *Society for Psychical Research* describes subject matter that includes paranormal healing, mediums, and near-death and out-of-body experiences.

More telling, perhaps, is that fact that parapsychologists have never advanced to the point that they can rule out certain phenomena as being fanciful and unlikely to exist. Yet, interest in some phenomena has waxed and waned and then waxed again. For instance, in the late 1800s and early 1900s, psychical researchers devoted much of their research to the study of mediums and their supposed communication with spirits. However, such inquiry was all but abandoned when no solid evidence was forthcoming and fraudulent mediums seemed to be the order of the day. One might have thought that that would be the end of it, but not so, for it is back with us once more. Recent studies of mediumistic communication with spirits are finding their way into the parapsychological literature (e.g., Beischel, 2007; Keen, Ellison, & Fontana, 1999). Again, psychologists at the beginning of the twentieth century (e.g., Coover, 1913) explored whether individuals can detect when they are unknowingly being stared at, and came to the conclusion that there is no such effect. At that point, research into "psychic staring" ceased, and it was no longer considered to be a psychic phenomenon. Now, it too is back for, once again, some parapsychologists are conducting research into psychic staring (e.g., Schlitz & LaBerge, 1997).

The hodgepodge of subject matter in parapsychology also makes it more difficult to attract mainstream scientists to the parapsychological research literature.

Elaborate studies involving careful attempts to control extraneous variables while focusing on a relatively narrow range of phenomena appear alongside relatively loose studies of psychic staring, spirit communications, and the psychic abilities of cockroaches (Schmidt, 1979), brine shrimp (Schmidt, 1974), and plants (Edge, 1978). It seems as if nothing is too bizarre for serious parapsychological consideration. No doubt, many mainstream scientists find it difficult to take seriously research about extrasensory perception when studies of psychokinesis operating backwards in time. The same goes for the so-called "checker effect" whereby data that has already been recorded can be altered psychically by the person who checks and analyzes it (e.g., Weiner & Zingrone, 1989). If one examines recent issues of the *Journal of Parapsychology*, American parapsychology's leading research journal, one finds research reports on such subjects as the effects of a "healer" on the growth of lettuce seeds (Roney-Dougal & Solfvin, 2003), a laboratory study of the *I Ching*, ("... *the significant sheep-goat effect does suggest that I Ching usage does involve some kind of paranormal process,*" Storm, 2006, p. 139), the influence of the earth's geomagnetic field on the retardation of the hemolysis of red blood cells (Palmer, Simmonds-Moore, & Baumann, 2006), and a discussion of methodology for the laboratory study of mediumistic communication (Beischel, 2007). Not only does this minimize the likelihood of being taken seriously by mainstream scientists, but this generosity in regard to what is appropriate subject matter both reflects and fosters a lack of focus on fundamental phenomena, whatever they may be.

NEGATIVE DEFINITION OF CONSTRUCTS

Not only does parapsychology have difficulty in deciding just what is its legitimate subject matter, but unlike the various domains of mainstream science, it deals exclusively with phenomena that are only negatively defined. Extrasensory perception? It can be said to occur only when all normal sensory communication can be ruled out. Psychokinesis? It is claimed to have occurred when an individual can produce effects on the physical environment without the application of any known force. Such definitions tell us not what the phenomena are, but only what they are not.

This total reliance on negative definitions means that a claimed demonstration of parapsychological effects must be accompanied by the assurance that no "normal" processes were in operation that could account for the data. The problem is, researchers are not always aware of all "normal" processes that might be at play. Given that the claim requires the assumption that all normal explanations have been ruled out, such claims understandably need much more scrutiny than is usually necessary in other areas of scientific research. Thus, a critical spotlight is focused onto possible design errors, methodological flaws, statistical oversights, over-interpretation of data, and at times, even fraud. This is only appropriate, in light of the negative definition of the phenomena. Those parapsychologists who criticize scientist-critics for devoting more effort to seeking out faults in parapsychological methodology than they do when vetting other areas of research somehow fail to appreciate the need for great caution in examining claims based on negative definitions, claims which stand in contradiction with what conventional science tells us about the world.

MISLEADING CONCEPT OF ANOMALY

Scientific discovery is driven by anomalies, that is, marked inconsistencies between theory and observation. Much attention has been given by philosophers of science to the role that such anomalies have played in bringing about major changes in scientific understanding. While it is not surprising that parapsychologists should like to frame their data in the mantle of scientific anomaly, the application of this term to parapsychological data is inappropriate. An anomaly in mainstream science is something that is both reliably observable and that stands in sharp contradiction to current scientific theory. A famous example is that of the precession of Mercury, which can be observed even by amateur astronomers. This precession was inconsistent with Newtonian mechanics, and yet it was clearly "real," in light of the reliability of observations. Scientists simply lived with this anomaly until Einstein's relativity theory came along and accommodated the precession and made sense of it. This success in dealing with the precession was an important factor leading to the acceptance of relativity theory and the subsequent paradigm shift in physics.

Anomalies in parapsychology are nothing of the sort. First of all, there is no well-articulated theory in parapsychology against which data can be judged to be anomalous. Just as important, even were such a theory to exist, there is no body of reliable observations that could be taken to constitute an anomaly.

Before leaving the subject of anomalies, one must wonder why it is, if parapsychological phenomena do really exist, that they do not present themselves in the very delicate experiments conducted in modern physics. Physicists differ in their predictions, expectations, moods, desires, and personalities, and yet no paranormal anomaly ever shows up in their careful, precise data. They find nothing that would suggest that the outcome of an experiment has been influenced by the mind, the mood, or the expectations of the experimenter.

LACK OF REPLICABILITY

Replication serves as a vital check in mainstream science; it leads to eventual confidence that a phenomenon is real. When it was claimed, for example, that nuclear fusion (so-called "cold" fusion) had been produced in tabletop laboratory apparatus (Fleischmann et al., 1990), a claim that flew in the face of physicists' beliefs that fusion can only occur at extremely high temperatures, hundreds of scientists immediately set out to try to replicate these startling results. In the end, failure to replicate combined with the discovery of apparent flaws in the original procedure consigned cold fusion to the scientific dustbin. (There are still some researchers who believe that there was indeed cold fusion involved, and they continue to pursue it. Regardless whether they ultimately prove to be correct, the point is that, without replicability by neutral others, scientists are not likley to pay much attention to the claims being made).

However, despite claims to the contrary, there has not been a single demonstration of paranormal phenomena that neutral scientists with the appropriate knowledge and skills can reproduce for themselves. Some parapsychologists acknowledge this problem: Watt and Irwin (2010) wrote that " . . . parapsychologists are not yet able to specify the testing conditions that would allow other researchers, skeptics included, to be able to demonstrate for themselves reasonably reliable evidence in support of the ESP hypothesis" (p. 58). And Parker (2010), in discussing psychokinesis (PK), concluded:

> Clearly PK cannot be considered in any sense demostable or "proven" on such shaky data as these. It becomes ironic that, despite all the enormous efforts, the best supporting data appear to come from studies of phenomena outside the laboratory, such as with so-called macro-PK and through the testing of specially selected individuals or groups. The purpose of the retreat to laboratory studies was to enable incontrovertible evidence of PK to be found, but this has not occurred. (p. 70)

MULTIPLICATION OF ENTITIES

"Ockham's razor"—"*Pluralitas non est ponenda sine neccesitate*" ("Plurality should not be posited without necessity")—refers to the generally accepted scientific practice of avoiding the introduction of new explanatory concepts when existing concepts are sufficient. Unfortunately for parapsychologists, their constructs cannot resist the blade of Ockham's razor. The constructs involve processes that are unheard of in normal science, processes that are vaguely-described and negatively defined, and that often provide *ad hoc* explanations that serve to explain away inconsistencies in the data or the absence of significant findings. The so-called *psi-experimenter effect* is one example. This "effect" is used to describe a situation where different parapsychologists have obtained dissimilar results after carrying out the same experiment, especially if one researcher obtained a statistically significant effect while the other did not. However, this "effect," which is in reality nothing other than a descriptive label, is then taken to reflect a quality of paranormal processes. When different researchers follow the same procedures but obtain disparate results in mainstream science, they do not suggest a new arcane force or process to account for it, but conclude that there are methodological problems in the empirical approach. The history of science has repeatedly taught that phenomena that are claimed to be observable but only by the motivated few, thereby rendering the observations impossible to replicate or falsify, are unlikely to be worthy of further study.

There are other such effects in parapsychology. For example, the *psi-missing effect* and the *decline effect* are invoked as explanations as to why significantly poorer results were obtained by an individual than were expected by chance, and the *sheep-goat effect* is claimed when those who believe that paranormal processes exist are found to be more successful in a parapsychological experiment than those without such belief. The invocation of such arbitrary constructs to explain away failed predictions and inconsistencies in the data raises a red flag to just about any scientist.

UNFALSIFIABILITY

Although it cannot be applied as a check in every area of science, falsifiability provides an important means for the vetting of most claims. Generally, a theory or claim that cannot be empirically falsified is of little or no use. I can tell you that I have an invisible elf sitting on my knee, and that only those whose hearts are pure can see him or detect his presence in any way. Such a claim cannot be falsified, for there is nothing that one can do to demonstrate that I am wrong. There is a similar problem in parapsychology, for there is no way to show that a parapsychological claim is false. If predicted parapsychological phenomena are not observed in a given experiment, this can be explained away, either by means of one of the *ad hoc* constructs discussed above, or simply in terms of the belief that such phenomena are capricious and not subject to the regularities observed in the normal world.

UNPREDICTABILITY

Predictability is a central part of scientific understanding. Scientists may not fully understand what underlies gravitational attraction, but they can predict its effects with great accuracy. All competent researchers will obtain similar results when studying gravitational influences. This reliable predictability infuses them with confidence that their concept of gravity is correct, even if it is limited.

That stands in strong contrast to the situation in parapsychology, where unpredictability is the order of the day. It is this unpredictability that makes replication so elusive. Add to that the fact that paranormal processes are apparently unaffected by distance or time or physical materials, they cannot be blocked or attenuated, and therefore parapsychologists cannot even tell us under what circumstances they will not occur. Some parapsychologists recognize the seriousness of this problem. Parapsychologist Adrian Parker (2003) referred to it as "an intractable problem in parapsychology. Until we can predict such outcomes ahead of time, the establishment of lawful relationships still evades us" (p. 127).

LACK OF PROGRESS

Every normal science builds over time. A student of physics or chemistry or biology or astronomy would be ill-advised to base his or her studies only on textbooks written a decade ago. While many fundamental principles remain unchanged, scientific knowledge and scientific methodology expands and becomes more refined over time. The development of more sophisticated methodology and equipment leads to ever more sensitive measurements, and this in turn produces refinements of theory and ultimately even more precise and reliable data.

Alas, this is not the situation in parapsychology. Even though parapsychologists have over the years developed new methodologies and have employed more sophisticated statistical analyses, effect sizes have not increased across the years. While some parapsychologists have devoted much of their professional lives to the pursuit of the paranormal—people such as such as Gurney, Myers, the Sidgwicks, the Rhines, Honorton, and many others—there is no stronger a scientific case for paranormal phenomena now than there was a century ago. Rather than taking this as a sign that the sought-after phenomena do not exist, parapsychologists choose instead to see this lack of progress as a reflection of the deep and continuing mystery that surrounds the paranormal.

METHODOLOGICAL WEAKNESSES

The conflict between parapsychologists and their critics is usually cast in disputes about the adequacy of methodology. Given that paranormal phenomena are only defined negatively, then it is absolutely critical that methodological flaws and statistical inadequacies can be ruled out. Yet, it is not easy to design and conduct parapsychological research that is free of methodological flaws, and one can never even be sure that one is aware of all possible flaws. Thus, it is not surprising that extremely few parapsychological studies are exempt from methodological criticism.

Sophisticated parapsychologists are aware of this problem. In defence, some of them try to flip the problem around, arguing that the onus falls upon a critic who discovers a methodological problem to demonstrate that the problem could account for the observed effect. Yet, this defence is weak in the extreme, and would be considered preposterous in mainstream science. The onus is on the researcher to eliminate the problem and run the experiment again. Naturally, given the replicability problem, parapsychologists generally are reluctant to follow such advice.

RELIANCE ON STATISTICAL DECISION-MAKING

Statistical analysis is a powerful tool for the analysis of data, but it can never speak to the existence or nonexistence of paranormal phenomena. Statistical decisions allow us to make reasoned explanations of empirical data, but in choosing those explanations, we are making a jump, an extrapolation, from the realm of numbers in the statistical world to the processes and events of the real world. Statistical conclusions can never tell us, for example, that extrasensory perception occurrred, but only that the results departed significantly from what one would expect on the basis of chance alone. A significant departure from chance in a guessing experiment might be attributed to any number of things: perhaps the participant employed extrasensory perception; or maybe there were flaws in the procedure or in the statistical analysis; or either the participant or the experimenter cheated but avoided detection; or Zeus exists and likes to taunt parapsychologists by producing extra-chance results in an unpredictable manner. The statistical process, the statistical decision cannot help us choose among such competing hypotheses. Therefore, in the absence of well-articulated theory and a body of replicable research to back it up, statistical departures from chance simply cannot give support to the existence of paranormal phenomena.

PROBLEM OF THEORY

I have made several references to the absence of well-articulated theory in parapsychology. Such theory plays a central role in normal scientific research. For example, astronomers no longer dispute the existence of black holes, even though they have not been (and presumably cannot be, because of their nature) directly observed. They have come to accept their existence because they were predicted by a mathematically precise theory that has proven itself in other domains, and their existence is consistent with a body of reliable but indirect observations.

Although parapsychology lacks formal theory supported by solid data that could provide such guidance, this does not mean that it has no theories at all. Many theories have been proposed, although none with the precision of general physical theories, including among others, Stanford's (1990) Conformance Behaviour Model; Decision Augmentation Theory (May, Utts, & Spottiswoode, 1995); Walker's (1984) quantum mechanical theory; Thermal Fluctuation Model (Mattuck, 1982), Schmidt's (1975) mathematical theory of psi, and Statistical Balancing Theory (Pallikari, 2003). However, each of these theories is really nothing more than an *ad hoc* effort to explain something the theoretician assumes to exist. Contrast this with normal science: the theory that predicted black holes had already proved its adequacy with regard to many other well-understood phenomena. It was not developed with the purpose of predicting or explaining black holes.

DISINTEREST IN COMPETING, NORMAL HYPOTHESES

Often when advocates and counteradvocates wrestle over the subject matter and the research of parapsychology, both sides often throw out the baby with the bathwater. After all, most people sooner or later have some very strange experiences in their lives that lack any obvious normal explanation. Parapsychologists are likely to support a paranormal explanation, while counteradvocates are more likely to challenge such explanations. In the meantime, the "experience" is real to the person, regardless of attributions concerning its cause. In a more reasonable world, one might expect that advocates and counteradvocates alike would want to focus their efforts on coming to understand such experiences, regardless of what the explanation turns out to be, but there is an obvious lack of interest within parapsychology to explore such non-paranormal explanations. This is regrettable for it adds weight to my contention that parapsychology represents beliefs in search of data, rather than data in search of explanation.

FAILURE TO JIBE WITH OTHER AREAS OF SCIENCE

Parapsychology by its very nature stands in contradiction to basic principles in mainstream science. There is nothing in physics or neurology that would allow for processes such as extrasensory perception or psychokinesis or other putative paranormal phenomena. This is unlike any area in normal science: biochemical knowledge does not violate the basic principles of physics; chemistry and genetics do not produce grossly conflicting results; biological data is in line with all three of those sciences; geology and astronomy work happily together. While there may be disputes between disciplines at the leading edges of scientific discovery, the diverse areas of science basically jibe with one another.

The failure of parapsychology to jibe with normal science does not in and of itself mean that parapsychology is in error. However, as the late and eminent neuropsychologist Donald Hebb (1978) pointed out, were parapsychology's claims to prove to be true, then there is something horribly and fundamentally in error in physics and in biology and in neuroscience. While that is not impossible, the evidence supporting the modern scientific overview in those disciplines is in most respects overwhelming, and thus it should not be surprising that most scientists will demand very strong and reliable evidence from parapsychologists before taking the reality of the paranormal seriously.

These 13 reasons to remain skeptical about the paranormal seem to me to be very reasonable, and at the very least, one should expect that parapsychological researchers interested in pursuing truth would acknowledge their reasonableness. Rather than arguing about such concerns, parapsychologists could instead focus on the need to run methodologically refined experiments that produce replicable data. Do so, and scientists will listen. That is, if the data are there.

It reflects a triumph of hope over experience that so many have continued to devote themselves to parapsychological research over such long periods of time despite both the absence of theoretical or empirical progress and the continuing rejection by mainstream science. However, given that it is impossible to prove that the paranormal does *not* exist, one might expect that such optimism, and the search that it fuels, will continue long into the future. After all, even if it is indeed the case that paranormal phenomena do not exist, it is difficult to conceive of anything that would lead most parapsychologists to come to that recognition. Instead, the belief in the reality of the paranormal that has sustained parapsychologists across the past century continues to flow in abundance.

As discussed above, the parapsychological quest is motivated not by scientific theory, nor by anomalous data produced in the course of mainstream science. Rather, it is motivated by deeply-held beliefs on the part of the researchers—belief that the mind is more than an epiphenomenal reflection of the physical brain, belief that it is capable of transcending the physical limits normally imposed by time and space. It is this belief in the possibility of such impossible things that sustains parapsychology and leaves it relatively undaunted by the slings and arrows of (yes, sometimes outrageous) criticism. And it is this belief that all too often blinds researchers to the possibility that extrasensory perception, psychokinesis, and other paranormal phenomena perhaps really are impossible after all.

REFERENCES

Alcock, J. E. (1981). *Parapsychology: Science or magic?* Oxford: Pergamon Press.

Alcock, J. E. (1986). Parapsychology's past eight years: A lack-of-progress report. In K. Frazier (Ed.), *Science confronts the paranormal* (pp. 20–27). Buffalo: Prometheus Books.

Alcock, J. E. (1987). Parapsychology: Science of the anomalous or search for the soul? *Behavioral and Brain Sciences, 10,* 553–565.

Alcock, J. E. (1990). *Science and super nature.* Buffalo, NY: Prometheus Books.

Alcock, J. E. (2003). Give the null hypothesis a chance. Reasons to remain doubtful about the existence of psi. In J. E. Alcock, J. Burns, & A. Freeman (Eds.), *Psi wars* (pp. 29–50). London: Imprint Academic.

Alcock, J. E. (2010). The parapsychologist's lament. In S. Krippner & H. Friedman (Eds.), *Mysterious minds: The neurobiology of psychics, mediums and other extraordinary people* (pp. 35–43). Santa Barbara, CA: Praeger.

Beischel, J. (2007). Contemporary methods used in laboratory-based mediumship research. *Journal of Parapsychology, 71,* 37–69.

Carter, C. (2006). Review of [*Extraordinary knowing: Science, skepticism, and the inexplicable powers of the human mind*] by E. L. Mayer. *Journal of Parapsychology, 70,* 391–399.

Coover, J. E. (1913). The feeling of being stared at. *American Journal of Psychology, 24,* 570–575.

Edge, H. L. (1978). Plant PK on an RNG and the experimenter effect. In W. G. Roll (Ed.), *Research in parapsychology 1977* (pp. 169–174). Metuchen, NJ: Scarecrow Press.

Eisenbud, J. (1946). Telepathy and problems of psychoanalysis. *Psychoanalytic Quarterly, 15,* 32–87.

Fleischmann, M., Pons, S. Anderson, M. W., Li, L. J., & Hawkins, M. (1990). Calorimetry of the palladium-deuterium-heavy water system. *Journal of Electroanalytical Chemistry, 287,* 293–348.

Hebb, D. O. (1978), Personal Communication, cited in Alcock, J. E. (1981), *Parapsychology: Science or Magic?* New York: Pergamon.

Irwin, H. J. (1989). On paranormal disbelief: The psychology of the sceptic. In G. K. Zollschan, J. F. Schumaker, & G. F. Walsh (Eds.), *Exploring the paranormal: Perspectives on belief and experience* (pp. 305–312). Bridgeport, Dorset, England: Prism Press.

Jeffers, S. (2003). Physics and claims for anomalous effects related to consciousness. *Journal of Consciousness Studies, 10,* 135–152.

Keen, M., Ellison, A., & Fontana, D. (1999). The Scole report. *Proceedings of the Society for Psychical Research, 58,* 220.

LeShan, L. (1966). Some psychological hypotheses on the non-acceptance of parapsychology as a science. *International Journal of Parapsychology, 8,* 367–385.

Mattuck, R. D. (1982). Some possible thermal quantum fluctuation models for psychokinetic influence on light. *Psychoenergetics, 4,* 211–225.

May, E. C, Utts, J. M., & Spottiswóode, S. J. P. (1995). Decision Augmentation Theory: towards a model of anomalous phenomena. *The Journal of Parapsychology, 59,* 195–220.

Pallikari, F. (2003). Must the "magic" of psychokinesis hinder precise scientific measurement? *Journal of Consciousness Studies, 10,* 199–219.

Palmer, J., Simmonds-Moore, C. A., & Baumann, S. (2006). Geomagnetic fields and the relationship between human intentionality and the hemolysis of red blood cells. *Journal of Parapsychology, 70,* 275–302.

Parker, A. (2003). We ask, does psi exist? But is this really the right question and do we really want an answer anyway? In J. E. Alcock, J. Burns, J., & A. Freeman (Eds.), *Psi wars* (pp. 111–134). London: Imprint Academic.

Parker, A. (2010). The mind-body problem and the issue of psychokinesis. In S. Krippner & H. Friedman (Eds.), *Mysterious minds: The neurobiology of psychics, mediums and other extraordinary people* (pp. 65–83). Santa Barbara, CA: Praeger.

Roney-Dougal, S. M., & Solfvin, J. (2003). Field study of an enhancement effect on lettuce seeds: A replication study. *Journal of Parapsychology, 67,* 279–298.

Schlitz, M., & LaBerge, S. (1997). Covert observation increases skin conductance in subjects unaware of when they are being observed: a replication. *Journal of Parapsychology, 61,* 185–195.

Schmidt, H. (1974). Animal PK tests with time displacement. *Journal of Parapsychology, 38,* 244–245.

Schmidt, H. (1975). Towards a mathematical theory of psi. *Journal of the American Society for Psychical Research, 69,* 301–320.

Schmidt, H. (1979). Search for psi fluctuations in a PK test with cockroaches. In W. G. Roll (Ed.), *Research in parapsychology 1977* (pp. 77–78). Metuchen, NJ: Scarecrow Press.

Society for Psychical Research (2009). Downloaded on January 5, 2009 from www.spr.ac.uk/expcms/index.php?section=63

Stanford, R. G. (1990). An experimentally testable model for spontaneous psi events. In S. Krippner (Ed.), *Advances in parapsychological research, 6* (pp. 54–167). Jefferson, NC: McFarland.

Storm, L. (2006). A parapsychological investigation of the I Ching: The relationship between psi, intuition, and time perspective. *Journal of Parapsychology, 70,* 121–142.

Tart, C. T. (1982). The controversy about psi: Two psychological theories. *Journal of Parapsychology, 46,* 313–320.

Tart, C. T. (1984). Acknowledging and dealing with a fear of psi. *Journal of the American Society for Psychical Research, 78,* 133–143.

Wren-Lewis, J. (1974). Resistance to the study of the paranormal. *Journal of Humanistic Psychology, 14,* 41–48.

Walker, E. H. (1984). A review of criticisms of the quantum mechanical theory of psi phenomena. *Journal of Parapsychology, 48,* 277–332.

Watt, C. A., & Irwin, H. J. (2010). Processes underlying the phenomena of mysterious minds: Laboratory evidence for ESP. In S. Krippner & H. Friedman (Eds.), *Mysterious minds: The neurobiology of psychics, mediums and other extraordinary people* (pp. 45–63). Santa Barbara, CA: Praeger.

Weiner, D. H., & Zingrone, N. L. (1989). In the eye of the beholder: Further research on the "checker effect." *Journal of Parapsychology, 53,* 203–231.

"The Head Shop" (© Dierdre Luzwick. Used by permission.)

CHAPTER 3

Parapsychology's Achilles Heel: Persistent Inconsistency

Ray Hyman

Some contemporary parapsychologists claim that the existence of psi has been conclusively demonstrated. They argue that the evidence for this claim meets strict scientific criteria. Furthermore, they state that the evidence is independently replicable. In contrast, other contemporary parapsychologists insist that the evidence for psi is capricious, elusive, and fails to meet accepted scientific standards. In particular, they bemoan the fact that the data cannot be replicated.

These contrasting positions pose a problem for anyone who wants to make a fair assessment of the status of parapsychology. If, indeed, the evidence meets scientific standards and supports the existence of psi, then the scientific community should take parapsychological claims seriously. On the other hand if the data are elusive and incapable of being replicated, the scientific and the general communities can safely dismiss or ignore the claims for psi. Science can deal only with data and evidence that are objective, lawful, and independently replicable.

This chapter will examine both the claims that psi has been scientifically demonstrated and the opposing claims that the evidence for psi is capricious and cannot be independently replicated. My conclusions about the status of parapsychology and its potential for becoming a serious field within science will be based on this examination.

THE CLAIM THAT PSI HAS BEEN DEMONSTRATED ACCORDING TO SCIENTIFIC STANDARDS

From the founding of the (British) Society for Psychical Research (SPR) in 1882 to the present, some psychical researchers and parapsychologists have claimed that psi has been demonstrated according to strict scientific protocols. Henry Sidgwick (1882), during his presidential address to the SPR, declared that the existing research had already demonstrated the existence of parapsychological phenomena. During the span from 1882 to today, many parapsychologists have made similar claims. Other parapsychologists, in the same time period, have acknowledged and lamented the fact that the evidence failed to meet acceptable scientific standards.

Two contemporary parapsychologists have been especially noteworthy in their insistence that the evidence for a "cognitive anomaly" is compelling. Professor Jessica Utts (1995) has written that, "Using the standards applied to any other area of science, it is concluded that psychic functioning has been well established" (p. 1). Dean Radin (1997) has put the claim more forcefully: " . . . we are forced to conclude that when psi research is judged by the same standards as any other scientific discipline, then the results are *as consistent* as those observed in the hardest of the hard sciences!"(italics in the original) (p. 58).

Utts and Radin relied on meta-analyses of existing databases in parapsychology to justify their claims. Utts argued that the inconsistencies among parapsychology experiments are more apparent than real. Because of low to moderate effect sizes, the number of trials or subjects in these experiments is insufficient to obtain significant results. Meta-analysis offers a convenient way to combine several experiments in the same domain into essentially one composite with a very large number of cases. They argued that this pooled effect size has sufficiently high power to guarantee a significant outcome if a real effect underlies the several experiments.

Unfortunately, this assumption is beset with several problems. I will only mention a few. A meta-analysis is basically an exploratory rather than a confirmatory procedure. The notion of replication (or reproduction) of an experiment in the regular sciences is a prospective (or predictive) one. A successful replication is one that achieves essentially the same result that was *predicted* on the basis of a previously conducted experiment. The parapsychologists who try to justify the replicability of psi results with meta-analysis are using a *retrospective* notion. They are arguing for successful replication if a set of already completed experiments show evidence of similar effect sizes whose combined average is significantly different from chance. Replicability implies the ability to predict successfully from the results of a meta-analysis to a new set of independent data. This is where parapsychological evidence falls woefully short.

The outcomes of the meta-analyses have deeper flaws. Within the sample of studies, the effect sizes are assumed to differ from each other according to a known distribution. And, of special importance, the individual effect sizes are assumed to be independent from one another. With the exception of the autoganzfeld experiments, the studies used in the meta-analyses in parapsychology have effect sizes that are highly heterogeneous. One implication is that the standard methods of testing the combined effect size such as Stouffer's Z and the exact binomial are inappropriate and greatly exaggerate the significance of the combined effect size. Another implication is that the combined effect size from these meta-analyses is a meaningless composite.

I could cite several more difficulties with using meta-analysis to justify the reproducibility of psi effects. But the issue becomes moot when we discover that virtually all the parapsychological domains in which meta-analyses have been conducted are subject to the decline effect. As Bierman (2001) has shown, there is a significant tendency of a series of experiments that begin with positive effect sizes to steadily decline, over time, to zero. This is one reason that many contemporary parapsychologists now admit that psi effects cannot be replicated.

Instead of conducting meta-analyses on already completed experiments on the ganzfeld, for example, the parapsychologists might have tried to directly replicate the autoganzfeld experiments with a study created for the stated purpose of replication. The study would be designed specifically for this purpose and would have adequate power. In fact, such studies have been carried out. An example would be Broughton and Alexander's (1997) attempt to deliberately replicate the autoganzfeld results with enough subjects to insure adequate power. This replication failed. From a scientific viewpoint this replication attempt is much more meaningful than the retrospective combining of already completed (and clearly heterogeneous) experiments.

An even more dramatic example is the attempt to replicate the outcome of years of random event generator (REG) experiments conducted at Princeton by Robert Jahn and his associates (Jahn et al., 2000). Although Jahn's laboratory collaborated in these experiments, several of the results were gathered at independent laboratories in Europe. This attempt at direct replication has been described by parapsychologists as the most massive replication ever attempted within parapsychology. This direct attempt, as have most such attempts within parapsychology, failed. Although Jahn initially tried to save the day by pointing to a number of unpredicted, but interesting secondary effects, the outcome eventually persuaded him to join those parapsychologists who admit that the evidence for psi cannot meet scientific standards. Indeed, these parapsychologists argue that it is an important property of psi that it eludes scientific scrutiny (Atmanspacher & Jahn, 2003).

ADMISSION THAT PARAPSYCHOLOGICAL EVIDENCE FAILS THE SCIENTIFIC TEST

Regardless of where they stand on the *scientific* adequacy of the evidence for psi, all parapsychologists seem to agree that an anomaly exists. Those who admit that the evidence for this anomaly is scientifically inadequate, propose that a critical property of psi is that it cannot be captured by the scientific method. Instead, they openly or implicitly request that parapsychological evidence be given a special exemption from having to meet current scientific standards. This is most clearly spelled out in Jahn and Dunne's (2008) plea to "Change the Rules!"

The Dutch parapsychologist, Dick Bierman, reanalyzed meta-analyses in para-psychological areas such as: (1) mentally influencing the fall of dice; (2) the ganz-feld psi experiments; (3) precognition with ESP cards; (4) psychokinetic influence on RNGs; and (5) mind over matter in biological systems (Bierman, 2001). He was looking at the relationship between effect size and the date of the study. In all the areas, he found a consistent trend for the effect sizes to decrease to zero over time. Bierman also discussed the dramatic failures at direct replication of psi experi-ments. He concluded "that this failure to replicate, rather than indicating that the original findings are due to statistical flukes or errors, suggests that when con-sciousness interacts with matter, an underlying reality arises. Efforts to 'push' anomalous phenomena observed in this intermediate reality into the objective one apparently destroy the phenomena ... " (p. 269).

The German physicist and parapsychologist, Walter von Lucadou (2001), expressed similar views: "The usual classical criteria for scientific evidence are effect oriented. Experimental results of parapsychology seem unable to fulfill these requirements. One gets the impression that an erosion of evidence rather than an accumulation of evidence is taking place in parapsychology" (p. 3).

Both Bierman and von Ludacou looked to quantum mechanics for an explan-ation for the failure for parapsychological data to replicate and the decline effect. Bierman speculated on the observer effect and von Ludacou focused on the Einstein-Podolsky-Rosen paradox. The idea is that when several individuals become interested in the outcome of an attempted replication, this suppresses the expression of psi.

Atmanspacher and Jahn (2003) framed the issue in terms of first and second order frameworks. Most physical sciences function well with first order frameworks in which theories refer to physical categories. Reproducibility of results, which is essential for scientific validity and progress, is conceptually straightforward when the scientists can operate completely within a first order framework. However, complex systems—especially systems that involve mind-matter interactions require working with a second order framework. With a second order framework the situation becomes complicated. Failure to replicate a parapsychological experi-ment within a first order framework may actually be a successful replication when considered within a second order framework.

Perhaps the most daring, or, to some readers, outlandish proposal concerning the inconsistencies of parapsychological data comes from J. E. Kennedy (2003). Kennedy supplied a comprehensive overview of the many ways in which the evi-dence for psi displays its frustratingly "capricious" nature. He covered such catego-ries as psi missing and negative reliability; the shift from intended effects to unintended secondary effects; erosion of evidence and decline effects; the inverse correlation of effect size with improved methodology; the lack of practical applica-tions of psi; and the general decline in funding and research in parapsychology. Kennedy reviewed various attempts to explain these inconsistent results. He found most of them lacking in terms of plausibility and/or empirical support.

The inspiration for his own explanation comes from some observations that William James wrote in 1909, a year before he died (James, 1909/1960). James was lamenting the lack of progress during his 25 years of involvement in psychical research. He wrote that, "I am theoretically no 'further' than I was at the beginning; and I . . . have been tempted to believe that the Creator has eternally intended this department to remain *baffling*, to prompt our hopes and suspicions all in equal measure, so that, although ghosts and clairvoyances, and raps and messages from spirits, are always seeming to exist and can never be fully explained away, they also can never be susceptible to full corroboration" (p. 310). I have long been familiar with this quotation, but I have never thought that James meant it literally; he was just using a metaphor to convey his degree of frustration.

Kennedy (2003), however, gave a literal interpretation to James' words. The following quotation summarizes Kennedy's position:

> This article focuses on the characteristics of psi that appear to indicate something like an intent or mechanism that actively prevents reliable psi manifestations. Terms such as actively evasive and self-obscuring emphasize the suppression of psi effects with little attention to the possibility that periods of impressive psi effects can sometimes occur, but such effects are unpredictable. The term unsustainable indicates that impressive psi effects can occur and may have predictable patterns, but the effects cannot be sustained and may become evasive. The general approach here is that these terms may offer differing connotations for a poorly understood property of psi. (p. 54)

Although Kennedy attempted to justify his belief in a form of "higher consciousness" that somehow is deliberately orchestrating the unsustainability of psi effects, many skeptics and scientists will view Kennedy's position as a return to the pranks of the ancient Greek gods. The anti-Darwinists promote "intelligent design"; Kennedy seems to be advocating "intelligent mischief."

SIMILARITIES OF PSI CLAIMS WITH OTHER FAILED CLAIMS OF ANOMALY

Parapsychological claims of a "communications anomaly" resemble failed claims of anomalies that have challenged scientific theories throughout the history of science. Claims of N-rays, mitogenetic radiation, polywater, Martian canals, and the like now occupy the scrap heap of science. Other claims of anomalies such as the apparent defects in the orbit of Uranus, continental drift, and meteorites survived the skeptical scrutiny of scientists and became incorporated into the scientific framework. The difference between the successful and the failed claims were that the successful claims were supported with evidence that was consistent and independently repeatable. Parapsychological claims depend upon evidence that is inconsistent and apparently non-replicable.

The parapsychologists who admit that their evidence is inconsistent and non-replicable argue that the pattern of inconsistencies in their data is an inherent property of psi. This argument, unfortunately, begs the question. In addition, the patterns of inconsistency that parapsychologists claim as a unique property of psi are similar to the patterns of inconsistency that plagued the other failed claims of anomaly. The other failed claims also exhibited a decline effect, an experimenter effect, and other indicators of what the parapsychologists claim to be unique to parapsychological evidence.

DIFFERENCES BETWEEN PSI CLAIMS AND CLAIMS
OF ANOMALIES WITHIN SCIENCE

One reason that some parapsychologists can claim to have demonstrated a cognitive anomaly (i.e., psi) based on scientific evidence is because they use terms such as "anomaly" and "replicability" in ways that differ in important ways from the manner these terms are used by the scientific community. An anomaly as understood by scientists is a detailed specification of how an observation or experimental outcome deviates from a scientific prediction. Both the claimed anomalies that were ultimately accepted and those that were rejected by the scientific community were precise in this sense. Consider the anomaly that resulted in the discovery of the planet Neptune in 1846 (Grosser, 1979; Hanson, 1962). Prior to this discovery, astronomers had noticed that the perceived orbit of Uranus deviated from the orbit calculated from Newtonian mechanics. Astronomers speculated on possible causes, including that Newton's inverse square law might not hold for the farther reaches of space. The mathematician and astronomer Urbain Le Verrier realized it was fruitless to speculate until the nature of the discrepancy (i.e., the anomaly) was clearly determined.

He began by assuming that Newton's laws were inviolate. This was a reasonable assumption because all previous challenges to Newton's laws had resulted in their vindication. Le Verrier reexamined both the old and later sightings of Uranus. He recalculated the orbit from the data and discovered that previous astronomers had made several errors. When he corrected the orbit for these errors, the size of the anomaly decreased, but it did not disappear. After considering a number of possibilities, he hypothesized that the perturbation was due to a previously undetected planet beyond Uranus. His task became that of calculating the size and orbit of this planet. Because of the several unknowns, this calculation—which Le Verrier had to do laboriously by hand—required considerable time and effort. When, finally, Le Verrier announced the size, distance from the sun, orbit, and predicted location for this hypothesized planet, he could not persuade the French and the British observatories to look for his planet. However, the German astronomer Johann Gottfried Galle, a few days after receiving the coordinates from Le Verrier, looked for and found the new planet very close to the predicted location.

Now consider a second example, which also involves Le Verrier. Prior to the discovery of Neptune, Le Verrier had discovered a perturbation in the orbit of Mercury. The discrepancy was very small, but, after careful investigation, Le Verrier could not dismiss it as an error. Le Verrier fresh from his triumph of reconciling the perturbation in Uranus's orbit with Newtonian mechanics, set about to do the same for the disturbance in Mercury's orbit. He worked on this problem for 13 years before he was ready to announce his prediction of a new planet closer to the sun than Mercury. This planet would help to account for the discrepancies in Mercury's orbit (Baum & Sheehan, 1997; Fernie, 1994; Fontenrose, 1973; Hanson, 1962). A few months later, Le Verrier announced the discovery of a new planet which he named Vulcan. Unlike the observations that confirmed the existence of Neptune, the sightings that were offered as evidence for Vulcan were inconsistent and most astronomers could not detect this planet. Eventually astronomers, with the exception of Le Verrier, who insisted on the existence of Vulcan until his death in 1877, decided that Vulcan did not exist. Not until 1915 when Albert Einstein published his general theory of relativity did astronomy finally have an explanation for the anomaly of Mercury's orbit.

In the case of the discovery of Neptune, both the specific discrepancy from the predicted orbit and the subsequent explanation for this discrepancy were based on reliable and replicable data. The discrepancies in the orbit of Mercury were also based on reliable and replicable observations. However, Le Verrier's claim of a new planet, Vulcan, failed to gain scientific approval because the latter claim could not be supported by reliable and replicable evidence.

When one compares how the concept of "anomaly" is used in these two examples, we see how the parapsychologists use the term in an importantly different way. The "anomaly" that the parapsychologists point to is simply a significant deviation from a chance base-line. Because the parapsychologists lack a positive theory to constrain what sorts of departures from chance should be indicators of psi, they lack any constraints as to what sorts of deviations count as evidence for psi and which do not. Because this laxness of definition does not exclude any discrepancy, this accounts for the patchwork quilt of parapsychological evidence. Any *glitch* in a body of data can count as evidence for psi. Nothing can count as evidence for the non-existence of psi. This, of course, provides parapsychology with a non-falsifiable claim.

It is this amorphous notion of anomaly that tempts parapsychologists to claim replicability when, according to conventional scientific practice, they have non-replicability. Consider the parapsychological claims that the autoganzfeld experiments successfully replicated the original ganzfeld database (Bem & Honorton, 1994). At least two parapsychologists now agree with my assertion that the autoganzfeld experiments *failed to replicate* the original ganzfeld data base (Bierman, 2001; Hyman, 1994; Kennedy, 2001). In the original database the average effect size was derived from studies that all used static targets. The autoganzfeld experiments used both static and dynamic (action video clips) targets. Only the dynamic targets produced a significant effect. The results on the static targets were consistent with chance and differed significantly from the results on the static targets in the original data base.

Apparently the amorphous nature of the assumed communications "anomaly" entices parapsychologists into claiming any significant outcome in a repeated experiment constitutes a successful replication of the first experiment regardless of the pattern of this outcome.

CONCLUSIONS: PERSISTENCE OF PARAPSYCHOLOGY DESPITE INCONSISTENT EVIDENCE

Many other considerations point to the failure of parapsychology to establish a scientific basis for its claimed anomaly after over a century of trying. Bierman (2001) and Kennedy (2003) have provided several illustrations of how parapsychological evidence persists in its elusive and capricious nature. Alcock (2003) listed additional reasons why parapsychology has failed in its claims to have demonstrated an "anomaly." Since the beginnings of modern science, many other claims of anomaly have failed to provide evidence that was consistent and replicable. All these failed claims now occupy the discard heap of science.

These other failed claims, once the evidence for them began to show inconsistencies and failures of replication, were scrapped a few years after they had initially been put forth. Somehow parapsychology has managed to continue pursuing its claims even after a long history of inconsistent and non-repeatable evidence. One reason could be that, unlike the other failed claims, the claims of parapsychology often arise outside the scientific community. The other failed claims arose within a particular scientific framework and occurred as a very specific pattern of deviation from a scientific prediction. These apparent anomalies arose as byproducts of research aimed at exploring and extending the reach of existing theories. In contrast, parapsychological research is aimed from the outset at finding an anomaly. The anomaly that parapsychologists seek is one that allegedly challenges all sciences, not just a particular theory within a given domain.

As I have pointed out, the claimed anomaly is also so amorphous and unconstrained by a positive theory that any glitch in a body of data can be used as evidence in its favor. Such freedom to use any deviation from chance as evidence for psi creates the situation of inconsistencies and failures to replicate. It also makes the case for psi non-falsifiable. Some parapsychologists apparently hope that future changes in scientific conventions will allow for parapsychological evidence, despite these limitations, to pass muster. We can, of course, expect many changes to occur in the future of science. We can expect major paradigm shifts; new and unexpected discoveries; new ideas about time, causality, genetics, and the brain; and many other surprises. However, we cannot expect that science will forego its reliance upon evidence that is objective, lawful, and public. Independent replicability is what assures these desiderata.

Parapsychologists, at various times, have theorized about the nature of psi. As I have indicated, these theories have never been developed sufficiently to connect with parapsychological research. With no clear ways to translate from theory to data and vice versa, the theories place no constraints upon what observations count as evidence for psi and the outcomes of parapsychology experiments place no constraints upon the theories. I have mentioned some of the consequences of having such a disconnect. I think it may be worthwhile to point to another consequence which should concern parapsychologists. I find it puzzling that I have never read any discussions about this issue. I have already discussed the variations in effect size *within* individual meta-analyses. The variation of effect sizes among meta-analyses in different domains of parapsychology is more striking. In a major meta-analysis of psychokinetic affects on RNGs, the mean effect size, although very significant, was only 0.00032. The mean effect size for the early ganzfeld telepathy experiments, by comparison, was 0.28 (Bierman, 2001). Other meta-analyses report effect sizes somewhere between these two extremes. In other words, different meta-analyses in parapsychology can obtain effect sizes such that some can be 875 times larger than others! Without a coherent theory, how can parapsychologists explain such results as representing a single phenomenon called psi? So even if the results from these different meta-analyses could become replicable, serious hurdles would still bedevil parapsychology in its quest to become a scientific discipline with a coherent and reliable phenomenon.

REFERENCES

Alcock, J. E. (2003). Give the null hypothesis a chance: Reasons to remain doubtful about the existence of psi. In J. E. Alcock, J. E. Burns, & A. Freeman (Eds.), *Psi wars: Getting to grips with the paranormal* (pp. 29–50). Charlottesville, VA: Imprint Academic.

Atmanspacher, H., & Jahn, R. G. (2003). Problems of reproducibility in complex mind-matter systems. *Journal of Scientific Exploration, 17,* 243–270.

Baum, R., & Sheehan, W. (1997). *In search of planet Vulcan: The ghost in Newton's clockwork universe.* New York: Plenum Trade.

Bem, D. J., & Honorton, C. (1994). Does psi exist? Replicable evidence for an anomalous process of information transfer. *Psychological Bulletin, 115,* 4–18.

Bierman, D. J. (2001). On the nature of anomalous phenomena: Another reality between the world of subjective consciousness and the objective world of physics? In P. van Locke (Ed.), *The physical nature of consciousness* (pp. 269–292). New York: Benjamins.

Broughton, R. S., & Alexander, C. H. (1997). Autoganzfeld II: An attempted replication of the PRL ganzfeld research. *Journal of Parapsychology, 61,* 209–226.

Fernie, J. D. (1994). In pursuit of Vulcan. *American Scientist, 82,* 412–415.

Fontenrose, R. (1973). In search of Vulcan. *Journey for the History of Astronomy, 4,* 145–158.

Grosser, M. (1979). *The discovery of Neptune.* New York: Dover. (Original work published 1962)

Hanson, N. R. (1962). Leverrier: The zenith and nadir of Newtonian mechanics. *Isis, 53*(3), 339–378.

Hyman, R. (1994). Anomaly or artifact? Comments on Bem and Honorton. *Psychological Bulletin, 115,* 19–24.

Jahn, R. G., & Dunne, B. J. (2008). Change the rules! *Journal of Scientific Exploration, 22,* 193–213.

Jahn, R., Dunne, B., Bradish, G., Dobyns, Y., Lettieri, A., Nelson, R., et al. (2000). Mind-machine interaction consortium: PortREG replication experiments. *Journal of Scientific Exploration, 14,* 499–555.

James, W. (1960). The final impressions of a psychical researcher. In G. Murphy & R. D. Ballou (Eds.), *William James on psychical research* (pp. 309–325). New York: Viking. (Original work published 1909)

Kennedy, J. E. (2001). Why is psi so elusive? A review and proposed model. *Journal of Parapsychology, 65,* 219–246.

Kennedy, J. E. (2003). The capricious, actively evasive, unsustainable nature of psi:
    A summary and hypotheses. *Journal of Parapsychology*, 67, 53–74.
Radin, D. (1997). *The conscious universe: The scientific truth of psychic phenomena.*
    San Francisco: Harper Edge.
Sidgwick, H. (1882). Presidential address. *Proceedings of the Society for Psychical Research*,
    1, 7–12.
Utts, J. (1995). *An assessment of the evidence for psychic functioning.* Retrieved June 7, 2009,
    from http://anson.ucdavis.edu/~utts/air2.html
von Lucadou, W. (2001). Hans in luck: The currency of evidence in parapsychology.
    Journal of Parapsychology, 65, 3–16.

CHAPTER 4

Reflections of a (Relatively) Moderate Skeptic

Christopher C. French

INTRODUCTION

The pages that follow contain my admittedly personal reflections upon the current state of parapsychology. Lest the reader feels it to be somewhat indulgent of me to engage in such personal reflections upon what is essentially a scientific question, I should perhaps justify my approach.

My main area of research is anomalistic psychology (e.g., French, 1992, 2001, 2009). The main aim of anomalistic psychology is to try to account for the kind of bizarre experiences that people often report and label as paranormal, but without assuming that psi necessarily exists. In the spirit of John Palmer's *progressive skepticism* (Palmer, 1986), it is an attempt to produce and empirically test non-paranormal accounts of ostensibly paranormal phenomena. One of the most striking, if not surprising, conclusions from research in this area is that our personal beliefs are crucial in determining how we interpret information, from the levels of basic perception and memory up to the level of judgments about complex sets of data. I do not believe that it is possible for human beings to be unbiased when it comes to judging controversial issues such as the existence of psi and I thus make no claim to be a neutral assessor of the evidence. I think I owe it to the reader, therefore, to be completely up-front about my current position with respect to the psi debate.

I am what Palmer (1986) would call a *conventional theorist* (i.e., I have a preference for non-paranormal rather than paranormal explanations of ostensibly paranormal events). However, I can honestly say that I lived much of my life as a believer in the paranormal. As a teenager, I was enthralled by the feats of Uri Geller and delighted that scientists had allegedly validated his claims. Parapsychological topics were rarely mentioned during my days as an undergraduate psychology student, but I read around a little. In particular, I found Eysenck's arguments in support of psi very persuasive (e.g., Eysenck, 1957). My conversion to skepticism can be explained by the reading of a single book, James E. Alcock's (1981) *Parapsychology: Science or Magic?* Alcock, a social psychologist, opened my eyes to the fact that there were some quite plausible non-paranormal explanations for ostensibly paranormal events. He also made me realize that there were books and papers written by skeptics, a fact that I had not really fully appreciated until then. I took out a subscription to *Skeptical Inquirer* and my conversion from true believer to extreme skeptic was complete!

Since that time, my attitudes have mellowed somewhat and I now prefer to think of myself as a moderate skeptic (although I am pretty certain that many parapsychologists would not agree!). I am still a conventional theorist, but I am very much in favor of the continuation of mainstream parapsychological research. Some areas of parapsychology have produced positive results that are a real challenge to critics and such evidence merits (although it rarely receives) serious consideration by the wider scientific community. Moderate parapsychologists on the other side of the psi debate recognize the value of the conventional theorists' approach. They willingly acknowledge that most paranormal claims are not true instances of paranormal forces in action. My only disagreement with such investigators is at the level of "gut feelings": Whereas they feel that paranormal forces probably do exist, I feel that they probably do not. But of course I could be wrong.

It should be noted that I have used the terms *believer* and *skeptic* throughout this essay even though there are good arguments for abandoning such value-laden terms in favour of such terms as *advocate* and *counteradvocate* (or, as already referred to, *conventional theorist*) when referring to proponents and critics of paranormal claims, respectively. My reasons for doing so are that the terms *believer* and *skeptic*, although imprecise, are in common usage to refer to these two points of view. My usage of the terms should obviously not be taken to imply that those who call themselves *skeptics* do not have beliefs or that those whom we commonly refer to as believers never adopt a skeptical approach to evidence. I agree with Palmer (1986) when he calls for skepticism to be adopted by both sides in the psi debate, insofar as both advocates and counteradvocates should adopt an attitude of critical but open-minded doubt whenever they are considering any unproven claims in this domain.

THE CURRENT STATE OF PARAPSYCHOLOGY

If one were approaching the subject of parapsychology for the first time, it would seem reasonable to attempt an initial assessment of the state of the field by consulting book-length reviews. If one were simply to enter the nearest bookshop and choose a popular treatment of the paranormal, one would almost certainly end up reading an uncritical account of allegedly demonstrated paranormal phenomena. But suppose that our hypothetical seeker after truth is a little bit more sophisticated than that and realizes that you cannot believe everything you read in books. She further appreciates that publishers may well give in to the temptation to sell more books by preferentially publishing those that pander to the public's desire to believe in matters paranormal rather than to critically assess the available evidence.

Such a reader may therefore seek out books written by well-qualified academics working in established university departments in preference to those written primarily for a popular readership. Unfortunately, such books do not speak with one voice with respect to the body of evidence pertaining to paranormal claims. Dean Radin (1997), for example, clearly believes that the scientific evidence in support of the existence of paranormal forces is overwhelming and that it is only ignorance and prejudice on the part of the wider scientific community that prevents the universal acceptance of this fact (see also Radin, 2006). In his words:

> The effects observed in a thousand psi experiments are not due to chance, selective reporting, variations in experimental quality, or design flaws. They've been independently replicated by competent, conventionally trained scientists at well-known academic, industrial, and government-supported laboratories worldwide for more than a century. (Radin, 1997, p. 275)

On the other hand, the long-standing critic of parapsychology David Marks (2000) concluded, after reviewing seven areas of parapsychological research: "My own beliefs are as they are—toward the extreme of disbelief—because the evidence as I see it warrants nothing more" (p. 308).

My own current position is somewhere between the two extremes represented by Radin and Marks. I find myself in fairly full agreement with the final paragraph of a third book-length review, this time by parapsychologists Harvey Irwin and Caroline Watt (2007):

> In the final analysis what fairly can be said of parapsychology? . . . [As] far as spontaneous cases are concerned it seems likely that there are numerous instances of self-deception, delusion, and even fraud. Some of the empirical literature likewise might be attributable to shoddy experimental procedures and to fraudulent manipulation of data. Be that as it may, there is sound phenomenological evidence of parapsychological experiences and experimental evidence of anomalous events too, and to this extent behavioral scientists ethically are obliged to encourage the investigation of these phenomena rather than dismissing them out of hand. If all of the phenomena do prove to be explicable within conventional principles of mainstream psychology surely that is something worth knowing[. . .]; and if just one of the phenomena should be found to demand a revision or an expansion of contemporary psychological principles, how enriched behavioral science would be. (pp. 260–261)

In addition to the controversy over the existence of psi, parapsychology has also long been the subject of criticism concerning its scientific status. Despite the fact that in 1969 the Parapsychology Association was admitted to the prestigious American Association for the Advancement of Science, many critics have condemned parapsychology to the status of pseudoscience (e.g., Alcock, 1981; Bunge, 1991; Radner & Radner, 1982). Different commentators sometimes give different reasons for their condemnation, but as Truzzi (1996) points out, there are real problems in trying to distinguish true science from pseudoscience. Edge, Morris, Palmer, and Rush (1986) argue that it is impossible to demarcate clearly between science and pseudoscience and that one should instead consider each discipline in terms of the degree to which it meets a number of benchmarks that characterize good science. While they acknowledge that parapsychology falls a little short on some of these benchmarks, they claim that it does not completely fail on any of them. I tend to agree (French, 2009). The best research in parapsychology appears to me to be at least as scientific as that in other areas of social science, including psychology. Of course, there are many examples of shoddy research in all disciplines but it is only fair to judge a discipline on the basis of its highest quality output. In other words, I do not think that experimental parapsychologists should change their basic approach too much. The best hope for the future of parapsychology lies in adhering as strictly as possible to the basic principles of science.

WHAT ARE THE PROBLEMS THAT PARAPSYCHOLOGY NEEDS TO SOLVE TO IMPROVE THE STATE OF THE FIELD?

I am not so presumptuous as to claim that the issues I am about to discuss represent a definitive list of the most important issues for parapsychology to address. I have simply taken the opportunity to reflect on the sort of evidence that might cause a moderate skeptic such as myself to cross that threshold from thinking that psi probably does not exist to thinking that it probably does.

I would agree with the late Robert Morris (2000) that further thought needs to be given to the strengths and limitations of meta-analysis. Parapsychologists such as Radin (1997) appear to have embraced meta-analysis as providing the royal road to scientific respectability. However, it is undoubtedly true that, although meta-analysis provides an extremely powerful tool when used appropriately, it is also open to abuse (see, e.g., Eysenck, 1994). This has been highlighted recently by the debate following the publication of Milton and Wiseman's (1999) meta-analysis of 30 ganzfeld studies carried out by seven different investigators. Although Bem and Honorton's (1994) original meta-analysis of 11 ganzfeld studies appeared to provide strong evidence of a replicable anomalous cognition effect, Milton and Wiseman's analysis did not (although it should be noted that some commentators have argued that this is because many of the more recent studies were process-oriented rather than proof-oriented; Bem, Palmer, & Broughton, 2001; Storm, 2000; Storm & Ertel, 2001).

Milton (1999) discussed many potential problems with the use of meta-analysis in parapsychology. Furthermore, the debate in response to this paper (Schmeidler & Edge, 1999) reveals a wide range of opinions regarding the appropriate use of such techniques. Parapsychologists are not only carrying out an essential service for their own discipline by attempting to resolve these issues but are also helping other disciplines that employ meta-analysis. They should be applauded for this. The conclusion cannot be avoided, however, that at this stage it would appear to be premature for parapsychology to put all its eggs into the meta-analytic basket (see also Utts, 1991, and associated commentaries).

Problems in interpreting meta-analyses of parapsychological studies were again highlighted when Bösch, Steinkamp, and Boller (2006) published a meta-analysis of 380 experimental investigations of psychokinesis (PK) employing random event generators (REGs). They concluded that there was a very small but significant overall effect size, which "even if incredibly small, is of great fundamental importance" (p. 517). However, they also noted that "study effect sizes were strongly and inversely related to sample size and were extremely heterogeneous" (p. 497). They argued that the most parsimonious explanation for the results was in fact in terms of publication bias. In other words, the apparently significant result of the meta-analysis was an artefact not a reflection of a genuine psi effect. Wilson and Shadish (2006), in commenting upon their analysis, did not accept that any significant effect, no matter how small, is fundamentally important. They suggested that PK researchers should focus on producing larger effects or on specifying the conditions under which they would be prepared to accept the null hypothesis. Radin et al. (2006), in their comment, argued against the publication bias explanation but did not convince Bösch et al. that such bias is an implausible explanation of the pattern of results found in the meta-analysis. However, the latter do acknowledge that their explanation cannot be proven prior to the introduction of compulsory registration of trials.

The fact that Milton and Wiseman's meta-analysis failed to replicate the results of Bem and Honorton's meta-analysis highlights a criticism that still continues to plague parapsychology—lack of replicability. It can be reasonably argued (e.g., Utts, 1991) that old-fashioned ideas of replication, based as they are upon misunderstandings of the concepts of statistical power and statistical significance, are in many ways inferior to the consideration of patterns of effect size across different experiments and experimenters. The latter is, of course, exactly the type of information that meta-analysis can provide. But given the legitimate doubts that exist regarding the use of meta-analysis, the fact that meta-analyses can fail to replicate each other, and the fact that the results of meta-analyses can be open to different interpretations, it appears that the replicability issue has not yet been resolved for parapsychology.

Several commentators (e.g., Edge et al., 1986) have quite rightly pointed out that, contrary to popular opinion, direct replications are quite rare in all areas of science, including psychology. Furthermore, many psychological effects reported in the literature have turned out to be difficult, sometimes impossible, to replicate. This often comes as a complete revelation to new postgraduate students who, having been raised upon a diet of practical classes based upon carefully chosen, very robust effects, are shocked to discover that often they cannot even replicate the basic effects that they intended to investigate in their own research. It is argued that it is therefore unfair to single out parapsychology as a discipline that has a particular problem in this respect. Is this another example of stricter standards being applied to parapsychology than to psychology? Indeed it is—but with good reason. In some important respects, the publication of an unreplicable effect in psychology simply matters less than it matters in parapsychology. I can perhaps illustrate this by citing an example from my own research in cognition and emotion.

In 1991 Anne Richards and I (Richards & French, 1991) published results in partial support of a novel prediction from Williams, Watts, MacLeod, and Mathews (1988) regarding the effect of anxiety on implicit memory. Unfortunately, despite our best efforts we were completely unable to replicate the basic effect using other measures of implicit memory. We submitted these negative findings to a number of journals but could not get the paper accepted. The motivation to write-up and submit negative findings in psychology is never very strong, as it is more or less certain that the "best" journals would not publish them. It is doubtful that we will ever find the time to re-submit them again. Publication bias for positive results is, in my opinion, a much bigger problem within psychology than parapsychology. Needless to say, we let colleagues know informally that we were unable to replicate the effect and that we now believe the original reported effect to be unreliable, but inevitably our initial paper is still cited as offering support for the prediction by Williams et al. (1988).

Why are such unreplicable effects less important in psychology than parapsychology? Firstly, because in the fullness of time a few papers with negative results will be published—and many other experimenters will also have failed to replicate the effects but not bothered to write-up their results. Thus, word will spread along the informal networks of researchers in this area. It may take some time, but eventually it will be generally accepted that this particular interesting hypothesis is not valid. But secondly—and much more importantly—whether or not the hypothesis is valid, no radical revision of our existing scientific world view would be required. In the case of tests of the psi hypothesis, positive results would require exactly such a radical revision. It is therefore much more important that we establish whether or not the claimed effects are replicable. As Pierre-Simon Laplace once said, "The weight of the proofs must be suited to the oddness of the facts."

Furthermore, although there are many claimed effects within the psychological literature that are unreplicable, there are many which are extremely robust (e.g., visual illusions, the Stroop effect, etc.). Parapsychologists do not, unfortunately, appear to be able to demonstrate any equally robust parapsychological effect. I guess we are back at the old-fashioned notion of replicability as referring to an effect which would be reasonably likely to be demonstrated by anyone who took the time and trouble to follow the appropriate procedures. Although it may not be a very sophisticated view of replicability, there is no doubt that if parapsychologists could find the magic formula to produce such effects it would a have a huge impact on the credibility and wider acceptance of their discipline.

It is sometimes argued by critics (e.g., Glymour, 1987; Wilson & Shadish, 2006) that the effect sizes typically found in parapsychology are so tiny that no sensible person would choose to consider them paranormal as opposed to being due to some (possibly unknown) combination of ordinary factors. This has never been an argument with which I have felt particularly comfortable. If an effect is replicable and (preferably) statistically significant, it deserves an explanation. It is notable that the effect sizes typically reported in apparently well-controlled parapsychological studies are orders of magnitude less than the effects typically claimed by self-professed psychics. The crucial importance of reliably producing a convincing demonstration of even a tiny psi effect under well-controlled conditions is that to many scientists, myself included, this would require the kind of radical revision of worldview that would make at least some of the larger scale paranormal claims seem more plausible. Even though I believe that small effect sizes should be taken seriously, it goes without saying that, if parapsychologists can find some way to amplify these weak effects, this would again add to the credibility of the discipline.

Furthermore, if a way could be found to increase effect sizes this would open up the possibility of practical applications for psi. Radin (1997), amongst others, has discussed possible practical applications of psi, including applications in medicine, military and intelligence work, crime detection, business, and technology. There is little doubt that considerable amounts of money have been invested by governments, technological industries, the military, and intelligence agencies in trying to develop such applications. So far, however, there are few obvious signs of success. The research program into remote viewing carried out by the Stanford Research Institute (later known as SRI International) and Science Applications International Corporation (SAIC) was funded over a period of 24 years at a total cost of around $20 million. Regardless of the quality of evidence relating to the existence of paranormal cognition produced by this program (for contrasting evaluations, see Utts, 1996a, 1996b, and Hyman, 1996), it is clear that the funding agencies decided that any effects found were too weak to have any useful practical applications. To my mind, this appears to be somewhat at odds with many accounts of this research, which claim that some amazingly accurate accounts were obtained. It strikes me as incredible that funding would be terminated for such a promising program (with the inherent risk that other nations would gain a lead in terms of psychic warfare) if the results produced were really so impressive.

Another potentially useful application of psi would be in investments or even casino gambling (again, see Radin, 1997). This would be doubly advantageous for parapsychology: Not only would it be one in the eye for skeptics, it would also provide a useful source of funding for future research! However, despite occasional claims of success with this type of application, no sustained program of this kind appears to have been successful over the long term.

Radin (1997) noted that several high-technology companies have invested in psi research, including Sony and Bell Laboratories. There is little doubt that if a practical technological device of some kind could be produced that relied on psi for its operation, skeptics would have to admit defeat—but yet again, despite the investment of resources, nothing has yet been produced.

In summary, then, I do not ask for much: just a reliable demonstration of psi with a large effect size (although I would settle for a moderate one), preferably of the kind that will have a useful practical application! Oh, and by the way, can it be ensured that it operates successfully in the presence of skeptics so that I can actually see it with my own eyes?

ONE PRACTICAL SUGGESTION FOR PARAPSYCHOLOGISTS

Morris (2000) reviewed ten problematic aspects of parapsychology and offered six strategies for parapsychology to adopt as it entered the twenty-first century. His paper is well worth reading. I would like to quote in full his fourth strategy, which I wholeheartedly endorse:

> We need to break down the divisions between "skeptic" and "researcher." Regardless of our views, most if not all of us have a tendency to critique any research we dislike, until we find flaws, and only minimally critique research having outcomes we prefer. The playing field needs to be leveled; some very poor methodology has appeared in print when the outcomes have been agreeable to editors. Given the extensive monitoring of our own research, it seems very appropriate to monitor as well the research and writings of members of the formal skeptical community. Just as we may have much to learn from informed, intelligent criticism, so do they, as certain of them increasingly acknowledge. With time, divisions may break down rather than become exaggerated, and we can all go on with our work. Ideally, of course, serious researchers always should be prepared to adopt a skeptical stance toward their own research and that which appears confirmatory. (Morris, 2000, p. 134)

In my opinion, it appears that over the last 30 years or so there has been some improvement in the relationship between informed skeptics and parapsychologists. One of the most fruitful examples of such cooperation was undoubtedly the joint communiqué produced by Hyman and Honorton in 1986 with respect to the ganzfeld controversy. This publication laid the foundation for the methodologically superior studies which were to follow by setting out agreed minimum standards for ganzfeld work. It is particularly encouraging that this joint paper was written as a direct result of the realization by Hyman and Honorton that, despite their profound disagreement over a few central points, there were actually a lot more issues upon which they fully agreed.

The improvement in mutual understanding between informed skeptics and experimental parapsychologists, coupled with methodological improvements in the actual experiments conducted, led to a definite change in attitude in some quarters. Two or three decades ago, the general attitude of informed skeptics appeared to be that there was nothing in the experimental psi database that could not easily be explained away in terms of shoddy methodology, failure to replicate, and occasional fraud by participants or experimenters. Subsequently, some informed skeptics went so far as to admit that there was *something* interesting in the data which required explanation, but they stopped short of actually endorsing the psi hypothesis. For example, consider this statement from Hyman (1996): "I agree with Jessica Utts that the effect sizes reported in the SAIC experiments and in the recent ganzfeld studies probably cannot be dismissed as due to chance. Nor do they appear to be accounted for by multiple testing, file-drawer distortions, inappropriate statistical testing or other misuse of statistical inference" (p. 39). He went on, "Having accepted the existence of non-chance effects, the focus now is upon whether these effects have normal causes" (p. 39).

His overall assessment of the state of evidence within parapsychology was also quite positive:

> I admit that the latest findings should make [parapsychologists] optimistic. The case for psychic functioning seems better than it ever has been. The contemporary findings along with the output of the SRI/SAIC program do seem to indicate that something beyond odd statistical hiccups is taking place. I also have to admit that I do not have a ready explanation for these observed effects. Inexplicable statistical departures from chance, however, are a far cry from compelling evidence for anomalous cognition. (Hyman, 1996, p. 43)

To avoid the risk of readers getting too carried away on a wave of optimistic euphoria, I should point out that not all subsequent assessments have been quite so positive. Marks (2000), for example, argued that the experimental protocols employed in the SAIC studies were not actually as tight as the published accounts may have led one to believe. In particular, Wiseman and Milton (1998; see also May, 1998) examined the protocol used in the first SAIC remote-viewing experiment and discovered a number of potential pathways for information leakage. The SAIC team then had difficulty in reconstructing the actual details of the protocol, producing no less than five different versions. As Wiseman and Milton (1999) pointed out, "These difficulties not only make an assessment of Experiment One extremely difficult, but also call into question whether the assessors commissioned to write a US-government sponsored report on the other studies in the SAIC program [i.e., Utts and Hyman] would have been given accurate information about their unrecorded details" (p. 3).

Although critiques such as those referred to before will often be perceived by parapsychologists as having a negative impact upon their field of activity, they are nonetheless essential if the field is to progress. Parapsychologists will simply have to accept the need to record their protocols with a level of accuracy and detail that would not be expected in other fields simply because their work will be subjected to such a high level of critical scrutiny. To reinforce the point made earlier, if psychological research were to be subject to the same level of critical scrutiny doubt would probably be cast upon many (but not all) of the effects reported—but so what? Few psychological claims are as inherently extraordinary from the standpoint of conventional science as any claim to have demonstrated psi.

Conventional theorists can of course contribute to parapsychology not only by presenting informed critiques of the published literature, but by actually engaging in experiments themselves. A nice example of this is the collaboration between Wiseman, a known skeptic, and Schlitz, a parapsychologist with a good track record for producing positive psi results. Wiseman and Schlitz (1997) investigated the claim that experimenters who believe in psi will tend to get positive results whereas those who do not, will not. Using the paradigm of remote detection of staring, this is exactly what they found when they carried out two studies using the same equipment and procedures, and drawing participants from the same pool. Unfortunately, no significant effects were obtained in a subsequent study designed to replicate and investigate these experimenter effects (Schlitz, Wiseman, Watt, & Radin, 2006). It remains unclear whether the pattern of results found in the most recent experiment reflects the true state of affairs (i.e., the results of the first two studies were artifactual and psi does not operate in this context) or whether a true psi effect was operating in the first two studies that failed to manifest in the third study for some unknown reason.

Informed skeptics are few and far between (you probably need to have a certain peculiar psychological profile to be passionately interested in things in which you do not believe!). But real skepticism is not about dismissing claims without having examined the evidence (French, 2005). It is about adopting an attitude of critical doubt and attempting to evaluate as fairly as our inevitable biases will allow the evidence both for and against the claims. Although a scientific approach cannot in practice eliminate all of the effects of our biases, it is the best approach we have to try to minimize them.

In the true spirit of progressive skepticism, if a critic cannot accept that a particular claimed paranormal effect could possibly be valid, he or she can always try to replicate it. If the effect does appear to replicate, the critic might well argue that it was an artifact produced by faults in the design of the experiment. However, to be able to demonstrate empirically that a particular methodological flaw in the original research is actually sufficient to artifactually produce positive results is much more convincing than simply pointing out that such flaws exist in a protocol. There is, of course, a problem with this approach. Given the possibility of experimenter effects referred to above, the conventional theorist may be doomed to always having to rely on second-hand accounts of paranormal effects and never be able to witness them directly.

Although my own research efforts are, as stated earlier, primarily in the area of anomalistic psychology, I am happy to supervise students who wish to carry out parapsychological studies. We never get positive results. For example, I had one postgraduate student who was unsuccessful in two attempts to replicate Bierman and Radin's (1997) presentiment effect and several to obtain Klintman's (1983) time-reversed interference effect. I have supervised undergraduate projects investigating telephone telepathy, the detection of unseen gaze, dowsing, and a range of other paranormal claims—all with negative outcomes. This raises the interesting possibility for possible future empirical study that a skeptical supervisor can inhibit psi even if the actual experimenter is sympathetic to the psi hypothesis! For the time being, we are simply grateful for the enlightened policy of many parapsychology journals with respect to negative findings and look forward to the day when, in due course, these studies will be included in future meta-analyses.

REFERENCES

Alcock, J. E. (1981). *Parapsychology: Science or magic? A psychological perspective*. Oxford: Pergamon Press.

Bem, D. J., & Honorton, C. (1994). Does psi exist? Replicable evidence for an anomalous process of information transfer. *Psychological Bulletin, 115*, 4–18.

Bem, D. J., Palmer, J., & Broughton, R. S. (2001). Updating the ganzfeld database: A victim of its own success? *Journal of Parapsychology, 65*, 207–218.

Bierman, D. J., & Radin, D. I. (1997). Anomalous anticipatory response on randomised future conditions. *Perceptual and Motor Skills, 84*, 689–690.

Bösch, H., Steinkamp, F., & Boller, E. (2006). Examining psychokinesis: The interaction of human intention with random number generators—a meta-analysis. *Psychological Bulletin, 132*, 497–523.

Bunge, M. (1991). A skeptic's beliefs and disbeliefs. *New Ideas in Psychology, 9*, 131–149.

Edge, H. L., Morris, R. L., Palmer, J., & Rush, J. H. (1986). *Foundations of parapsychology: Exploring the boundaries of human capability*. Boston: Routledge & Kegan Paul.

Eysenck, H. J. (1957). *Sense and nonsense in psychology*. Harmondsworth: Penguin.

Eysenck, H. J. (1994). Meta-analysis and its problems. *British Medical Journal, 309*, 789–792.

French, C. C. (1992) Factors underlying belief in the paranormal: Do sheep and goats think differently? *The Psychologist, 5*, 295–299.

French, C. C. (2001). Why I study anomalistic psychology. *The Psychologist, 14*, 356–357.

French, C. C. (2005). Scepticism. In J. Henry (Ed.), *Parapsychology: Research into exceptional experiences* (pp. 80–89). London: Routledge.

French, C. (2009). Anomalistic psychology. In M. Cardwell, L. Clark, C. Meldrum, & A. Wadeley (Eds.), *Psychology A2 for AQA A* (4th ed., pp. 472–505). London: Collins.

Glymour, C. (1987). ESP and the big stuff. *Behavioral and Brain Sciences, 10*, 590.

Hyman, R. (1996). Evaluation of a program on anomalous mental phenomena. *Journal of Scientific Exploration, 10*, 31–58.

Hyman, R., & Honorton, C. (1986). A joint communiqué: The psi ganzfeld controversy. *Journal of Parapsychology, 50*, 351–364.

Irwin, H. J., & Watt, C. A. (2007). *An introduction to parapsychology* (5th ed.). Jefferson, NC: McFarland.

Klintman, H. (1983). Is there a paranormal (precognitive) influence in certain types of perceptual sequences? Part I. *European Journal of Parapsychology, 5*, 19–49.

Marks, D. (2000). *The psychology of the psychic* (2nd ed.). Amherst, NY: Prometheus.

May, E. C. (1998). Response to "Experiment one of the SAIC remote viewing program: A critical re-evaluation." *Journal of Parapsychology, 62*, 309–318.

Milton, J. (1999). Should ganzfeld research continue to be crucial in the search for a replicable psi effect?Part I. Discussion paper and introduction to an electronic mail discussion. *Journal of Parapsychology, 63*, 309–333.

Milton, J., & Wiseman, R. (1999). Does psi exist? Lack of replication of an anomalous process of information transfer. *Psychological Bulletin, 125*, 387–391.

Morris, R. L. (2000). Parapsychology in the 21st century. *Journal of Parapsychology, 64*, 123–137.

Palmer, J. (1986). Progressive skepticism: A critical approach to the psi controversy. *Journal of Parapsychology, 50*, 29–42.

Radin, D. (1997). *The conscious universe: The scientific truth of psychic phenomena.* New York: HarperEdge.

Radin, D. (2006). *Entangled minds: Extrasensory experiences in a quantum reality.* New York: Simon & Shuster.

Radin, D., Nelson, R., Dobyns, Y., & Houtkooper, J. (2006). Reexamining psychokinesis: Comment on Bösch, Steinkamp, and Boller (2006). *Psychological Bulletin, 132*, 529–532.

Radner, D., & Radner, M. (1982). *Science and unreason.* Belmont, CA: Wadsworth.

Richards, A., & French, C. C. (1991). Effects of encoding and anxiety on implicit and explicit memory performance. *Personality and Individual Differences, 12*, 131–139.

Schlitz, M., Wiseman, R., Watt, C., & Radin, D. (2006). Of two minds: Sceptic-proponent collaboration within parapsychology. *British Journal of Psychology, 97*, 313–322.

Schmeidler, G., & Edge, H. (1999). Should ganzfeld research continue to be crucial in the search for a replicable psi effect? Part II. Edited ganzfeld debate. *Journal of Parapsychology, 63*, 335–388.

Storm, L. (2000). Research note. Replicable evidence of psi: A revision of Milton's (1999) meta-analysis of the ganzfeld databases. *Journal of Parapsychology, 64*, 411–416.

Storm, L., & Ertel, S. (2001). Does psi exist? Comments on Milton and Wiseman's (1999) meta-analysis of ganzfeld research. *Psychological Bulletin, 127*, 424–433.

Truzzi, M. (1996). Pseudoscience. In G. Stein (Ed.), *The encyclopedia of the paranormal* (pp. 560–574). Amherst, NY: Prometheus.

Utts, J. (1991). Replication and meta-analysis in parapsychology. *Statistical Science, 6*, 363–382.

Utts, J. (1996a). An assessment of the evidence for psychic functioning. *Journal of Scientific Exploration, 10*, 3–30.

Utts, J. (1996b). Response to Ray Hyman's report of September 11, 1995, "Evaluation of a program on anomalous mental phenomena." *Journal of Scientific Exploration, 10*, 59–61.

Williams, J. M. G., Watts, F., MacLeod, C., & Mathews, A. (1988). *Cognitive psychology and emotional disorders.* Chichester, England: Wiley.

Wilson, D. B., & Shadish, W. R. (2006). On blowing trumpets to the tulips: To prove or not to prove the null hypothesis—Comment on Bösch, Steinkamp, and Boller (2006). *Psychological Bulletin, 132*, 524–528.

Wiseman, R., & Milton, J. (1998). Experiment one of the SAIC remote viewing program: A critical re-evaluation. *Journal of Parapsychology, 62*, 297–308.

Wiseman, R., & Milton, J. (1999). "Experiment one of the SAIC remote viewing program: A critical re-evaluation": Reply to May. *Journal of Parapsychology, 63*, 3–14.

Wiseman, R., & Schlitz, M. J. (1997). Experimenter effects and the remote detection of staring. *Journal of Parapsychology, 61*, 197–207.

CHAPTER 5

How I Became
a Psychic for a Day

Michael Shermer

On Wednesday, January 15, 2003, I filmed a television show with Bill Nye in Seattle, Washington, for a new Public Broadcasting Service science series entitled "The Eyes of Nye." This 30-minute segment focused on psychic claimants who allegedly can foresee the future, talk to the dead, and describe the personality traits of a person they have never met before. Although I have analyzed these claims and have written about them in *Skeptic* and *Scientific American* (e.g., Shermer, 2002), I have had very little experience in actually attempting to simulate so-called psychic readings myself. Bill and I thought it would be a worthwhile test of the effectiveness of the technique, as well as the receptivity of people to it, to see how convincing I could be armed with some knowledge of basic psychological principles.

Since the day of the taping was set just two days before, I had little time to prepare for my performance. This made me especially nervous, because I consider psychic readings as a form of acting and good acting takes talent and practice. I made matters even harder on myself by convincing Bill and the producers that we should use a number of different psychic modalities including Tarot cards, palm reading, astrology, and psychic mediumship, under the assumption that these are all "props" used to stage a psychodrama often called "cold reading" (reading someone "cold" without any prior knowledge of their personal history).

I "read" five different people, all women whom the production staff had selected and about whom I was told absolutely nothing other than the date and time of

An earlier version of this chapter was published in *Skeptic*, 10(1), 48–55, 2003.

their births (in order to prepare an astrological chart). I had no contact with any of the women until they sat down in front of me for the taping, and there was no conversation between us until the cameras were rolling. The setting was a sound stage at KCTS, the PBS affiliate station in Seattle. Since sound stages can have a rather formal feel to them, and because I believe that the set-up for a convincing psychic reading is vital to generate receptivity in subjects, I instructed the production staff to set up two comfortable chairs with a small table between them, with a lace cloth covering the table, candles on and around the table, all sitting on a beautiful Persian rug. Soft colored lighting and incense provided a "spiritual" backdrop. This was meant to be a demonstration of how psychic claimants attempt to do readings, not a scientific "experiment" with controlled conditions.

THE PARTIAL FACTS OF COLD READINGS

My primary source for all of these readings was Ian Rowland's (2003) insightful and encyclopedic *The Full Facts Book of Cold Reading*. There is much more to the cold reading process than I had previously understood before reading this book carefully to prepare for my performance.

Rowland stressed the importance of the pre-reading set-up to "prime" the subject into being sympathetic to the reading. He suggested adopting a soft voice, a calm demeanor, and sympathetic and non-confrontational body language: a pleasant smile, constant eye contact, head tilted to one side while listening, and facing the subject with legs together (not crossed) and arms unfolded. I opened each reading by introducing myself as Michael from Hollywood, calling myself a "Psychic Intuitor." I explained that my "clients" come to see me about various matters that might be weighing heavily on their hearts and minds. I added that everyone has the gift of intuition, but that I have improved mine through practice.

I also noted that "we psychics" cannot predict the future perfectly—setting up the pre-emptive excuse for later misses—by explaining how we look for general trends and "inclinations" (an astrological buzz word). I built on this disclaimer by adding a touch of self-effacing humor meant also to initiate a bond between us: "While it would be wonderful if I were a hundred percent accurate, you know, no one is perfect. After all, if I could psychically divine the numbers to next week's winning lottery I would keep them for myself!"

Since I do not do psychic readings for a living, I do not have a deep backlog of dialogue, questions, and commentary from which to draw, so I outlined the reading into the following themes that are easy to remember, the main subject areas that people want to talk about when they go to a psychic: Love, Health, Money, Career, Travel, Education, Ambitions. I also added a personality component, since most people want to hear something about their "inner selves." I used the Five Factor Model of Personality (Costa & McCrae, 1992), also known as the "Big Five," that has an easy acronym of OCEAN: *Openness to experience, Conscientiousness, Extraversion, Agreeableness,* and *Neuroticism*. Since I have been conducting personality research with my colleague Frank Sulloway (e.g., Shermer, 2002), it was easy for me to riffle through the various adjectives used by psychologists to describe these five personality traits. For example: *Openness to Experience* (fantasy, feelings, likes to travel), *Conscientiousness* (competence, order, dutifulness), *Agreeableness* (tender-minded versus tough-minded), *Extraversion* (gregariousness, assertiveness, excitement seeking), and *Neuroticism* (anxiety, anger, depression).

I began with what Rowland called the "Rainbow Ruse" and "Fine Flattery," and what similar writers more generally call a Barnum reading (offering something for everyone, as P.T. Barnum always did). I opened my readings with this general statement:

> You can be a very considerate person, very quick to provide for others, but there are times, if you are honest, when you recognize a selfish streak in yourself. I would say that on the whole you can be a rather quiet, self-effacing type, but when the circumstances are right, you can be the life of the party if the mood strikes you.
>
> Sometimes you are too honest about your feelings and you reveal too much of yourself. You are good at thinking things through and you like to see proof before you change your mind about anything. When you find yourself in a new situation you are very cautious until you find out what's going on, and then you begin to act with confidence.
>
> What I get here is that you are someone who can generally be trusted. Not a saint, not perfect, but let's just say that when it really matters, you are someone who does understand the importance of being trustworthy. You know how to be a good friend.
>
> You are able to discipline yourself so that you seem to be in control to others, but actually you sometimes feel somewhat insecure. You wish you could be a little more popular and at ease in your interpersonal relationships than you are now.
>
> You are wise in the ways of the world, a wisdom gained through hard experience rather than book learning.

According to Rowland—and he was spot on with this one—the latter statement was flattery gold. Every one of my subjects nodded furiously in agreement, emphasizing that this statement summed them up to a tee.

After the general statement and personality assessment, I went for specific comments lifted straight from Rowland's list of high probability guesses. These include items found in the subject's home:

> A box of old photographs, some in albums, most not in albums;
> Toys, books, mementoes from childhood;
> Pack of cards, maybe with a card missing;
> Notepad or message board with missing matching pen;
> Books about a hobby no longer pursued;
> Drawer that is stuck or doesn't slide properly;
> Watch or clock that no longer works;

And peculiarities about the person:

Scar on knee;
Number 2 in the home address;
Childhood accident involving water;
Photos of loved ones in purse;
Wore hair long as a child, then had a shorter haircut.

I added one of my own to great effect: "I see a white car." All of my subjects were able to find a meaningful connection to a white car. As I was reading this list on the flight to Seattle the morning of the reading, I was amazed to discover how many flight attendants and people around me validated them.

Finally, Rowland reminded his ersatz psychics that if the set-up is done properly people are only too willing to offer information, especially if you ask the right questions. Here are a few winners:

"Tell me, are you currently in a long-term relationship, or not?"
"Are you satisfied in terms of your career, or is there a problem?"
"What is it about your health that concerns you?"
"Who is the person who has passed over who you want to try to contact today?"

While going through the Barnum reading I remembered to pepper the commentary with what Rowland called "incidental questions," such as:

". . . now why would that be?"
". . . is this making sense to you?"
". . . so to whom might this refer to?"
". . . what might this link to in your life?"
". . . can you see why this might be the impression I'm getting?"

With this background, all gleaned from a single day of intense reading and note taking, I was set to perform.

THE TAROT CARD READING

My first subject was a 21-year old woman, for whom I was to do a Tarot Card reading. To prepare myself, I bought a Tarot deck created by Hermann Haindl and produced by U.S. Games Systems in Stamford, Connecticut, at the Alexandria II New Age book store in Pasadena, California. I read through the pamphlet that came with the Haindl deck, itself glossed from a two-volume narrative that presumably gives an expanded explanation of each card. The $16.00 deck is a sleek, elegantly illustrated collection of 78 cards, each of which is replete with

Figure 5.1. The Author as a Tarot Card Psychic

an astrological symbol, a Rune sign, a Hebrew letter, I Ching symbols, and a compilation of mythic characters.

I selected a total of ten cards including, for dramatic effect, the death card for my presentation.

At a total of 78 cards there was no way that I could memorize all the "real" meanings and symbols, so the night before I sat down with my family and read through the instruction manual. We did a reading together, going through what each of the 10 cards I had selected to use is supposed to mean. My daughter then quizzed me on them until I had them down pat. I used what is called the "Hagall Spread," where you initially lay out four cards in a diamond shape, then put three cards on top and three more on the bottom. The individual cards in the spread is supposed to indicate various life issues, such as "The General Situation," "Spiritual History," "The Helper," and "The Teacher."

However, by the time of the reading, I forgot all of this, so I made up a story about how the center four cards represent the present, the top three cards represent the future, and the bottom three cards are the characters that are going to help someone get to that future. I was glad, however, that I had memorized

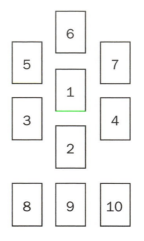

Figure 5.2. The Hagall Spread of Tarot Cards

the meanings of the symbols and characters on the cards I used because my subject told me that she had previously done Tarot card readings herself. (Since the card reader is supposed to have the client shuffle the Tarot cards ahead of time to insert her "influence" into the deck, I palmed my memorized cards and then put them on top of the newly shuffled deck.)

Since this subject was my first reading I was somewhat stiff and nervous, so I did not stray far from the standard Barnum reading. I worked my way through the Big Five personality traits fairly successfully (from which I correctly guessed that she was a middle child) and did not hazard any risky guesses. Since she was a college student, I figured she was indecisive about her life, so I offered several trite generalities: "You are uncertain about your future but excited about the possibilities," "You are confident in your talents yet you still harbor some insecurities," "You strike a healthy balance between head and heart," and so forth.

Tarot Cards are a great tool because they provide the cold reader with a prop to lean on, something to reference and point to, and something for the subject to ask about. I purposely put the "Death" card in the spread because that one seems to make people anxious. This gave me an opportunity to pontificate about the meaning of life and death, that the card actually represents not physical death but metaphorical death. I told them that transitions in life are a time of opportunity—the "death" of a career and the "rebirth" of another career. The bait was set and the line cast. I had only to wait for the fish to bite.

After each reading the producers conducted a short taped interview with the subjects, asking them how they thought the reading went. This young lady said she thought the reading went well, that I had accurately summarized her life and personality, but that there were no surprises, nothing that struck her as startling. She had experienced psychic readings before and that mine was fairly typical. I felt that the reading was mediocre at best but I was just getting started.

THE PALM READING

My second reading was on a young woman aged 19. Palm reading is the best of the psychic props because, as in the Tarot cards, there is something specific to reference, but it has the added advantage of making physical contact with the subject. I could not remember what all the lines on a palm are supposed to represent, so while I was memorizing the Tarot Cards, my daughter did a Google image search for me and downloaded this palm chart.

I mainly focused on the Life, Head, Heart, and Health lines, and for added effect added some blather about the Marriage, Money, and Fate lines. Standard statements include:

- If the Head and Lifelines are connected it means that there was an early dependence on family.

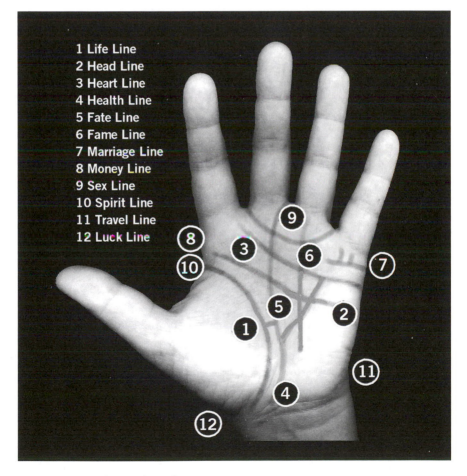

Figure 5.3. A Palm Reading Chart

- The degree of separation between the Head and Heart lines indicates the degree of dependence or independence between the head and the heart for making decisions.
- The strength of the Head line indicates the thinking style—intuitive or rational.
- Breaks in the Head line may mean there was a head injury, or that the subject gets headaches, or that something happened to the head at some time in the subject's life.

One web page I downloaded included some material about the angles of the thumbs to the hand that was quite useful. The reader has the subject rest both hands palm down on the table, and then observe whether they are relaxed or tight and whether the fingers are close together or spread apart (i.e., this purportedly indicates how uptight or relaxed someone is, how extraverted or introverted they are, how confident or insecure they feel, etc.). According to one palm reader, a small thumb angle "reveals that you are a person who does not rush into doing things. You are cautious and wisely observe the situation before taking action." In the same way, there are a variety of descriptions for what an average and a large thumb angle is supposed to mean. Since they are all equally unspecific, conveniently, you can use any description with anyone. According to the various palm reading practitioners, the psychic is supposed to comment on the color and texture of the skin, hair on the back of the palm, and general shape of the hands. The psychic should also take note of the shape of the fingers; the fingertips represent spiritual or idealistic aspects of the person, the middle phalanges everyday and practical aspects, and the lower phalanges the emotional aspects. I found it most effective to rub my fingers over the mounds of flesh on each finger segment while commenting on her personality.

For this reading I threw in a few high probability guesses, starting with the white car. It turns out that this subject's 99-year-old grandmother had a white car, which gave me an opening to comment about the special nature of her relationship with her grandmother, which was enthusiastically affirmed. Then I tried the out-of-date calendar, which did not draw an affirmative response, so I recovered by backing off toward a more general comment: "Well . . . what I'm getting here is something about a transition from one period in your life to another," which elicited a positive affirmation that she was thinking of switching college majors.

This subject's assessment of my reading was slightly more positive than the first subject's, as was my own self-evaluation, but no one was yet floored. I was still gathering steam for the big push to come.

THE ASTROLOGICAL READING

My third subject was another young lady, age 20, and was my toughest "read" of the day. She gave monosyllabic answers to my incidental questions for extracting information, and did not seem to have anything going on in her life that required much in the way of psychic advice. I downloaded an astrological chart from the Internet (below). It was constructed some time ago for a man named John, born May 9, 1961. My subject was born September 3, 1982. I didn't have a clue as to what the chart was supposed to mean, but I began by explaining that "the stars incline but do not compel." Then I made up a scenario about how the conjunction of having a rising moon in the third house and a setting sun in the fifth house is an indication that she has a bright future, and that her personality is a healthy balance between mind and spirit, intellect and intuition. Her nods indicated agreement.

I tossed out a number of high probability guesses and got about half of them right (including the line about wearing her hair longer at a younger age), then closed the reading by asking her if she had any questions. She said that she had applied for a scholarship in a foreign student exchange program in England, and wanted to know if she was going to get it. I responded that the important issue was not whether she was going to get it or not, but how she would deal with getting it or not, and that I was highly confident that her balanced personality would allow her to handle the outcome. This seemed to go over well. In the

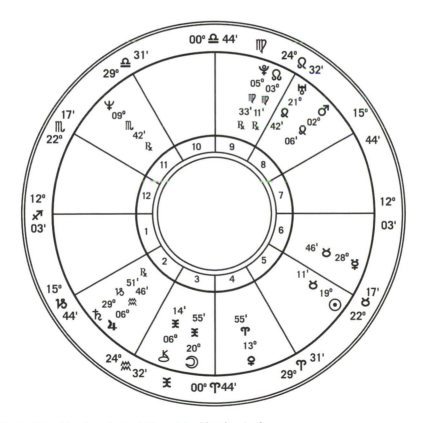

Figure 5.4. The Astrological Chart Used by the Author

post-reading interview she was much more positive than I anticipated, considering how stilted the reading was, so I suppose we can count this one as a success as well.

PSYCHIC READING

My fourth subject was a 58-year-old woman, for whom I was to do a straight cold reading with no props. I began with the Barnum reading, but did not get far into it before it became apparent that she was more than a little willing to talk about her problems. She wanted to get straight to the specific issues on her mind that day. She was overweight and did not look particularly healthy, but since I didn't want to say anything about her weight I said I was picking up something about her concerns with her health and diet, guessing, since this was still early January, that she probably made a New Year's resolution about losing weight and starting a new exercise program. Bingo!

This subject then opened up about her recent back surgery and other bodily ailments. I tried a number of high probability guesses that worked quite well, especially the box of photographs, broken gadgets around the house, and the short hair/long hair line, all hits, especially the hair, which she explained she changes constantly. I said I was getting something about a scar or scrape on her knees, and that left her slack jawed. She said that she had not scraped her knees since childhood, but just the week before had fallen down and tore them up pretty badly. Swish!

Although I was able to glean from the conversation that she had recently lost her mother, and a few minutes of generic comments from me about her mother staying close to her in her memory left her in tears, she really had come to find out about her son. What was he going to do? A minute of discussion revealed that he was a senior in high school, so I assumed that, as his mother, she was worried about him going to college. Nothing but net! What in particular was she worried about? He was thinking of going to the University of Southern California, so I jumped in before she could explain, and surmised that it was because USC is located in downtown Los Angeles, not exactly the safest neighborhood in the area.

In the post-reading interview, this subject praised my psychic intuition to the hilt and Bill and his producers were beside themselves with glee at what great dramatic television this was going to make.

TALKING TO THE DEAD

My last subject was a woman age 50, who turned out to be my best reading. She had told Bill's producer that she had something very specific she wanted to talk about, but did not offer a clue as to what it was. It didn't take me long to find out. When I introduced myself and shook her hand, I noticed that her hands were exceptionally muscular and her palms sweaty. This was a high-strung, nervous person who was obviously anxious and agitated. I assumed that someone near to her had died (the proper phrase among many psychics is "passed into spirit"), and that she wanted to make contact. "I'm sensing several people that have passed over, either parents or a parent-like figure to you." It was her father who died, and she clearly had unfinished business with him.

From the ensuing conversation I discovered that her father had died when she was 27, so I deduced that it must have been a sudden death and that she did not have the opportunity to make her peace with him (both hunches were correct). Finally, I accurately deduced that she was sad because she would have liked to have shared her many life experiences over the past two decades with her father, "such as having a child." Wrong—she is childless. Without missing a beat I offered this riposte: "Oh, what I mean is . . . giving birth to a new idea or new business." A three-pointer from downtown! This was an entrepreneurial woman whose father was a successful businessman with whom she would have loved to share this success.

It wasn't long before my charge was nearly sobbing. This was an emotionally fragile woman of whom I could have easily taken advantage by jumping in with some comforting line such as, "Your father is here with us now and he wants you to know that he loves you." Instead I said, "Your father would want you to keep him in your heart and your memories, but that it is time now to move on." I wanted to give her something specific, as well as lighten up the reading because it was getting pretty glum, so I said "and it's okay to throw away all those boxes of his stuff that you have been keeping but want to discard." She burst out laughing and confessed that she had a garage full of her father's belongings that she had long wanted to dispose of but was feeling guilty about doing so. This exchange was, I hoped, a moral message that violated no trust on my part and still had the desired effect for our show.

In the post-reading interview this subject said that she had been going to psychics for over ten years trying to resolve this business with her father, and that mine was the single best reading she had ever had. Wow! That made my psychic day.

DISCLOSURE

I am not a psychic and I do not believe that precognition, telepathy, clairvoyance, or any of the other forms of alleged psychic manifestation have any factual basis. The fact that I could do reasonably well with only one day of preparation shows just how vulnerable people are to these very effective nostrums. Give me six hours a day of practice for a couple of months and I have no doubt that I could easily host a successful syndicated television series and increase by orders of magnitude my current bank balance. I cannot do this for one simple reason—it is unethical. I have lost both of my parents—my father suddenly of a heart attack in 1986, my mother slowly from brain cancer in 2000—and I cannot imagine anything more insidiously insulting than constructing a fantasy that they are hovering nearby, awaiting some self-proclaimed psychic conduit to reveal to me breathtaking insights about scarred knees, broken appliances, and unfulfilled desires. For me, it would be nothing less than wanton depravity.

REFERENCES

Costa, Jr., P. T., & McCrae, R. R. (1992). *NEO PI-R Professional Manual; Revised NEO Personality Inventory (NEO PI-R); and NEO Five-Factor Inventory (NEO-FFI)*. Odessa, FL: Psychological Assessment Resources.

Rowland, I. (2003). *The full facts book of cold reading*. London: Author. (Available from www.ianrowland.com)

Shermer, M. (2002, May). The exquisite balance. *Scientific American*, p. 24.

CHAPTER 6

Persistent Denial: A Century of Denying the Evidence

Chris Carter

> It seems clear that Hyman and James Alcock proceeded on an intentional path to discredit the work in parapsychology ... What, we may ask, are they afraid of? Is protecting scientific orthodoxy so vital that they must deny evidence and suppress contrary opinion?
>
> Colonel John Alexander (U.S. Army, retired, 1989)

The controversy over the existence of psychic phenomena, now commonly called *psi*, has been raging for centuries. But it is only in the last 100 years that psychical researchers, now commonly called parapsychologists, have been mostly confined to their laboratories in order to gather experimental evidence. The anecdotal evidence is easy to question and dismiss, and so the critics have demanded—quite reasonably—reliable *experimental* evidence for the existence of psi. Has such evidence been provided?

In direct contradiction of Ray Hyman's (Hyman, 1996a) insistence that psi research is characterized by a "lack of consistently replicable results" (p. 35), I argue that consistent, replicable evidence has in fact been provided. If this were any other field of inquiry, the controversy would have been settled by the data decades ago. However, parapsychology is *not* like any other field of inquiry. The data of parapsychology challenge deeply held worldviews, worldviews that are concerned not only with science, but also with religious and philosophical issues. As such, the evidence arouses strong passions, and for many, a strong desire to dismiss it. I argue that this controversy cannot be properly understood without placing it in a larger historical, cultural, and social context.

We should be astonished that this controversy has continued for as long as it has. And in the minds of many, it continues with no end in sight. I am convinced that the key to a rational resolution of this matter lies in realizing that this controversy is *not* primarily about evidence, but rather about competing worldviews. This means that our analysis of the controversy must be broadened far beyond data sets and significance levels. The engineer George Hansen (2007), who has extensively researched the skeptical movement, recently wrote:

> Professional parapsychology is currently dominated by psychologists and physicists. They are largely unfamiliar with the concepts, tools, and methods of analysis developed in the humanities and social sciences. As such, they fail to comprehend the extent of their predicament, and the reasons for their marginality. (p. 11)

Unless we view this controversy from a broader perspective, I fully agree with Hansen's statement that the situation is "unlikely to change any time soon" (p. 11).

It is impossible to fully understand this controversy without realizing that it has a strong ideological component. The ideology involved is a product of the unique history of Western civilization. Until the eighteenth century, the great majority of our philosophers and scientists took for granted the existence of psychic phenomena. Among educated men, all of this changed with the dawn of the Scientific Revolution, spanning the period between the birth of Galileo Galilei in 1564 and the death of Sir Isaac Newton in 1727. During this period the universe came to be viewed as a gigantic clockwork mechanism, operating as a self-regulating machine in accordance with inviolable laws.

These views became prevalent in the eighteenth century, during what became known as the Enlightenment, which can be thought of as the ideological aftermath of the Scientific Revolution. Its most striking feature was the rejection of dogma and tradition in favor of the rule of reason in human affairs, and it was the precursor of modern secular humanism. Inspired by the dazzling success of developments in physics, prominent spokespeople such as Denis Diderot and Voltaire argued for a worldview based upon an uncompromising materialism that left no room for any intervention of mind in nature, whether human or divine. The science of Newton, Galileo, and Johannes Kepler had given birth to a new *metaphysics*—philosophical assumptions about the nature of reality—which simply could not accommodate the reality of psi phenomena.

The horrors of the religious wars, the witch hunts, and the Inquisition were still fresh in peoples' minds, and the new scientific worldview can be seen partly as a reaction against the ecclesiastical domination over beliefs that the Church had held for centuries. By 1700, many educated men and women considered such things as "second sight" to be incredible at best, and vulgar superstition at worse. Lingering widespread belief in the reality of these phenomena was considered to be the unfortunate legacy of a superstitious, irrational, pre-scientific era.

Parapsychology is the scientific study of these "anomalous" phenomena, considered anomalous in the sense that they seem to defy a purely materialistic explanation.

THE MODERN CRITICS

The current counteradvocates of parapsychology are those who see themselves as heirs of the Enlightenment, guardians of rationality who must at all costs discredit any dangerous backsliding into superstition. Until the mid-1970s, critics and debunkers of "paranormal" claims were disorganized, as they did not have a formal organization with which to advance their point of view. This situation troubled Paul Kurtz, who was then editor of *The Humanist* (the bi-monthly magazine of the American Humanist Association). With Kurtz as editor, *The Humanist* vigorously criticized so-called "paranormal" ideas of all kinds, defined as everything from religious faith to popular occultism to the findings of academic parapsychology, and treated them all as irrational superstition. Kurtz and his secular humanist associates believed favorable media coverage of unorthodox topics dangerously promoted irrationality and superstition.

Kurtz began to explore the idea of founding an organization to challenge what he saw as the uncritical coverage of "paranormal" and "occult" ideas in the media. The Committee for the Scientific Investigation of Claims of the Paranormal (CSICOP) was thus formed in 1976 at a meeting of the American Humanist Association (in 2006 CSICOP shortened its name to the Committee for Scientific Inquiry, CSI). Ray Hyman and James Alcock were among the early academicians who were members of CSICOP, and today are members of CSI.

Under the editorship of Kendrick Frazier, the magazine *Skeptical Inquirer* became CSICOP's organ of propaganda. In a 1989 issue of the *Journal of Scientific Exploration*, Henry Bauer reported an exchange of letters with Frazier in which the *Skeptical Inquirer*'s editor argued that "the magazine's purpose is not to consider what the best evidence for anomalous claims might be but to argue against them" (Bauer, 1989, p. 9).

The revolutionary new science that began in the seventeenth century, with its mechanistic and materialistic assumptions, gave intellectuals the tools to effectively challenge the authority of Church and scripture, and to replace it with an appeal to human reason and secular values. In the new worldview given birth by classical science there was little if any room for the action of a seemingly immaterial mind, and by corollary, for telepathy, second-sight, and other "paranormal" phenomena that were now dismissed as vulgar superstition. It is this worldview that is defended by modern secular humanists, which they rightly see as threatened by the claims of parapsychology. For many secular humanists the widespread acceptance of these claims would be the first step in a return to religious fanaticism, superstition, and irrationality.[1]

Not all critics of parapsychology—or even members of CSI—would consider themselves secular humanists. But many members of CSI hold views about religion that are antagonistic toward putative psychic phenomena. The psychologist Alcock—one of the most prominent counteradvocates—has made several attempts to associate parapsychology with religion in order to discredit its status as a branch of science, even at one point referring to parapsychology as "the spiritual science" (Alcock, 1985). Elsewhere, in a book titled *Parapsychology: Science or Magic?* Alcock (1981) wrote:

> In the name of religion human beings have committed genocide, toppled thrones, built gargantuan shrines, practiced ritual murder, forced others to conform to their way of life, eschewed the pleasures of the flesh, flagellated themselves, or given away all their possessions and become martyrs. .... An examination of the origins and functions of religion . . . is a useful starting point for the study of modern parapsychology. (p. 7)

And if he were writing this today, he would no doubt provide several more examples of religiously-motivated atrocities. But we can just as easily find examples of atrocities committed in the name of non-religious ideologies, which I define as faith-based belief systems that motivate a social agenda. Consider the misery inflected upon millions in the twentieth century by the ideologies of fascism and communism. Turning from one faith-based belief system to another is unlikely to solve the problem of fanaticism.

Despite Alcock's attempts to associate parapsychology with religion, religious people are often just as hostile to parapsychology as are the secular humanists. Adrian Parker (2003) pointed out, "Paradoxically, many of the claims of the paranormal are still seen as either a devilish challenge to Christianity or as an affront to Humanism. Some scientists may even have a hidden agenda in defending one or the other of these faiths" (p. 130).

There seems to be a growing realization that ideological factors play a crucial role in several scientific controversies. The philosopher Tyler Burge (1993) has argued that the naturalistic view of the world is more like a political or religious ideology than like a position supported by evidence, and that materialism is an article of faith. More to the current point, the neuroscientist Mario Beauregard (2007) has written:

> Materialists have conducted a running war against psi research for decades, because *any* evidence of psi's validity, no matter how minor, is fatal to their ideological system. Recently, for example, self-professed skeptics have attacked atheist . . . Sam Harris for having proposed, in his book titled *The End of Faith* (2004), that psi research has validity. Harris is only following the evidence. But in doing so, he is clearly violating an important tenet of materialism: materialist ideology trumps evidence. (p. xii)

And this is no laughing matter. Ideological correctness, quite apart from corrupting the nature of free scientific inquiry, also takes a heavy personal toll on those who dare to violate it. David Hess (1992) has documented several cases in which psi researchers have been denied jobs, promotions, and tenure. Of the 20 researchers interviewed by Hess, 13 reported some cases of prejudice because of their research interests. In one particularly dramatic case, a hostile department chairman allegedly destroyed a junior colleague's data from a precognition experiment. However, Hess (1992) did find a few psi researchers who did not report any adverse affects on their careers, and wrote that these "few exceptions seem to be explained by extenuating circumstances, as in the case of psi researcher B, whose experience is primarily with non-Western culture" (p. 7).

MATERIALISM

As I have described in my book, *Parapsychology and the Skeptics* (Carter, 2007), the doctrine of materialism is one of the implications of taking classical physics to be a complete description of all of nature, including human beings.[2] It is essentially the idea that all events have a physical cause: in other words, that all events are caused by the interaction between particles of matter and force fields. It follows from this that mind has no causal role in nature but is at most merely a useless by-product produced by the brain; and, so in short, all that matters is matter.

Considered as a scientific hypothesis, materialism makes a bold and admirable prediction: psychic abilities such as telepathy simply do not exist. If they are shown to exist, then materialism is refuted.[3] Of course, in practice followers of a theory do not always admit defeat so easily, as the philosopher of science Karl Popper (1974) reminded us:

> We can always immunize a theory against refutation. There are many such immunizing tactics; and if nothing better occurs to us, we can always deny the objectivity—or even the existence—of the refuting observation. Those intellectuals who are more interested in being right than in learning something interesting but unexpected are by no means rare exceptions. (p. 983)

However, religious fundamentalists are often antagonistic to parapsychology. As Parker pointed out, immunizing a theory against refutation turns it into an ideology, a belief held as an article of faith: a belief whose truth is simply not questioned, because it is considered so important.[4] This is just what the critics of parapsychology have done, for as I show below, the counteradvocates have gone to extraordinary lengths to try to dismiss and explain away the data. In any other field of inquiry the collective evidence would have been considered extremely compelling decades ago.

THE EARLY YEARS

The year 1882 marks a milestone in psi research: in this year the Society for Psychical Research was founded in London. The early membership included many distinguished scholars and scientists of the late Victorian era. Early experimental work primarily involved the reproduction of drawings at a distance, and it was one of the founders, Frederic Myers, who coined the term "telepathy"—Greek for "distant feeling." However, the work of the Society drew criticism from many scientists of the time, as it was seen as incompatible with the materialist doctrine that was then becoming prevalent. A particularly dogmatic response to the Society's work came from the physiologist Hermann von Helmholtz, who remarked that "Neither the testimony of all the Fellows of the Royal Society, nor even the evidence of my own senses, would lead me to believe in the transmission of thought from one person to another independently of the recognized channels of sense. It is clearly impossible."[5]

But the work continued at a vigorous pace. However, the statistical apparatus necessary to properly evaluate psi experiments was not fully in place until the 1920s, due to the work of R. A. Fisher and other pioneer statisticians. By this time, J. B. Rhine was setting up the first university laboratory to be devoted exclusively to parapsychological research.

By 1934 Rhine was ready to publish his findings, and this he did in a book titled *Extra-Sensory Perception*, thereby introducing the acronym "ESP" to the English language. Rhine's book was greeted by some as the start of a new era, and several laboratories at other universities readily adopted the card-guessing methodology. For the first time ever, the scientific community was faced with a body of evidence for psychic phenomena collected through conventional experimental methods.

But acceptance would not come easily. Critical articles began to appear, challenging almost every aspect of the evaluative techniques and experimental conditions. Between 1934 and 1940 approximately 60 critical articles by 40 authors appeared, primarily in the psychological literature. Many of the earliest criticisms focused on the statistical methods Rhine had used; the debate went back and forth, until the statistician Burton Camp (1937), then president of the Institute of Mathematical Statistics, settled the issue by stating that "the statistical analysis is essentially valid. If the Rhine investigation is to be fairly attacked, it must be on other than mathematical grounds" (p. 305).

The criticisms then focused on the methodology of the experiments, with allegations that the use of ordinary sensory cues could account for the results. Many of the critics were silenced in 1940 after Rhine published *Extra-Sensory Perception after Sixty Years*. ESP-60 (as it came to be known) showed how results from the six best parapsychology experiments could not easily be explained away and parapsychology gained a measure of acceptance. Other laboratories initiated ESP research without fear of ridicule, and independent replications began to be reported.

The parapsychologist Charles Honorton (1975) performed a detailed statistical review of the early experiments, and came to this conclusion:

> By 1940 nearly one million experimental trials had been reported under conditions which precluded sensory leakage. The results were independently significant in 27 of the 33 experiments. By the end of the 1930s there was general agreement that the better-controlled ESP experiments could not be accounted for on the basis of sensory leakage. (p. 107)

There has been a widespread belief that most of the positive results came from Rhine's laboratory at Duke University, and that most of the experiments performed elsewhere failed to confirm Rhine's results (Hansel, 1980). Honorton (1975) investigated this claim, and wrote:

> A survey of the published literature between 1934 and 1940 fails to support this claim. [The table below] shows all the published experimental reports during this period. Inspection of this table reveals that a majority (61 percent) of the outside replications report significant results (p < .01) and that the proportion of significant studies was not significantly greater for the Duke University group. (pp. 109–110)

Since 1940 most of the criticisms on the early results have focused on the possibility of fraud. One of the most prominent critics was the psychologist C. E. M. Hansel (1980), who wrote that "It is wise to adopt initially the assumption that ESP is impossible, since there is a great weight of knowledge supporting this point of view" (p. 22). Hansel provided no documentation at all for this assumption. Instead, he went on to develop elaborate fraud scenarios to explain how each experiment *could* have been accomplished by fraud. The fact that as late as 1980 Hansel was still developing his elaborate fraud scenarios (some involving the experimenters themselves!) shows the lengths a scoffer must be prepared to go in order to explain away the early experimental results.[6] Perhaps the term "debunker" is more appropriate than "scoffer." "Scoffing" is trivial dismissal; debunking is committed opposition. Creating fraud scenarios is debunking, not scoffing.

And note Hansel's assumption that "ESP is impossible" echoes the remark made 100 years earlier by Helmholtz. The latter may perhaps be forgiven, as this misconception is based on outdated classical physics and metaphysics, with their assumptions of locality, mechanistic causation, and materialism.

However, adherence to obsolete metaphysics (today much more common among psychologists and biologists than physicists) is one explanation why the

Table 6.1
Breakdown of Experimental ESP Studies (1934–1939)

	# Studies[a]	# Studies Reported Significant (p < .01)	Percent Significant
Duke group	17	15	88
Non-Duke	33	20	61
Total	50	35	70

[a]Includes all English-language studies involving assessment of statistical significance of data, 1934–1939 inclusive. X^2 (Duke versus non-Duke X significant versus nonsignificant) = 1.70 (1 df).
Source: Honorton, 1975, p. 110.

controversy has continued for as long as it has. Back in 1951, psychologist Donald Hebb (1951) wrote:

> Why do we not accept ESP as a psychological fact? *Rhine has offered enough evidence to have convinced us on almost any other issue.* . . . Personally, I do not accept ESP for a moment, because it does not make sense. My external criteria, both of physics and of physiology, say that ESP is not a fact despite the behavioral evidence that has been reported. I cannot see what other basis my colleagues have for rejecting it . . . Rhine may still turn out to be right, improbable as I think that is, and my own rejection of his view is— in the literal sense—prejudice. (p. 45, emphasis added)

Four years later, George Price (1955), then a research associate at the Department of Medicine at the University of Minnesota, published an article in the prestigious journal *Science* that began:

> Believers in psychic phenomena . . . appear to have won a decisive victory and virtually silenced opposition. . . . This victory is the result of careful experimentation and intelligent argumentation. . . . Dozens of experimenters have obtained positive results in ESP experiments, and the mathematical procedures have been approved by leading statisticians. . . . Against all this evidence, almost the only defense remaining to the skeptical scientist is ignorance. (p. 359)

But Price then argued "ESP is incompatible with current scientific theory" and asked:

> If, then, parapsychology and modern science are incompatible, why not reject parapsychology? . . . The choice is between believing in something "truly revolutionary" and "radically contradictory to contemporary thought" and believing in the occurrence of fraud and self-delusion. Which is more reasonable? (p. 367)

Here we have two critics in effect *admitting* that if this were any other field of inquiry—that is, one with results less threatening to a worldview based on seventeenth century science, less threatening to an ideology with its roots in an eighteenth century struggle between secular and religious members of society—then the experimental data would have carried the day by 1950.

THE GANZFELD CONTROVERSY

But of course the controversy continued, and 30 years later, parapsychologists reported impressive results with a new procedure. The ganzfeld, as it was named, has most often been used to test for telepathic communication between a sender and a receiver. The receiver is subjected to sensory deprivation in an acoustically sealed room, and is asked to simply relax and describe whatever thoughts and images come to mind. At the end of the session the receiver is shown a set of four pictures or video clips, one of which was viewed by the sender. The receiver's task is to determine which target was viewed by the sender. So, if chance alone is operating, we would expect receivers to correctly guess which target was used about 25 percent of the time (Bem, Palmer, & Broughton, 2001; Broughton & Alexander, 1997).

Charles Honorton was one of the originators of the ganzfeld technique in the 1970s, and in 1982 presented his results: a 35 percent over-all hit rate, which seemed impressive. But Ray Hyman disagreed, arguing that because of methodological problems, the actual results were close to chance level. This disagreement led to a debate, the opening rounds of which were carried in two full issues of the *Journal of Parapsychology* in 1985 and 1986.

The debate centered on 28 studies from ten different laboratories.[7] Out of the 28 studies, 23 had results greater than chance expectation, and 43 percent of the 28 studies yielded significant results. The over-all hit rate was 35 percent (with 25% expected by chance). The odds against these results happening by chance alone were a billion to one (Bem & Honorton, 1994; Honorton, 1993).

Hyman (e.g., 1991) agreed with Honorton that neither sensory leakage nor selective reporting could explain the results (selective reporting refers to the possibility that only successful studies were reported, also known as the "file drawer" problem). Contrary to what all ten other contributors to the debate concluded, Hyman continued to insist that there was a positive relationship between inadequate randomization and study outcome, but he finally agreed that "the present database does not support any firm conclusion about the relationship between flaws and study outcome" (Hyman & Honorton, 1986, p. 353).

In the end, Hyman and Honorton (1986) coauthored a joint communiqué, which concluded:

> We agree that there is an overall significant effect in this data base that cannot reasonably be explained by selective reporting or multiple analyses. We continue to differ over the degree to which the effect constitutes evidence for psi, but we agree that the final verdict awaits the outcome of future experiments conducted by a broader range of investigators and according to more stringent standards. (p. 351)

One of Honorton's colleagues pointed out that "Honorton was especially interested in getting Hyman to agree publicly to these criteria, as skeptics are notorious for changing the rules of the game after all previous objections have been met and new experiments continue to provide significant results" (Radin, 1997, p. 85). The stage was set to see if future ganzfeld experiments would provide similar results. But before the results of new ganzfeld experiments were revealed, a rather disturbing incident occurred.

The National Research Council Report

"Perhaps our strongest conclusions are in the area of parapsychology" continued the speaker, reading the prepared statement. The room was quiet as the speaker paused for slight dramatic effect and then went on. "The committee finds no scientific justification from research conducted over a period of one hundred thirty years for the existence of parapsychological phenomena." (as cited in Broughton, 1991, p. 322)

The paragraph above is an account of a statement read by John Swets to a roomful of journalists at a December 1987 press conference. Swets had chaired a committee created by the National Research Council (NRC) to investigate various techniques of enhancing human performance in which the U.S. Army was interested. He had called the press conference to announce the results of this two-year, nearly half-million dollar project.

Three years earlier, the U.S. Army Research Institute (ARI) had asked the NRC, a branch of the National Academy of Sciences, to evaluate various techniques of enhancing human performance such as sleep learning, guided imagery, meditation, and telepathy and clairvoyance. To help ensure fairness, ARI normally appoints an unbiased observer to monitor research contracts. But in this case, they appointed George Lawrence, a civilian army psychologist with a history of opposition to psi research; along with Ray Hyman, he was instrumental in getting a Pentagon funded parapsychology project at Stanford canceled in 1972 (Alexander, 1989, p. 12).

Because the NRC is often asked to evaluate controversial areas of science, it has an explicit policy requiring any committee it assembles to be composed of a balanced panel: the policy even requires members to affirm that they have no conflicts of interest for or against subjects they are asked to study. This is meant to ensure that reviews are fair and unbiased. However, when the NRC began to form subcommittees to investigate the different areas, they appointed Ray Hyman to head the parapsychology subcommittee. At the time Hyman held this position, he was an active member of the executive council of CSICOP. In addition, no one with parapsychology research experience sat on the subcommittee.

The only psi studies evaluated in the report were the ganzfeld experiments; the NRC evaluation was not based on an additional examination, but rather on the same meta-analysis conducted by Hyman. Although two years earlier he had agreed with Honorton that "there is an overall significant effect in this data base that cannot reasonably be explained by selective reporting or multiple analysis" and that "significant outcomes have been produced by a number of different investigators" (Hyman & Honorton, 1986, p. 352), neither of these points is mentioned in the report. At the press conference Hyman announced that the "poor quality of psi research was 'a surprise to us all—we believed the work would be of much higher quality than it turned out to be'" (News & Comment, 1987, p. 1502).

The NRC committee requested several reports from outside experts, but no parapsychologist was consulted. Instead, they commissioned psychologist James Alcock to prepare a report. Alcock was also a member of CSICOP and was widely known for his books and articles criticizing parapsychological research.

The psychologist Robert Rosenthal of Harvard University was also asked to prepare a report. Rosenthal was world-renowned as an expert in evaluating controversial research claims in the social sciences and, along with Monica Harris, prepared a report on the quality of research in all five controversial areas studied by the committee. In direct contradiction to Hyman's remark at the press conference, Harris and Rosenthal (1988) wrote that, of the five areas "only the ganzfeld ESP studies meet the basic requirements of sound experimental design" (p. 53). Their report concluded:

> The situation for the ganzfeld domain seems reasonably clear. We feel it would be implausible to entertain the null (that is, conclude the results are due to chance) given the combined p (probability) from these 28 studies. . . . When the accuracy rate expected under the null is ¼, we estimate the obtained accuracy rate to be about 1/3. (p. 51)

In other words, Harris and Rosenthal concluded that the ganzfeld results were not simply due to chance, and that the accuracy rate was about 33 percent, when 25 percent would be expected if chance alone were responsible.

Incredibly, the committee chair John Swets phoned Rosenthal and asked him to withdraw the section of his report that was favorable to parapsychology! Rosenthal refused. In the final NRC report the Harris-Rosenthal paper is cited only in the several sections dealing with the *non*-parapsychology topics. There is no mention of it in the section dealing with parapsychology.[8]

The excerpt at the beginning of this essay is from an article written the following year by Colonel John Alexander (U.S. Army, retired). Alexander was involved with the army's investigation of many of the subjects the NRC committee was asked to examine, and it seems worthwhile here to quote at length from the article he (Alexander, 1989) wrote as a challenge to the NRC report:

> I was a briefer to the NRC committee members as they researched the EHP Report. I have served as chief of Advanced Human Technology for the Army Intelligence and Security Command (1982–1984) and, during the preparation of the EHP Report, was director of the Advanced Systems Concepts Office at the U.S. Army Laboratory Command. I believe I am personally well qualified to review the committee's findings.
>
> Many organizations in the Army had already been experimenting with various techniques to enhance human performance and frequently they had reported some very exciting results. . . . It was felt by several in the top leadership of the Army that contracting such an august body as the NRC . . . would provide a credible report on which the stewardship of the public funds

for Army research allocations in the field of enhancing human performance could be based.

The task of administering the contract fell to ARI. It was they who proposed that Dr. George Lawrence, a civilian army psychologist with a background in biofeedback, be assigned as the Contracting Officers' Technical Representative (COTR). A COTR is normally an unbiased observer who does not participate in the study and who is there to ensure that the study is technically sound. Unfortunately . . . Lawrence was far from unbiased. He had a prior history in the field of being firmly and publicly in opposition to several of the areas to be studied. . . .

Prior to the formal organization of the EHP board, Lawrence told me in personal conversation in 1984 that he was seeking to get [Dr. Ray] Hyman on the EHP committee, an effort at which he proved to be successful. The issue to be raised concerning the credibility of the EHP Report here is that the *only* person assigned to the committee who had had any previous familiarity with the parapsychological research literature was Ray Hyman—who was known from the outset to have his mind already made up. . . .

Thus, I questioned from the beginning the issues of "bias" and "objectivity" as they related to the committee's constitution. For it seems clear that Lawrence, and then Hyman and James Alcock . . . proceeded on an intentional path to discredit the work in parapsychology. . . . Throughout the parapsychology section of the EHP Report, the committee referred only to those published articles that supported its position and ignored material that did not. . . .

What, then, are we to conclude about the EHP report? . . . First, it is significant that a determined group of psi debunkers could find no "smoking gun" and no "plausible alternative" to the psi hypothesis. . . . Second, we should worry about the fact that the highest scientific court in the land operated in such a biased and heavy-handed manner, and that there seems to be no channel for appeal or review of their work. (Alexander, 1989, pp. 10–15)

HAVE THE GANZFELD RESULTS BEEN REPLICATED?

Since the National Research Council Report, several other laboratories in different countries have reported successful replications. These are discussed in some detail in my book (Carter, 2007, pp. 62–67). In summary, it is clear that the ganzfeld findings have been successfully replicated to a reasonable scientific standard and charges to the contrary are obfuscations of this fact (e.g., Office of Technology Assessment, 1989; Parker, 2000; Schlitz & Honorton, 1992; Wright & Parker, 2003).

THE MATERIALIST'S LAMENT

Alcock's (2010) "The Parapsychologist's Lament" contains many factual and conceptual errors requiring rebuttal. I will deal with them in the order in which they occur. In this essay's first sentence, he asked the loaded question: "Why, parapsychologists ask, does parapsychology continue to be rebuffed by mainstream science?" (p. 35). But is parapsychology really rebuffed by mainstream science? Parapsychology has been an affiliate of the American Association for the Advancement of Science (AAAS) since 1969. In contrast, not one of the so-called skeptical organizations—including the one Alcock belongs to—is affiliated with the AAAS.

Also, surveys show that a large proportion of scientists accept the possibility that telepathy exists. Two surveys of over 500 scientists in one case, and over 1,000 in another, both found that the majority of respondents considered ESP "an established fact" or "a likely possibility": 56 percent in one and 67 percent in the other (Evans, 1973; Wagner & Monet, 1979). These polls suggest that most scientists are curious and open-minded about psi. This however, does not seem to be the case in one field: psychology. In the former study 53 percent of the "ESP is impossibility" responses came from psychologists, although psychologists made up only 6 percent of the total sample. Only 3 percent of natural scientists considered ESP "an impossibility," compared to 34 percent of psychologists. Later in this paper I will address why psychologists in particular seem predisposed to this view; contrary to what Alcock (2010) insisted, it has nothing to do with "the weakness of the data" (p. 35). As mentioned earlier, in 1951 psychologist Donald Hebb wrote that "Rhine has offered enough evidence to have convinced us on almost any other issue" (p. 45).

In the same essay, Alcock (2010) write that "I have met many [scientists] who have initially shown interest in parapsychological claims, only to have this interest dissipate after a close look at the data or after carrying out their own experiments (e.g., Freedman et al., 2003)" (pp. 35–36). In fact, Stanley Jeffers is one of the very few skeptics to ever try his own experiments. He tried on two occasions to repeat PK experiments reported by others, and failed. But in 2003 Jeffers coauthored a third study in which he finally reported a repeatable, significant PK effect (Freedman et al., 2003).

Ambiguous Definition of Subject Matter

Alcock (2010) asked: "What is the subject matter of parapsychology?" (p. 36). Well, one could easily ask, what is the subject matter of psychology? Indeed, the same argument has been so contentious within the American Psychological Association (APA) that it ended up splitting into two organizations: the APA and the Association for Psychological Science (APS). Why has Alcock applied a double-standard?

Alcock (2010) stated: "Even the most bizarre notions are tolerated, and there seems to be no 'horizon of the ridiculous' beyond which claims can be ignored" (p. 36). But who is clever enough to know what can safely be ignored? How often in history have strange and unexpected claims been ignored merely because the horizon of the ridiculous was set too low? The famed debunking of the existence of rocks that fall from the sky and of continental drift are only two examples.

Negative Definition of Constructs

Alcock (2010) wrote, "Definitions of parapsychological phenomena tell us not what the phenomena are, but only what they are not" (p. 37). But as Radin (2006) replied, this complaint "confuses the method of detection with the phenomenon itself. As a positive definition, psi is a means by which information can be gained from a distance without the use of the ordinary senses" (p. 284).

Misleading Concept of Anomaly

Alcock (2010) said: "When parapsychologists speak of 'anomalies,' something altogether different is involved. First of all, there is no coherent, well-articulated theory against which particular observations stand in contrast" (p. 37).

I actually agree with Alcock on this point. An anomaly is, as Thomas Kuhn (1996) argued, a violation of expectations: that is, a result or finding that is opposite of that predicted by your theory. But as many modern physicists have pointed out, nothing in quantum mechanics is compromised or contradicted by the findings of parapsychology. Hence, it is misleading to speak of psi phenomena as anomalies. I will return to this point later.

Alcock (2010) stated:

> Incidentally, one wonders why, if parapsychological phenomena are genuine, they do not present as genuine anomalies in the very delicate experiments conducted in modern physics. Despite physicists' differing predictions, expectations, moods, desires, and personalities, their data do not show any such anomaly that would suggest that the mind of the experimenter has affected the outcome of an experiment. (p. 37)

The results of the PK experiments of physicist Helmut Schmidt contradict the last part of this statement (Carter, 2007). Also, the Nobel laureate Wolfgang Pauli was reported by several colleagues as being responsible for certain unintended psychokinetic effects in laboratories he visited, and for fear of the "Pauli effect" the experimental physicist Otto Stern banned Pauli from his laboratory in Hamburg despite their friendship. According to his biographer, Pauli was convinced that the effect named after him was real. He reported that Markus Fierz, a close colleague, as saying "Pauli himself thoroughly believed in his effect" (as cited in Enz, 2002, p. 150).

Lack of Replicability

Alcock (2010) wrote that "parapsychologists have not yet produced a single successful experiment that neutral scientists can reproduce for themselves" (p. 38). The ganzfeld data clearly shows this "skeptical" mantra to be erroneous. He went on to say Irwin and Watt (2007) concluded that "parapsychologists are not yet able to specify the testing conditions that would allow other researchers, skeptics included, to be able to demonstrate for themselves reasonably reliable evidence in support of the ESP hypothesis" (p. 38). On the basis of a single experiment this is true. On the basis of many experiments it is not true. The psi effects are small, but when dealing with a small to medium effect it takes hundreds or sometimes thousands of trials to establish statistical significance. Pointing to small individual studies in parapsychology that do not find an effect is applying a double standard that other branches of science are not required to meet.

"Replication on demand" is a problem not exclusive to psi research, but found throughout the life sciences. Commenting on experiments in conventional psychology, Seymour Epstein (1980) wrote in a prominent psychology journal: "Not only are experimental findings often difficult to replicate when there are the slightest alterations in conditions, but even attempts at exact replication frequently fail" (p. 790). The sociologist Harry Collins (1985) conducted an extensive study of replication in science and concluded: "Experiments hardly ever work the first time; indeed, they hardly ever work at all" (p. 40).

Multiplication of Entities

Alcock (2010) wrote that "the so-called *psi-experimenter effect* is invoked when different parapsychologists have obtained dissimilar results after carrying out the same experiment, particularly if one researcher obtained an apparent parapsychological effect while the other did not" (p. 38). Here again he applied a double standard: the effect is basically the same as Rosenthal's (2002) experimenter's expectancy effect, which is well accepted in psychology. Briefly, this refers to the idea that experimenter's expectations can be subtly conveyed to the participants so as to create a self-fulfilling prophecy, and it has been demonstrated in hundreds of experiments outside of parapsychology.

Unfalsifiability

Alcock (2010) has written that "when others cannot replicate a parapsychologist's results, this is taken as another manifestation of the psi-experimenter effect" (p. 39). If by "others" Alcock means his fellow counteradvocates, then the truth of the matter is that very few of them have attempted their own experiments; criticizing from the sidelines is by far the rule. However, I have documented instances in which two prominent counteradvocates who are the main exceptions to this rule actually found statistically significant evidence for psi, and both then went to extraordinary lengths to deny it (Carter, 2007, pp. 69–82).

Alcock (2010): "Scientists have learned through long and hard experience that effects that are observable only by the motivated few, thereby making the claim impossible to falsify, are unlikely to be worthy of any further study" (p. 39). If this were true, it would rule out the use of expertise in any realm. While science requires independent replication, which has been demonstrated in psi research, this does not mean that unmotivated individuals should be able to conduct any arbitrary experiment. It can take years of training to learn how to properly conduct some experiments. The fact that I lack the technical expertise to attempt to replicate Edwin Hubble's findings that light from distant galaxies is "red-shifted" does not mean his claim that the universe is expanding is thereby impossible to falsify.

Unpredictability

Alcock (2010) wrote: "Prediction is a keystone of science. . . . Even though scientific understanding of the nature of gravity is far from complete, the effects of gravity can be easily measured by anyone; they occur in an orderly and predictable fashion for any researcher" (p. 39).

I find it astonishing that a psychologist would compare the predictability of human behavior and performance with the relatively simple phenomenon of gravity. In both Newton's and Einstein's theories, only two categories of simple, easily-measured variables are involved: distance and mass. None of the human sciences enjoy this luxury.

Alcock (2010) insisted: "Parapsychological effects appear unpredictably" (p. 39). Not true. The ganzfeld is an exemplar case that shows if you replicate certain conditions, then generally you will find evidence for telepathy. You might not see it in an individual trial, but neither in an fMRI or EEG evoked potential study will you see the predicted effect every single time. But in all three cases we can use statistics to extract signal from noise. In neuroscience studies the signal is an electrical or hemodynamic response. In a telepathy test it is a correspondence between the target information sent by one person and the accurate impressions of the receiver.

Lack of Progress

Alcock (2010) wrote that "the scientific case for psi is no stronger now than it was a century ago" (p. 39). It only remains that way if one completely ignores meta-analyses on the empirical side, and developments in quantum entanglement on the theoretical side (Radin, 2006).

Methodological Weaknesses

Alcock (2010) stated, "Parapsychological studies that are free of obvious methodological flaws are relatively few and far between" (p. 40). This echoes the remark of his fellow counteradvocate Ray Hyman at the NRC press conference cited above, in which Hyman announced that the "poor quality of psi research was 'a surprise to us all' " (News & Comment, 1987, p. 1502).

As mentioned above, Harvard psychologist Robert Rosenthal prepared a report on the quality of research in all five controversial areas studied by the committee. In direct contradiction to Alcock's and Hyman's remarks, Harris and Rosenthal (1988) wrote that, of the five areas "only the Ganzfeld ESP studies meet the basic requirements of sound experimental design"[9] (p. 53).

Rupert Sheldrake (1999a) surveyed papers in leading science journals to discover what proportion in different fields took precautions for experimenter effects and used blind assessments of data. The highest proportion by far was found in parapsychology (85%), followed by medical science (24%) and psychology (7%).

Finally, if Rhine's work had "obvious methodological flaws" then Hansel would not have had to resort to constructing elaborate *fraud scenarios* to explain away Rhine's results 40 years later.

Reliance on Statistical Decision-Making

Alcock (2010) said:

> Modern parapsychological research depends to a very large extent on the power of sophisticated statistical analysis to reveal tiny but statistically significant departures from chance that would otherwise likely go unnoticed. There is nothing wrong with that in principle. What is wrong, however, is that such a departure is then considered to be evidence in support of the psi hypothesis. (p. 40)

I must admit I find this statement strange. First Alcock admitted there are "statistically significant departures from chance," and conceded there is nothing wrong with this "in principle" but then stated that it is wrong to use such data as evidence. Using statistically significant departures from chance to support hypotheses is commonly done in many branches of science, such as medical research, biology, economics, and psychology, to mention only four.

Alcock (2010) added: "Statistical significance can never tell us anything about what caused the departure. It could be due to any number of things—perhaps psi, perhaps methodological flaws, or fraud, or statistical error" (p. 40). Methodological flaws, fraud, and statistical error were ruled out, as Hyman admitted, in the ganzfeld debate (Carter, 2007, chapter 7). And as we saw earlier, Burton Camp (1937), then president of the Institute of Mathematical Statistics, ruled out statistical error in 1937 (p. 305).

Problem of Theory

Alcock (2010) wrote: "Parapsychology is devoid of any well-articulated theory" (p. 40) and then immediately contradicted himself by mentioning several. One of the theories he mentioned is Evan Harris Walker's quantum mechanical theory, which predicted retroactive-PK effects, later found to exist (Walker, 1984, p. 321; see also, Schmidt, Morris, & Rudolph, 1986). However, Alcock argued that "none of these theories serves to advance parapsychology, for they represent ad hoc efforts to explain something that is only assumed to exist" (p. 40).

Reports of phenomena such as telepathy and precognition come from virtually all cultures, and stretch back to the dawn of history. Their existence has been corroborated by hundreds of experiments in the laboratory. They are not "only assumed" to exist. And the Nobel prize-winning physicist Brian Josephson has written that "if psychic phenomena had not been found experimentally, they might have been predicted by an imaginative theoretician" (as cited in Puharich, 1979, p. 4).

Disinterest in Competing, Normal Hypotheses

Alcock (2010) told us that, "There is no doubt that most people have some very strange experiences in their lives" (p. 41) that they attribute to the paranormal, but "there is an obvious disinclination within parapsychology to explore non-paranormal explanations" (p. 41). But anyone who reads the ganzfeld debate between Hyman and Honorton can easily see that this accusation is unreasonable (Carter, 2007); parapsychologists are well aware of conventional explanations for these experiences. They are accounted for by proper experimental designs, and results are still obtained when such explanations can be ruled out.

Failure to Jibe with Other Areas of Science

Finally, we come to the most fundamental fallacy in the materialist belief system. Alcock (2010) concluded that the claims of parapsychology:

> stand in defiance of the modern scientific worldview. That by itself does not mean that parapsychology is in error, but as the eminent neuropsychologist Donald Hebb [1978] pointed out, if the claims of parapsychology prove to be true, then physics and biology and neuroscience are horribly wrong in some fundamental respects. (p. 41)

In a similar vein, Hyman (1996b) wrote that the results that parapsychologists seek allegedly challenge all sciences, not just a particular theory within a given domain. But neither Alcock nor Hebb (1951) ever bothered to explain *how* the claims of parapsychology "stand in defiance" of science, or *how* "physics and physiology say that ESP is not a fact." Indeed, it is rare for a counteradvocate to ever back up this criticism with specific examples. On those rare occasions that they do (Carter, 2007, pp. 131–136), they invariably invoke the principles of classical physics, which have been known to be fundamentally incorrect for almost a century.

However, a number of leading physicists such as Henry Margenau, David Bohm, Brian Josephson, and Olivier Costa de Beauregard have repeatedly pointed out that nothing in quantum mechanics forbids psi phenomena. Costa de Beauregard (1975) even maintained that the theory of quantum physics virtually *demands* that psi phenomena exist, and Walker (1979) developed a theoretical model of psi based upon the orthodox von Neumann formulation of quantum mechanics.

Hyman's (1996b) argument (in the *Skeptical Inquirer*) that the acceptance of psi would require that we "abandon relativity and quantum mechanics in their current formulations" is, thereby, shown to be erroneous. Contrast Hyman's statement with that of theoretical physicist Costa de Beauregard (1975, 1979), who observed "relativistic quantum mechanics is a conceptual scheme where phenomena such as psychokinesis or telepathy, far from being irrational, should, on the contrary, be expected as *very rational*" (p. 101).

As mentioned earlier, adherence to an outmoded metaphysics of science seems much more prevalent among psychologists than physicists. In the survey mentioned earlier, only 3 percent of natural scientists considered ESP "an impossibility," compared to 34 percent of psychologists. Counteradvocates such as the psychologist Susan Blackmore (1989) are fond of saying that the existence of psi is incompatible "with our scientific worldview"—but with *which* scientific worldview? Psi is certainly incompatible with the old scientific worldview, based on Newtonian mechanics and behaviorist psychology. It is not incompatible with the emerging scientific worldview based upon quantum mechanics and cognitive neuroscience.

But even before quantum mechanics began to supersede classical mechanics in the 1920s, many physicists were much more open to investigating psi phenomena than most psychologists seem today. An astonishing number of the most prominent physicists of the nineteenth century expressed interest in psychical research including: William Crookes, inventor of the cathode ray tube, used until recently in televisions and computer monitors; J. J. Thomson, who won the Nobel Prize in 1906 for the discovery of the electron; and Lord Rayleigh, considered one of the greatest physicists of the late nineteenth century and winner of the Nobel Prize in physics in 1904. Of course, for their efforts in investigating these and other unusual phenomena, these scientists were often criticized and ridiculed mercilessly by their colleagues.

The great psychologist Gardner Murphy (1969), a president of the American Psychological Association, and later of the American Society for Psychical Research, urged his fellow psychologists to become better acquainted with modern physics, not only for its relevance to parapsychology but to psychology in general.

> ... the difficulty is at the level of physics, not at the level of psychology. Psychologists may be a little bewildered when they encounter modern physicists who take these phenomena in stride, in fact, take them much more seriously than psychologists do, saying, as physicists, that they are no longer bound by the types of Newtonian energy distribution, inverse square laws, etc., with which scientists used to regard themselves as tightly bound. ... Psychologists probably will witness a period of slow, but definite, erosion of the blandly exclusive attitude that has offered itself as the only appropriate scientific attitude in this field. The data from parapsychology will be almost certainly in harmony with general psychological principles and will be assimilated rather easily within the systematic framework of psychology as a science when once the imagined appropriateness of Newtonian physics is put aside, and modern physics replaces it. (p. 527)

The Psychology of the Dogmatic Critic

A candidly written book by the clinical psychologist Elizabeth Mayer (2007) provides a revealing glimpse into the psychology of the dogmatic critic. While reading the book I was struck several times by the similarities between the opinions of
Mayer and the counteradvocate Blackmore. In both women's writings there is
the same view of science as a monolithic body of conclusions that tell you in
advance what is and is not possible.

There is also the same profound fear of psi experiences. Blackmore (1996) had
to face the fact that others were reporting positive results. One day she was asked
to witness a telepathy experiment involving children:

> We observed for some time, and the children did very well. They really
> seemed to be getting the right picture more often than chance would
> predict. I began to get excited; even frightened. Was this really ESP happen-
> ing right in front of my eyes? Or was there an alternative explanation? . . .
> Somehow I just couldn't accept that this was psi, and I was to go on arguing
> about the method used in future years. Was it just perversity? A refusal to
> accept my own failures? A deep fear of psi? Whatever it was, it led me into
> constant confusion. I just didn't seem able to accept that other people could
> find psi while I could not. (p. 88)

Similarly, Mayer (2007) participated in a ganzfeld experiment as a
"receiver"—a participant trying to guess what image the "sender" is trying to
send—and scored an apparent match with the distant target.

> And at that moment the world turned weird. I felt the tiniest instant of
> overwhelming fear. It was gone in a flash but it was stunningly real. It was
> unlike any fear I've ever felt. My mind split. . . . The feeling was terrifying.
> My mind had slipped out from under me and the world felt out of control.
> (pp. 206–207)

However, unlike Blackmore, Mayer did not give up. Blackmore (2000) claimed
to have officially retired from parapsychology, complaining that "I am just
too tired—and tired above all of working to maintain an open mind" (p. 55).
Instead, Mayer created her own psychoanalytic theory of why so many critics dog-
matically dismiss all evidence of psi: a Freudian theory of unconscious fear, in this
case a fear that our beliefs may be wrong. Near the end of her life, she learned that
psi is not ruled out by modern physics, and her fear evaporated (p. 254).

Hyman often seemed to display a similar irrational attitude. Schwartz (2002)
related:

> Professor Ray Hyman has told me, "I do not have control over my beliefs."
> He had learned from childhood that paranormal events are impossible.
> Today he finds himself amazed that even in the face of compelling theory

and convincing scientific data, his beliefs have not changed. His repeated disappointments with past genuine frauds prevent him from accepting genuine science today. (p. 224)

There is nothing rational about being terrified that our beliefs may be partly wrong. Nor is there anything rational about holding beliefs that are impervious to evidence. The quality of the data in parapsychology is not the issue: the real issue is the devastating implications of the data for a cherished ideological belief system.

HOW WISEMAN NULLIFIES POSITIVE RESULTS, AND WHAT TO DO ABOUT IT

Psychologist Richard Wiseman is a well-known critic of parapsychology, frequently appearing in the British media to debunk psychic research. In this section I will first respond to some of the criticisms Wiseman advances in an article he wrote for *The Skeptical Inquirer* in 2010 and then demonstrate how, on several occasions, he has attempted to nullify the positive results of various parapsychological experiments.

To begin with, Wiseman (2010) wrote, "After more than sixty years of experimentation, researchers have failed to reach a consensus about the existence of psi" (p. 36). But who exactly does he mean by "researchers"? Does he include committed critics and debunkers such as himself? And furthermore, it is contrary to the idea of science as an objective method of inquiry to suggest that it operates according to "consensus." Science in its purest and most effective form does not operate by consensus of opinion, but rather by the testing of theories against evidence, and by the evaluation of this evidence in a fair and impartial manner. Of course, scientists are human, and frequently political and ideological concerns interfere with the ideal operation of the scientific enterprise. But the renowned scientists we remember are often considered great precisely *because* they opposed the prevailing consensus of their time, such as Galileo (who was bitterly opposed by the Aristotelian academics) and Alfred Wagener (ridiculed for decades by other geographers for his theory of continental drift).

If scientific research stopped every time a consensus failed to be reached, it would be impossible for theories and paradigms to be overthrown, and scientific progress would grind to a halt.

In another section of his article, Wiseman wrote: "Parapsychologists frequently create and test new experimental procedures in an attempt to produce laboratory evidence for psi. Most of these studies do not yield significant results" (p. 27). How does Wiseman know that most of these studies yield non-significant results? He provided not a shred of evidence for these claims, yet continued:

Once in a while one of these studies produces significant results. Such studies frequently contain potential methodological artifacts, In part because they are using new procedures that have yet to be scrutinized by the research community. (p. 37)

Again, Wiseman offers no supporting evidence for these claims. However, a search through journals such as the *Journal of Parapsychology* and the *Journal of the Society for Psychical Research* shows that negative results from new experimental procedures are often reported. A case in point is the article by Simmonds-Moore and Moore (2009) in the *Journal of the Society for Psychical Research* (concerning the possible influence of gender role on a psi experiment). The authors go on for 21 pages describing the details of their experiment, only to conclude: "Psi scoring in the group as a whole was not significantly different from mean chance expectation" (p. 129). There is nothing wrong with trying new experimental procedures, as this has led in the past to breakthrough techniques, such as the ganzfeld.

Wiseman remarked that "The evidential status of these positive findings is impossible to judge because all too often they have emerged from a mass of non-significant studies" (p. 37). Here he refers to what is known as the "file-drawer" problem: the likelihood that successful studies are more likely to be published than unsuccessful studies, which are more likely to end up discarded in someone's file drawer.

It has long been believed that in all fields there may be a bias in favor of reporting and publishing studies with positive outcomes. Given the controversial nature of their subject, parapsychologists were among the first to become sensitive to this problem, and in 1975 the Parapsychological Association adopted a policy opposing the withholding of nonsignificant data, a policy unique among the sciences. In addition, Blackmore (1980) conducted a survey of parapsychologists to see if there was a bias in favor of reporting successful ganzfeld results, and concluded that there was none.

Still, since it is impossible in principle to know how many unreported studies may be sitting in file drawers, meta-analysis provides a technique to calculate just how many unreported, non-significant ganzfeld studies would be needed to reduce the reported outcomes to chance levels. In the ganzfeld debate between Hyman and Honorton, Hyman had raised the possibility that the positive results were due to selective reporting. However, once Honorton calculated that the results could only be explained away by a ratio of unreported-to-reported studies of approximately fifteen to one, it is not surprising that Hyman concurred with Honorton that selective reporting could not explain the significance of the results (Hyman & Honorton, 1986, p. 352).

Regarding follow-up studies of successful experiments, Wiseman complained:

> However, any failure to replicate can be attributed to the procedural modifications rather than to the nonexistence of psi. Perhaps the most far-reaching version of this "get out of a null effect free" card involves an appeal to the "experimenter effect," wherein any negative findings are attributed to the psi inhibitory nature of the researchers running the study. (p. 37)

It is somewhat hypocritical for Wiseman to dismiss appeals to experimenter effects, especially remarks about psi-inhibitory effects, since one of the best documented studies demonstrating this effect involves Wiseman himself

(Wiseman & Schlitz, 1997). Wiseman and Marilyn Schlitz ran identical studies in the same location using the same equipment, in order to see if participants could detect whether or not the experimenter was staring at them. Wiseman's results were not significantly different from chance, while experiments involving Schlitz produced results significantly higher than chance would predict.

Throughout Wiseman's career, he has tended to adopt a "heads I win, tails you lose" approach to parapsychology's research findings, viewing null results as evidence against the psi hypothesis, whilst ensuring that positive results do not count as evidence for it. In support of the latter part of this statement, I present here three such cases:

A Dog That Knew When Its Owner Was Coming Home

One of Wiseman's most highly publicized experiments concerned a dog named Jaytee. His owner, Pamela Smart, claimed that the dog could anticipate her arrival home. Pam's parents noticed that Jaytee seemed to anticipate Pam's return, even when Pam returned at completely unpredictable times. It seemed as though Jaytee would begin waiting by the window at about the time she set off on her homeward journey.

In April 1994 Pam read an article in the *Sunday Telegraph* about research into animals that seem to know when their owners were coming home, being undertaken by biologist Rupert Sheldrake. She contacted Sheldrake and volunteered to take part in his research.

After receiving a grant from the Lifebridge Foundation of New York, Sheldrake (1999b) began videotaped experiments with Jaytee in May 1995. Between May 1995 and July 1996, 30 videotapes were made of Jaytee's behavior under natural conditions while Pam was out and about. Pam's parents were not told when she would be returning, and Pam usually was not sure herself. The results showed that Jaytee waited at the window far more when Pam was on her way home than when she was not, and this difference was highly statistically significant (Sheldrake, 2000).

The researchers discovered early that Jaytee responded even when Pam set off at randomly selected times. This was an important discovery, as it seemed to clearly rule out an explanation based upon routine, or expectations based upon the behavior of her parents. Consequently, 12 more experiments were videotaped in which Pam returned home at random times, determined by the throw of dice after she had left her home.

The results clearly show that Jaytee was at the window far more when Pam was on her way home than during the main period of her absence (55% versus 4%). The difference is statistically significant, implying odds against chance of over 10,000 to one.

Following a televised segment of this experiment, several reports about this research appeared in European television and newspapers. Journalists sought out a critic to comment on the results, and the obvious choice for many was Wiseman who suggested a number of possible explanations, such as routine times of return and selective memory that Sheldrake had already tested and eliminated. However, rather than debate the issue, Sheldrake simply invited Wiseman to perform some tests of his own. Pam and her family kindly agreed to help him.

In his four experiments, Wiseman and his associate (1998) videotaped Jaytee, while his assistant, Matthew Smith, went out with Pam and videotaped her. They went out to pubs or other places five to eleven miles away, and returned at times selected randomly by Smith once they were out. Smith himself knew in advance when they would be returning, but did not tell Pam until it was time to go. Wiseman, back in the apartment, did not know when they would be returning. Furthermore, Pam and Smith traveled by taxi or by Smith's car, in order to eliminate the possibility that Jaytee was listening for the sound of a familiar vehicle. Three of Wiseman's experiments with Jaytee were performed in the flat of Pam's parents, similar to the experiments Sheldrake had conducted. The fourth experiment was performed in the flat of Pam's sister, but Jaytee fell ill during the experiment (Wiseman, Smith, & Milton, 2000).

As in Sheldrake's experiments, Jaytee was at the window much more when Pam was on her way home than during the main period of her absence (78% versus 4%). In these three experiments, the sample size was small but the results were still statistically significant. In other words, Wiseman had replicated Sheldrake's results.

However, much to Sheldrake's astonishment, in 1996 Wiseman addressed a series of conferences announcing that he had refuted the "psychic pet" phenomenon, and later appeared on a series of television shows claiming to have refuted Jaytee's abilities. How did he justify his conclusions? Simple: Wiseman used an arbitrary criterion for success in the experiment, a criterion that enabled him to ignore most of the data he had gathered. If Jaytee went to the window "for no apparent reason" at any time during the experiment, Wiseman simply ignored all the rest of the data and declared the experiment a failure (Wiseman, Smith, & Milton, 2000). These "failures" occurred during the 4 percent of the time Jaytee was at the window when Pam was absent. After these "failures," the rest of the data was ignored, even though Jaytee was at the window 78 percent of the time when Pam was on her way home.

Sheldrake met with Wiseman in September 1996 and pointed out to Wiseman that his data showed the same pattern as the data Sheldrake had gathered. Sheldrake made it clear that far from refuting Sheldrake' results, Wiseman's own data replicated them. He even gave Wiseman copies of graphs showing Wiseman the data from his own experiments.

By Wiseman's standards, only the fourth experiment—the one performed in Pam's sister's apartment—was a partial success; because only in this trial did Jaytee go to the window "for no apparent reason" for the first time during the period Pam was on her way home. (The videotape record showed that his visit to the window coincided *exactly* with Pam setting off on her way home.) However, Wiseman did not consider the fourth trial a success because Jaytee did not stay there for at least two minutes, but instead left the window and vomited.

Over the next two years, Wiseman repeatedly told the media that he had discredited the dog's ability to anticipate his owner's return. For instance, on a British television program called *Strange but True*, that aired on November 1, 1996, he said of Jaytee: "In one out of four experiments he responded at the correct time—not a very impressive hit rate, and it could just be a coincidence."

Wiseman dismissed Sheldrake's analysis of his data, calling it *post hoc* (Latin for "after this"), implying that it is somehow unscientific to analyze data someone else has collected. However, it is important to remember that Sheldrake applied exactly the same analysis to his own data two months *before* Wiseman arrived on the scene and for two years afterward.

As mentioned, Wiseman used an arbitrary criterion for success in the experiment, a criterion that enabled him to ignore most of the data he had gathered. An analogy would be if Wiseman had set out to test the claim that smokers have a greater risk of developing lung cancer; set the criterion that smokers must show a greater frequency of developing lung cancer within two years of starting to smoke; used this criterion to ignore all the rest of the data, and then announced to the press that his experiment shows that smokers do *not* have a greater risk of developing lung cancer.

During the controversy that followed, Blackmore (1999) came to Wiseman's aid in a newspaper article, claiming that there was a fatal flaw in Sheldrake's experiment.

> Sheldrake did 12 experiments in which he beeped Pam at random times to tell her to return. Now surely Jaytee could not be using normal powers, could he? No. But there is another simple problem. When Pam first leaves, Jaytee settles down and does not bother to go to the window. The longer she is away, the more often he goes to look. (p. 18)

Blackmore's point is simply that Jaytee spends more and more time by the window the longer Pam is out, and so of course he spends more time by the window as Pam is on her way home, but not because of any telepathic ability. But anyone who looks at the actual data can easily see that Blackmore's comment misses the mark. For instance, during the short absences, Jaytee spent the most time by the window when Pam was on her way home, but there was no comparable increase in time spent at the window in this same period during the medium and long absences. Sheldrake (2000) also made a series of videotapes on evenings when Pam was not coming home until very late, or staying out all night. These tapes served as controls.

Once again, a close examination of the evidence shows the need to treat the claims of the counteradvocates with skepticism. In April 2004, Wiseman was still making this claim on his Web site (see www.richardwiseman.com). Here we have a case in which Wiseman replicated a successful psi experiment, and (at least from my perspective) was only able to maintain his position by arbitrarily ignoring most of his own data.

Wiseman's Challenge to the Ganzfeld Experiments

In 1999 Wiseman and Julie Milton challenged Honorton's claims of replication with the autoganzfeld. The challenge appeared in the form of a short article by the two psychologists, in which they presented the results of 30 ganzfeld studies completed since 1987, the starting date chosen so that "the studies' designers would have had access to Hyman and Honorton's (1986) guidelines for ganzfeld research" (Milton & Wiseman, 1999, p. 388). These 30 studies were retrieved from 14 papers written by ten different principle authors from seven laboratories, comprising altogether 1,198 sessions. No criteria were used to select the studies; the authors simply followed a policy "of including in our database all psi studies that used the ganzfeld technique" (p. 388).

The combined hit rate for these 30 studies is 27.5 percent, just below the 95 percent confidence intervals of the first two major studies. At the end of their article Milton and Wiseman (1999) concluded:

> The new ganzfeld studies show a near-zero effect size and a statistically non-significant overall [total]. This failure to replicate could indicate that the autoganzfeld's results were spurious. ... Alternatively, the differences in outcome between the autoganzfeld studies and the new database could have been due to the latter not being carried out under psi-conducive conditions. Whatever the reason, the autoganzfeld results have not been replicated by a "broader range of researchers." The ganzfeld paradigm cannot at present be seen as constituting strong evidence for psychic functioning. (p. 388)

However, Milton and Wiseman had not considered sample size. Dean Radin (2006) simply added up the total number of hits and trials conducted in those 30 studies (the standard method of doing meta-analysis) and found a statistically significant result with odds against chance of about 20 to 1 (pp. 118, 317). Not only that, but Milton and Wiseman did not include a large and highly successful study by Kathy Dalton (1997) due to an arbitrary cut-off date, even though it was published almost two years before Milton and Wiseman's paper, had been widely discussed among parapsychologists, was part of a doctoral dissertation at Milton's university, and was presented at a conference attended by Wiseman two years before Milton and Wiseman published their paper.

The Natasha Demkina Case

In September 2004 Wiseman alleged that a Russian girl who claimed to be gifted in "psychic medical diagnosis" had failed a test that he and his colleagues had designed. From my perspective, however, the girl had scored at a level above chance.

Natasha Demkina, then 17 years old, claimed that she could look deeply inside peoples' bodies and spot when something was wrong. As part of a broadcast on the Discovery Channel, Natasha was given a set of seven cards, with a medical condition indicated on each. Medical subjects with these seven conditions (one of which was "no condition"), each bearing an identifying number, stood in a row and Natasha had to mark each card with the number of the person whom she thought had the condition indicated on the card. Under the tightly-controlled conditions imposed by the experimenters, she identified four of the seven correctly. The odds of getting four hits or more out of seven by chance are more than 50 to 1. Another way of expressing this would be to say the probability that Natasha displayed no genuine psychic ability but merely was lucky is less than 2 percent.

However, Wiseman declared the test a "failure." He was able to do this because the experimental protocol, to which Natasha and her agent had agreed, stated: "If Natasha correctly matches fewer than five target medical conditions, then the Test Proctor will declare that results are more consistent with chance guessing and does not support any belief in her claimed abilities."

Accordingly, it was announced that Natasha had "failed the test." However, Josephson, a Nobel laureate in physics, investigated Wiseman's claims about this test and stated his disagreement on his Web site (See: www.tcm.phy.cam.ac.uk/~bdj10/propaganda/). A four out of seven success rate is considered to be of at least borderline significance in many psychological studies when one out of seven would represent chance results.

Keith Rennolls, professor of Applied Statistics at the University of Greenwich, wrote a letter that appeared in the *Times Higher Education Supplement*. In part it reads:

> I have reviewed Professor Josephson's arguments, published on his web page, and find them to be scientifically and statistically correct. In contrast, the statement of Professor Wiseman . . . , "I don't see how you could argue there's anything wrong with having to get five out of seven when she agrees with the target in advance", demonstrates a complete lack of understanding of how experimental data should be interpreted statistically. The experiment is woefully inadequate in many ways. The chance of the observed 4 successes 7 subjects by pure guessing is 1 in 78, an indication of a significantly non-random result, as claimed by Professor Josephson. (Rennolls, 2004, p. 1)

Here we have a case in which Wiseman was only able to maintain his position by ignoring the fact that the girl scored at a level accepted in some scientific experiments as significantly above what chance alone would predict.

What can be done about this? Readers need to be aware of Wiseman's history of dismissing positive results, and checking to see if either technique has been used whenever he appears in the media to debunk the work of parapsychological researchers. Readers also need to remember that many controversies in science have a strong ideological component, and so what is presented as proper science is occasionally—upon closer inspection—nothing of the sort. And finally, regarding the assertion that consensus has no proper place in science, readers need to keep in mind the words of physicist Max Planck (1950), one of the founding fathers of quantum mechanics who sadly remarked in his autobiography:

A new scientific truth does not triumph by convincing its opponents and making them see the light, but rather because its opponents eventually die, and a new generation grows up that is familiar with it. (pp. 33–34)

CONCLUDING REMARKS

At the start of my responses to Alcock (2010) I had argued that parapsychology is not "rebuffed by mainstream science," and that most scientists are curious and open-minded about psi. However, despite the willingness of many scientists to express favorable opinions toward psi research, parapsychology courses are *not* routinely taught at universities, there are only a few laboratories conducting full-time psi research in the United States, and only a handful of such labs exist in the entire world. One explanation for this is that critical opinions of psi seem more common among the administrative elite than among ordinary working scientists. The sociologist James McClenon (1984) surveyed the council and selected section committees of the American Association for the Advancement of Science (AAAS) in 1981. He found that these scientists were more skeptical of ESP than scientists in general, with just fewer than 30 percent believing that ESP was "an established fact" or "a likely possibility." Surveyed members in the social sciences (where parapsychology courses would normally be categorized) were even more skeptical (20% believers) than those in the natural sciences (30% believers). Worried about the reputations of their schools and labs, administrators may be reluctant to express favorable opinions of psi research than many ordinary working scientists.

The attitudes of those who run the scientific establishment is surely one reason why, throughout its history, the resources devoted to psi research have been extremely meager. Psychologist Sybo Schouten (1993) compared the funding directed toward parapsychology between 1882 and 1982, finding that it was approximately equal to the expenditures of *two months* of conventional psychological research in the United States in 1983. The other reason funding is difficult to come by is that many private and public funding agencies have no wish to be associated with what the counteradvocates call "pseudo-science." Is it any wonder that academic administrators and funding agencies feel this way?

It is no wonder when scientific journals continue to publish hostile attacks on the scientific validity of parapsychology. For instance, the prominent journal *Nature* published the following in a commentary by psychologist and CSI member David Marks (1986):

Parascience has all the qualities of a magical system while wearing the mantle of science. Until any significant discoveries are made, science can justifiably ignore it, but it is important to say why: parascience is a pseudo-scientific system of untested beliefs steeped in illusion, error, and fraud. (p. 124)

George Hansen (2007) has written, "Within academe, derision and ridicule enforce the taboo—and CSI serves as an agent of enforcement" (para. 6). Parapsychology is the only scientific discipline for which there is an organization of critics actively trying to discredit its work. As this organization no longer performs any research of its own, the true nature of CSI seems to be that of a scientific vigilante organization defending a narrow brand of scientific fundamentalism, attempting to influence the media, and through it, public opinion. Many writers have pointed out that true skepticism involves the practice of *doubt*, not of simple *denial*, and so according to this criterion CSI does not truly qualify as an organization of skeptics.

A central theme of my work has been that this debate is not primarily about evidence, but about frameworks of understanding; or to be precise, about scientific and philosophic assumptions that cannot accommodate the reality of psi. One hundred years ago classical physics was widely assumed—with certainty—to be correct and complete. The dogmatism of the current counteradvocates is, in part, a legacy of this outmoded science, whose implications are contradicted by the existence of psi.

How then, can we account for the fear that psi research generates in some critics? How can we explain their persistent denial, to the point of ignoring, even suppressing evidence? *What, we may ask, are they afraid of?* Their thinking must go something like this: If we admit to the reality of psi, then our scientific assumptions are shown to be false. If we admit this, what will then happen to society? If we open the door a crack, what will come through? The collapse of science? Prayer in schools, holy wars, religious persecution, *even a theocracy?* We simply cannot let that happen!

But such hysteria is misplaced. Although belief in the reality of psi phenomena is widespread among the general public, polls have also shown that over 90 percent of the public regard scientists as having "considerable" or even "very great" prestige (Clark, 1990, p. 425). As Jerome Clark (1990) has written, "Some observers view CSICOP's claims about 'anti-science' components of paranormal interest not only as a rhetorical strategy, but also as an equation (explicitly stated in the literature) of the Humanist vision with the scientific vision" (p. 425). And finally, as noted above, nothing in modern physics would be compromised by the existence of psi.

For my part, I am impressed by how many contemporary physicists and philosophers—especially younger ones—are rejecting the doctrine of materialism.[10] If my instincts are correct, then in the next few decades materialism will join fascism and communism on history's ash heap of discredited ideas.

It seems fitting to conclude this essay with a quote from Charles Honorton (1993), pioneer of the ganzfeld experiments. Shortly before his sudden death at age 46 in 1992, Honorton wrote his classic article "Rhetoric over Substance," which he concluded with these words:

> There is a danger for science in encouraging self-appointed protectors who engage in polemical campaigns that distort and misrepresent serious research efforts. Such campaigns are not only counterproductive, they threaten to corrupt the spirit and function of science and raise doubts about its credibility. The distorted history, logical contradictions, and factual omissions exhibited not in the arguments of the critics represent

neither scholarly criticism nor skepticism, but rather counteradvocacy masquerading as skepticism. True skepticism involves the suspension of belief, not disbelief. In this context we would do well to recall the words of the great nineteenth century naturalist and skeptic, Thomas Huxley: "Sit down before fact like a little child, be prepared to give up every preconceived notion, follow humbly to wherever and to whatever abysses nature leads, or you shall learn nothing." (p. 214)

NOTES

1. There is an apocalyptic strain to some of the Committee's writing. For instance, the announcement of the founding of CSICOP stated: *"Perhaps we ought not to assume that the scientific enlightenment will continue indefinitely . . . like the Hellenic civilization, it may be overwhelmed by irrationalism, subjectivism, and obscurantism"* (Kurtz, 1976, p. 28).

2. Newton did not subscribe to this view, but instead followed Descartes on this matter. As mentioned above, this doctrine was popularized by Newton's followers, such as Voltaire and Diderot, both of whom were strongly motivated by opposition to religion.

3. Note that materialism can be refuted independently of parapsychology. See Beauregard, 2007, pp. 125–153; Carter, 2007, pp. 110–122; Popper and Eccles, 1977, pp. 98–99.

4. Modern secular humanism has its roots in the metaphysical assumptions thought to follow from classical science, one of which is materialism. But of course it is possible to believe in the sub-ideology of materialism without considering oneself a secular humanist.

5. This remark was made to William Barrett (1904), Professor of Physics in the Royal College of Science in Dublin, and one of the early founders of the Society for Psychical Research (p. 329).

6. One is reminded of Henry Sidgwick's famous remark in his first address to the British Society for Psychical Research: "We have done all we can when the critic has nothing left to allege except that the investigator is in the trick." (Sidgwick, 1882, p. 12)

7. This debate is discussed in great detail in chapter 7 of *Parapsychology and the Skeptics* (Carter, 2007).

8. According to Alexander, Swets even tried to have Rosenthal's report dropped from the supporting documentation available with the report. Evidently he failed, as the Harris and Rosenthal report is available from the National Academy Press.

9. Rosenthal has also said that "ganzfeld research would do very well in head-to-head comparisons with mainstream research. The experimenter-derived artifacts described in my 1966 (enlarged edition 1976) book *Experimenter Effects in Behavioral Research* were better dealt with by ganzfeld researchers than by many researchers in more traditional domains." (personal communication, February 2009)

10. Also, Whitehead (2004) has presented survey results that support a shift among consciousness researchers from materialist toward non-materialist views (p. 70).

REFERENCES

Alcock, J. E. (1981). *Parapsychology: Science or magic?* New York: Pergamon.

Alcock, J. E. (1985). Parapsychology: The spiritual science. *Free Inquiry, 5*(2), 25–35.

Alcock, J. E. (2010). The parapsychologist's lament. In S. Krippner & H. Friedman (Eds.), *Mysterious minds: The neurobiology of psychics, mediums and other extraordinary people* (pp. 35–44). Santa Barbara, CA: Praeger.

Alexander, J. A. (1989). Enhancing human performance: A challenge to the report. *New Realities, 9*(4), 10–15, 52–53.

Barrett, W. F. (1904). Address by the President. *Proceedings of the Society for Psychical Research, 18,* 323–350.

Bauer, H. (1989). Arguments over anomalies: II. Polemics. *Journal of Scientific Exploration, 3,* 1–14.

Beauregard, M. (2007). *The spiritual brain.* New York: Harper Collins.

Bem, D., & Honorton, C. (1994). Does psi exist? *Psychological Bulletin, 115,* 4–18.

Bem, D., Palmer, J., & Broughton, R. (2001). Updating the Ganzfeld database: A victim of its own success? *Journal of Parapsychology, 65,* 207–218.

Blackmore, S. (1980). The extent of selective reporting of ESP Ganzfeld studies. *European Journal of Parapsychology, 3,* 213–219.

Blackmore, S. (1989). Confessions of a parapsychologist. In T. Schultz (Ed.), *The fringes of reason: A whole earth catalog* (pp. 70–74). New York: Harmony Books.

Blackmore, S. (1996). *In search of the light: The adventures of a parapsychologist.* Amherst, NY: Prometheus Books.

Blackmore, S. (1999, August 27). If the truth is out there, we've not found it yet. *The Times Higher Education Supplement,* p. 18.

Blackmore, S. (2000, November 4). Into the unknown. *New Scientist, 2263,* p. 55.

Broughton, R. (1991). *Parapsychology: The controversial science.* New York: Ballantine Books.

Broughton, R. S., & Alexander, C. H. (1997). AutoGanzfeld II: An attempted replication of the PRL Ganzfeld research. *Journal of Parapsychology, 61,* 209–226.

Burge, T. (1993). Mind-body causation and explanatory practice. In J. Heil & A. Mele (Ed.), *Mental causation* (pp. 97–120). Oxford, England: Clarendon Press.

Camp, B. H. (1937). Statement from the "notes" section. *Journal of Parapsychology, 1,* 305.

Carter, C. (2007). *Parapsychology and the skeptics.* Pittsburgh, PA: Sterlinghouse Books.

Clark, J. (1990). Skeptics and the new age. In J. G. Melton, J. Clark, & A. Kelly (Eds.), *New age encyclopedia* (pp. 417–427). Detroit: Gale Research.

Collins, H. H. (1985). *Changing order: Replication and induction in scientific practice.* Beverly Hills, CA: Sage.

Costa de Beauregard, O. (1975). Quantum paradoxes and Aristotle's twofold information concept. In L. Oteri (Ed.), *Quantum physics and parapsychology* (pp. 91–102). New York: Parapsychology Foundation.

Costa de Beauregard, O. (1979). The expanding paradigm of the Einstein theory. In A. Puharich (Ed.), *The Iceland papers* (pp. 161–191). Amherst, NY: Essentia Research Associates.

Dalton, K. (1997). Exploring the links: Creativity and psi in the ganzfeld. In *Proceedings of Presented Papers of the Parapsychological Association 40th Annual Convention* (p. 119–134). Durham, NC: Parapsychological Association.

Enz, C. P. (2002). *No time to be brief, a scientific biography of Wolfgang Pauli.* Oxford, England: University Press.

Epstein, S. (1980). The stability of behavior. II. Implications for psychological research. *American Psychologist, 35,* 790–806.

Evans, C. (1973, January). Parapsychology—what the questionnaire revealed. *New Scientist, 25,* p. 209.

Freedman, M., Jeffers, S., Saeger, K., Binns, M., & Black, S. (2003). Effects of frontal lobe lesions on intentionality and random physical phenomena. *Journal of Scientific Exploration, 17,* 651–668.

Hansel, C. E. M. (1980). *ESP and parapsychology: A critical re-evaluation*. Buffalo, NY: Prometheus. (Original work published 1966)

Hansen, G. (2007, October 23). CSICOP to CSI: *The stigma of the paranormal*. Retrieved on September, 23, 2009 from www.paranormaltrickster.blogspot.com/2007/10/csicop-to-csi-stigma-of-paranormal.html

Harris, M., & Rosenthal, R. (1988). *Human performance research: An overview*. Washington, DC: National Academy Press.

Hebb, D. O. (1951). The role of neurological ideas in psychology. *Journal of Personality, 20*, 39–55.

Hess, D. J. (1992). Disciplining heterodoxy, circumventing disciplines: Parapsychology, anthropologically. In D. J. Hess & L. Layne (Eds.), *Knowledge and society: The anthropology of science and technology* (Vol. 9, pp. 223–252). Greenwich, CT: JAI Press.

Honorton, C. (1975). Error some place! *Journal of Communication, 25*, 103–116.

Honorton, C. (1993). Rhetoric over substance: The impoverished state of skepticism. *Journal of Parapsychology, 57*, 191–214.

Hyman, R. (1991). Comment. *Statistical Science, 6*, 389–392.

Hyman, R. (1996a). Evaluation of program on anomalous mental phenomena. *Journal of Scientific Exploration, 10*, 31–58.

Hyman, R. (1996b). The evidence for psychic functioning: Claims vs. reality. *Skeptical Inquirer, 20*(5), 24–26.

Hyman, R., & Honorton, C. (1986). A joint communiqué: The psi Ganzfeld controversy. *Journal of Parapsychology, 50*, 351–364.

Irwin, H. J., & Watt, C. (2007). *Introduction to parapsychology* (5th ed.). Jefferson, NC: McFarland.

Kuhn, T. (1996). *The structure of scientific revolutions* (3rd ed.). Chicago: University of Chicago Press.

Kurtz, P. (1976, March/April). Committee to scientifically investigate claims of paranormal and other phenomena. *The Humanist*, p. 28.

Marks, D. F. (1986). Investigating the paranormal. *Nature, 320*, 119–124.

Mayer, E. L. (2007). *Extraordinary knowing: Science, skepticism, and the inexplicable powers of the human mind*. New York: Bantam Dell.

McClenon, J. (1984). *Deviant science: The case of parapsychology*. Philadelphia: University of Pennsylvania Press.

Milton, J., & Wiseman, R. (1999). Does psi exist? Lack of replication of an anomalous process of information transfer. *Psychological Bulletin, 125*, 387–391.

Murphy, G. (1969). Psychology in the year 2000. *American Psychologist, 24*, 523–530.

News & Comment. (1987). Academy helps Army be all that it can be. *Science, 238*, 1501–1502.

Office of Technology Assessment. (1989). Report of a workshop on experimental parapsychology. *Journal of American Society for Psychical Research, 83*, 317–339.

Parker, A. (2000). A review of the Ganzfeld work at Gothenburg University. *Journal of the Society for Psychical Research, 64*, 1–15.

Parker, A. (2003). We ask does psi exist? But is this the right question and do we really want an answer anyway? *Journal of Consciousness Studies, 10*, 111–134.

Planck, M. (1950). *Scientific autobiography*. London: Williams & Norgate.

Popper, K. (1974). Replies to my critics. In P.A. Schlipp (Ed.), *The philosophy of Karl Popper* (Part II). Chicago: Open Court Publishing Company.

Popper, K., & Eccles, J. (1977). *The self and its brain*. New York: Springer International.

Price, G. R. (1955). Science and the supernatural. *Science, 122,* 359–367.

Puharich, A. (Ed.). (1979). *The Iceland papers.* Amherst, NY: Essentia Research Associates.

Radin, D. (1997). *The conscious universe: The scientific truth of psychic phenomena.* San Francisco: HarperCollins.

Radin, D. (2006). *Entangled minds.* New York: Pocket Books.

Rennolls, K. (2004, December 17). Distorted vision 3: Brian Josephson's arguments are scientifically and statistically correct. *Times Higher Education.* Retrieved from http://www.timeshighereducation.co.uk/story.asp?storyCode=193121&sectioncode=26

Rosenthal, R. (2002). Covert communication in classrooms, clinics, courtrooms, and cubicles. *American Psychologist, 57,* 839–849.

Schlitz, M., & Honorton, C. (1992). Ganzfeld psi performance with an artistically gifted population. *Journal of American Society for Psychical Research, 86,* 93–98.

Schouten, S. A. (1993). Are we making progress? In L. Coly & J. D. S. McMahan (Eds.), *Psi research methodology: A re-examination* (pp. 295–322). New York: Parapsychology Foundation.

Schwartz, G. (2002). *The afterlife experiments.* New York: Pocket Books.

Schmidt, H., Morris, R., & Rudolph, L. (1986). Channeling evidence for a PK effect to independent observers. *Journal of Parapsychology, 50,* 1–15.

Sheldrake, R. (1999a). How widely is blind assessment used in scientific research? *Alternative Therapies, 5*(3), 88–91.

Sheldrake, R. (1999b). *Dogs that know when their owners are coming home.* New York: Crown.

Sheldrake, R. (2000). A dog that seems to know when his owner is coming home: Videotape experiments and observations. *Journal of Scientific Exploration, 14,* 233–255.

Sidgwick, H. (1882). Presidential address. *Journal of the Society for Psychical Research, 1,* 8, 12.

Simmonds-Moore, C., & Moore, S. (2009). Exploring how gender role and boundary thinness relate to paranormal experiences. *Journal of the Society for Psychical Research, 73,* 129–149.

Wagner, M., & Monet, M. (1979). Attitudes of college professors toward extra-sensory perception. *Zetetic Scholar, 5,* 7–16.

Walker, E. H. (1979). The quantum theory of psi phenomena. *Psychoenergetic Systems, 3,* 259–299.

Walker, E. H. (1984). A review of criticisms of the quantum mechanical theory of psi phenomena. *Journal of Parapsychology, 48,* 277–332.

Whitehead, C. (2004). Everything I believe might be a delusion. Whoa! Tucson 2004: Ten years on, and are we any nearer to a science of consciousness? *Journal of Consciousness Studies, 11,* 68–88.

Wiseman, R. (2010). "Heads I win, tails you lose": How parapsychologists nullify null results. *Skeptical Inquirer, 34* (1), 36–39.

Wiseman, R., & Schlitz, M. (1997). Experimenter effects and the remote detection of staring. *Journal of Parapsychology, 61,* 197–207.

Wiseman, R., Smith, M., & Milton, J. (1998). "Can animals detect when their owners are returning home? An experimental test of the 'psychic pet' phenomenon." *British Journal of Psychology, 89,* 453–462.

Wiseman, R., Smith, M., & Milton, J. (2000). The "psychic pet" phenomenon: A reply to Rupert Sheldrake. *Journal of the Society for Psychical Research, 64,* 46–49.

Wright, T., & Parker, A. (2003). An attempt to improve ESP scores using real time digital Ganzfeld technique. *European Journal of Parapsychology, 18,* 69–75.

PART TWO

Rebuttals

"Pandora" (© Dierdre Luzwick. Used by permission.)

CHAPTER 7

The Critic's Lament: When the Impossible Becomes Possible

Dean Radin

> When a distinguished but elderly scientist states that something is possible he is almost certainly right. When he states that something is impossible, he is very probably wrong.
>
> A. C. Clarke

Thoughtful critiques are essential for advancing the state of the art in all scientific disciplines. Informed assessments of parapsychology have been especially helpful over the years in sharpening research methods and analyses. I found the chapter by Christopher French to be laudable in this regard, except for a few points that I will elaborate on below. The other chapters were less illuminating.

From these chapters we learn that investigating psychic phenomena is difficult, so it would be best to give it up and do something easier. We are told that parapsychology is disturbingly different from "normal" science because psi is impossible, thus any evidence offered in support of it is necessarily flawed. We are relieved to hear that there is no academic prejudice despite the complete absence of even a single degree program in parapsychology among recognized universities. And finally, in a spectacular stroke of Machiavellian chutzpah, we learn that it is reprehensible to deceive people, but what the heck, let's do it anyway.

Beyond such foolishness, I was struck by two general observations. First, the state of criticism has stagnated. Complaints hurled today are largely the same as those recited a century ago. By contrast, the empirical evidence, experimental designs, and methods of analysis in parapsychology have kept up with scientific progress in many fields, and as a result the evidence in favor of psi has progressively improved. This does not bode well for the critics' position. Second, arguments that psi phenomena are impossible are based on an understanding of the physical world that might have been appropriate to the seventeenth century, but not the twenty-first century.

CHRISTOPHER FRENCH'S CHAPTER

This chapter strikes a commendable balance of criticism and openness to new ideas. It provides a good model for how to critique controversial science without collapsing into simplistic dogma or encouraging the imagination to coagulate. This is not to say that I agree with all of French's comments. For example, he writes that although Bem and Honorton's original 1994 meta-analysis of eleven ganzfeld studies appeared to provide strong evidence of a replicable anomalous cognition effect, Milton and Wiseman's 1999 analysis did not. And again, later we are told that the fact that Milton and Wiseman's meta-analysis failed to replicate the results of Bem and Honorton's 1994 meta-analysis highlights a criticism that still continues to plague parapsychology—a lack of replicability.

If these statements were true, the critic's line of reasoning might carry some weight. But is it really true that the Milton/Wiseman (M/W) meta-analysis failed to replicate the Bem/Honorton (B/H) outcome? The answer is no, it is not true. As I have pointed out (Radin, 2006, p. 118), and later confirmed by statistician Jessica Utts in a conference presentation attended by both Richard Wiseman and Ray Hyman, when the M/W database is evaluated using the same method as B/H (i.e., as a simple hit/miss statistic) it results in a significantly positive outcome. The reason the M/W meta-analysis purportedly failed is because the authors used an unweighted statistic that did not take into account each study's sample size. If they had performed the correct analysis, M/W would have reached a conclusion that was diametrically opposed to the "failure" trumpeted in the title of their paper. Unfortunately, the skeptical mythos has uncritically adopted the wrong conclusion, and as such this may become an instance where myth is more comfortable than reality, and so the fictional story sticks.

There is another problem. Meta-analyses were developed to objectively assess whether a given class of effects were repeatable. Meta-analyses of some psi experiments, such as Bem and Honorton's (1994), provide highly significant evidence for an independently repeatable effect. That one analysis should have settled the psi repeatability question long ago. But critics disagree. Why? Because, for them, the repeatable experiment is no longer sufficient. Instead, the goal post has moved and now we are seeing concerns about the *repeatability of repeatability*.

While some argue that extreme levels of repeatability are required when it comes to assessing anomalies, insisting on meta-repeatability is a whole new game. To win this game, all the critic needs to do is to keep conducting meta-analyses until one fails, and then stop and announce that the effect is not repeatable. French is impressed by an apparent (albeit false) failure, as are other critics, but he is not impressed by (nor does he mention) subsequent meta-analyses that continue to show statistically robust, repeatable effects.

French continues to tell us that the crucial importance of reliably producing a convincing demonstration of even a tiny psi effect under well-controlled conditions is that to many scientists, himself included, this would require the kind of radical revision of worldview that would make at least some of the larger scale paranormal claims seem more plausible. I will address this issue in more detail later, but for now I will simply state that a radical revision in our worldview has already been with us for 80 years; but because that worldview presents such a radical departure from everyday common sense, it is only now beginning to penetrate into the awareness of the psychological sciences. The "new" worldview is based upon our most comprehensive understanding of the physical world to date, namely, quantum theory.

Some critics seem determined to dismiss this association out of hand, imagining that valid connections between exotic physics and the human psyche are unwarranted, or impossible. I would argue that this is a grave misunderstanding of quantum formalisms, and a growing number of physicists agree (e.g., Rosenblum & Kuttner, 2006). Indeed, many disciplines are beginning to show a new openness to quantum concepts, not merely to jump on a bandwagon with enticing new jargon, but because quantum-inspired models are proving to be pragmatically useful in solving otherwise intractable problems. For example, in 2009, a special issue of the *Journal of Mathematical Psychology*, which is not known for being sympathetic to new age babble, was entirely devoted to the topic of "quantum cognition."

Finally, French writes that although his own research efforts are primarily in the area of anomalistic psychology, he is happy to supervise students who wish to carry out parapsychological studies, but that they never get positive results. I have read similar assertions before. My reaction is: Really? Never? Surely he meant that they never get "statistically significant" results, because otherwise obtaining only studies that go opposite to a directional hypothesis would imply a stupendously significant negative effect.

So let us assume French meant that he never obtained statistically significant outcomes (two-tailed). But even then, one would expect to see at least one significant study at $p < 0.05$ purely by chance now and then, so if say, he had conducted 20 studies, approximately one *ought* to have been significant. So perhaps he only supervised a few experiments, and a significant study had yet to show up by chance. But no, that cannot be the case because just a few experiments could not possibly provide confidence about the existence or non-existence of psi. To gain confidence about anomalies, critics keep telling us that they require extreme levels of meta-repeatability.

Then perhaps he conducted many more than 20 studies. But if that were the case, it seems reasonable to ask whether a meta-analysis would show an overall positive trend. Even if not one individual study had reached statistical significance, if they tended to go in the same direction then French's collection of studies would still be astronomically significant. Or perhaps the distribution of effect sizes might have showed significant variance. The bottom line is that glib state-ments like they "never get positive results" are rhetorical devices that we should never accept at face value.

RAY HYMAN'S CHAPTER

From Hyman's perspective, the "anomaly" that the parapsychologists point to is simply a significant deviation from a chance baseline. He uses this position to justify why psi anomalies are not like "real" scientific anomalies. But this argu-ment has two major problems. First, a significant deviation from chance is not "simply" anything. It is a genuine anomaly in need of an explanation. Obviously if the observed hit rate in a forced-choice test was 32 percent, and chance expectation was 25 percent, then the 7 percent above chance outcome is not merely a meaningless glitch. It is a wildly unexpected outcome. In the case of the ganzfeld experiments, the overall hit rate as of 2009, with over 4,000 trials reported from a dozen laboratories over four decades, is 32 percent. This 7 percent positive effect is *extremely* significant, confidently excluding chance as an explan-ation. More to the point, the deviation is also exactly what the experiments were designed to show in the first place, presuming telepathy is real. The second prob-lem with Hyman's statement is that it overlooks classes of psi experiments that explicitly compare experimental versus control conditions, such as the physiologically-based studies known as DMILS (distant mental interactions with living systems).

Hyman then repeats a mantra commonly heard in critical thinking classes, but in the process he steps into a fallacy. He writes that parapsychological claims of a "communications anomaly" resemble failed claims of anomalies that have chal-lenged scientific theories throughout the history of science. Claims of N-rays, mitogenetic radiation, polywater, Martian canals, and the like now occupy the scrap heap of science, according to Hyman.

The "scrap heap of science" assumes that observations once dismissed as mis-taken are necessarily wrong for all time, allowing no possibility that the observa-tions were correct but not sufficiently robust to win the debate of the day. History shows that the permanent scrap heap assumption is an exceedingly unwise bet. For example, not long ago the list of scrap-worthy ideas also included heavier than air flying machines and continental drift. Those ideas and practically every-thing else in science that we accept today was, at one time, considered new-fangled, laughable nonsense. Fortunately science marches on, and generations of critics who confidently declared this or that to be "impossible" are soon forgotten.

So, what about Hyman's examples? Of the four he mentions, only N-rays remains on the provisional "scrap heap." All of the others are now topics of respect-able scientific discussion. Mitogenetic radiation, first reported in the 1920s, is now being vigorously studied in the form of biophotons (Trushin, 2004; Voeikov & Belousov, 2005). The idea of "Martian canals" is no longer unthinkable because water has been detected on Mars (and on the moon). Polywater is being discussed in terms of autothixotropy, a term used to describe a weak gel-like behavior that can develop in water (Vybíral & Voráček, 2007). More generally, water is now known to display different properties based not just on its chemical composition, which was a long-held dogma, but also on its structure (Roy et al., 2005).

My point is that critics who are enamored of the *status quo* often find challenging observations unsettling, so they are quick to consign anomalies to an imagined scrap heap where they can be ignored. This over-eager reaction accomplishes just one thing: It prematurely thwarts potential scientific breakthroughs. History is rife with such failures of imagination. Examples include:

> If the motion of the earth were circular, it would be violent and contrary to nature, and could not be eternal, since nothing violent is eternal. It follows, therefore, that the earth is not moved with a circular motion. *St. Thomas Aquinas, 1270*
>
> Animals, which move, have limbs and muscles; the earth has no limbs and muscles, hence it does not move. *Scipio Chiaramonti, Prof. of Philosophy and Mathematics, University of Pisa, 1633*
>
> The so-called theories of Einstein are merely the ravings of a mind polluted with liberal, democratic nonsense which is utterly unacceptable to German men of science. *Dr. Walter Gross, 1940.*
>
> (as cited in Cerf & Navasky, 1998)

Later, Hyman is amazed to find that he has never read any discussions about the variation of effect sizes among meta-analyses in different domains of parapsychology. He adds that different meta-analyses in parapsychology can obtain effect sizes such that some can be 875 times larger than others!

The reason he never read such discussions is because the idea is nonsense. It is tantamount to assuming that all medical studies involving humans ought to result in similar effect sizes because the target organisms in each case are the same. Obviously the effect size one obtains depends on what is being measured, and how. But all this aside, are there discussions of effect sizes in studies designed to look at *the same* underlying phenomenon? Yes, there are. I have compared effect sizes in ESP card tests, dream telepathy, ganzfeld telepathy, and remote perception experiments, and I found that they are indeed nearly identical (Radin, 1997, p. 110).

Hyman continues, recalling Bierman's (2001) statement that there is a significant tendency of a series of experiments that begin with positive effect sizes to steadily decline, over time, to zero, and that this is one reason that many contemporary parapsychologists now admit that psi effects cannot be replicated. Hyman presents Bierman's (2001) statement as evidence of a "regression to the mean" effect, which, if psi does not exist, would eventually lead to null results. But this is a misrepresentation of Bierman's position, who wrote: "However, [regression to the mean] doesn't fit the data because the mean of . . . study 2 and further on, should show a mean null effect size. In almost all the examples given in the previous chapter, this is not the case" (p. 275).

In any case, I doubt that "many" contemporary parapsychologists would agree with Hyman's interpretation. They might acknowledge, as I do, that effects can be difficult to replicate due to many unknown variables. But that they decline to zero effect sizes? No. Meta-analyses demonstrate that this is not the case. Indeed, if Hyman had continued his citation of Bierman (2001), he would have added that after declining, many effect sizes are observed to *rebound* and become positive again. In addition, serial position effects and declines in meta-analytical effect sizes are commonly observed in many scientific disciplines (Radin, 2006, pp. 121–125).

JAMES ALCOCK'S CHAPTER

Alcock repeatedly emphasizes his belief that psi violates the laws of physics. He writes that if the parapsychologists are demonstrated to be correct, the laws of physics as we know them will have been shown to be terribly wrong in some very important respects. Later he asserts that while the scientists are likely to attribute this state of affairs both to the absence of persuasive data and to the incompatibility of parapsychological claims with modern scientific theory, parapsychologists on the other hand typically attribute it to dogmatism rooted in the belief that paranormal phenomena are impossible because their existence would violate the laws of physics.

This last statement suggests a regrettable prejudice, which leads to a blithe assertion that is, frankly, preposterous. Alcock claims that it is simply wrong to claim that parapsychology's entry into the hallways of science is barred by scientific bigotry.

If this statement were true, then why does Alcock find it necessary to distinguish between what the parapsychologists say versus what "the scientists" say? Why do public opinion surveys consistently show that the majority of the world's population is interested in psi, and yet out of the thousands of institutions of higher learning around the world, over 99 percent of them do not employ a single faculty member known for his or her interest in this topic? Academia is usually quick to respond to the public's interest, offering accredited courses in areas ranging from basket weaving to videos games. So where are the degree programs offered in parapsychology? Why is it virtually impossible for a junior faculty member at a mainstream university to gain tenure if his or her research interest is in parapsychology (McClenon, 1984)? Why did the National Science Foundation, in its annual *Science and Engineering Indicators* report include parapsychology as an example of pseudoscience, thereby guaranteeing instant rejection of any grant proposals involving psi?[1] Why do some academics literally snort in derision when someone mentions an interest in parapsychology? Could there be any clearer evidence of bigotry than the fact that Alcock is completely oblivious to this prejudice?

Alcock continues to note that there have been a number of scientists over the years who have taken an interest in parapsychological matters, to the extent that they have conducted their own research, but then later abandoned it when their data showed no evidence of paranormality (e.g., Jeffers, 2003). The implication is that Jeffers is a proper "scientist," not one of those muddle-headed "parapsychologists." Unfortunately, he picked a poor example, because in fact Jeffers *did* obtain significant evidence for psi. Jeffers was a coauthor on an experiment that showed a significant psi effect precisely where it was predicted to appear, and it was successfully repeated (Freedman et al., 2003).

Not only does parapsychology have difficulty in deciding just what its legitimate subject matter is, writes Alcock, but, he adds, unlike the various domains of mainstream science, it deals exclusively with phenomena that are only negatively defined. Even if this assertion were true, so what? Negative definitions are common in many disciplines, ranging from physics, where concepts like dark energy and matter are defined by what they are not, to psychology, where concepts like inattentional blindness, implicit cognition, and unconscious processing are defined by contrast to conscious awareness, i.e., to what is not conscious. In any case, a positive definition of telepathy is easy to state: "A means of communication between people who are isolated by distance or shielding." Likewise, precognition may be defined as "a means of perception through time." Psychokinesis as "mind/matter interactions." And so on.

Then Alcock presents us with a Catch 22: "Anomalies" in parapsychology are nothing of the sort. First of all, there is no well-articulated theory in parapsychology against which data can be judged to be anomalous. Just as important, even were such a theory to exist, there is no body of reliable observations that could be taken to constitute an anomaly. In other words, you're damned if you have a theory, and damned if you don't. This "experimenter's regress" has been extensively discussed by Collins (1992). It is an illegitimate, unfalsifiable criticism.

Why is it, continues Alcock, if parapsychological phenomena do really exist, that they do not present themselves in the very delicate experiments conducted in modern physics? Physicists differ in their predictions, expectations, moods, desires, and personalities, and yet no "paranormal" anomaly ever shows up in their careful, precise data.

This may seem like a reasonable question, except for two important problems: First, most physicists don't set out to look for paranormal effects. On the rare occasion when they do, they sometimes *do* find these effects, as mentioned above in the case of Jeffers. And even in more conventional research physicists regularly discard unexpected "outliers." Some will throw away as much as 45 percent of their data when measurements do not conform to theoretical expectations (Radin, 1997, pp. 53–55). What causes these outliers? Could they be "paranormal"? Psychokinesis experiments suggest that some of them might be.

Second, Alcock wrongly assumes that expectation bias and other factors do not influence results of physics experiments. As Jeng (2006) explains, "The impression one gets from the history in physics textbooks is that [expectation] plays virtually no role, but this may be misleading" (p. 580). Jeng reviewed the historical record, which shows that the theoretical expectations of Sir Isaac Newton, Robert Millikan, James Maxwell, Albert Einstein, etc., strongly influenced what they and other physicists ultimately measured and published.

The same is true for Gregor Mendel and Louis Pasteur in biology and for famous scientists in many other disciplines. The point is that cognitive biases are ubiquitous and unavoidable in all human affairs, including science.

Alcock continues his critical litany claiming that there is an obvious lack of interest within parapsychology to explore non-paranormal explanations. This is regrettable for it adds weight to my contention that parapsychology represents beliefs in search of data, rather than data in search of explanation. This statement seems oblivious to the fact (a) that psi experiments are specifically designed to exclude "non-paranormal" explanations; (b) that articles reporting these experiments regularly include extensive discussions of possible alternative explanations; and; (c) that critics, such as Ray Hyman, who have reviewed several classes of psi experiments agree that they cannot propose plausible alternatives to psi. In addition, "belief in search of data" is a theory-based approach, which is presumably what Alcock and other critics keep insisting upon, whereas "data in search of an explanation" is empiricism, which is what parapsychology is largely about. If parapsychologists are damned for following both the former *and* the latter, then Alcock's critique is focused not on what parapsychologists actually *do*, but on what he believes parapsychology *is*.

And that belief is revealed unambiguously in his closing statement: Were parapsychology's claims shown to be true, then there is something horribly and fundamentally in error in physics and in biology and in neuroscience. In other words, Alcock's beliefs about parapsychology are motivated by what he believes is possible. Given that many of his beliefs about parapsychology are at best highly questionable, and some are plain wrong, what if his conception of what is physically possible is also wrong?

MICHAEL SHERMER'S CHAPTER

This chapter reveals the lengths some will go to prove a point, even if it requires maintaining a stark incongruity with their own beliefs. Shermer describes how he colluded with a television program to create an elaborate deception designed to fool five unwitting women into believing that he was psychic. After describing this process in some detail, he congratulates himself on how easy it was to foist the deception, and then concludes by stating that he would never host a television program that did this sort of thing regularly for one simple reason—it is unethical. He adds, it would be nothing less than wanton depravity.

At last, this is something on which we can fully agree. It is indeed reprehensible to deliberately set out to deceive the innocent. But this is exactly what Shermer set out to do! His chapter does not state if he required an informed consent from the individuals who participated in this sham, or whether he provided a post-session debriefing to explain why he had foisted the trick in the first place. If this were an experiment conducted in an academic setting, and executed as described, it would be rejected by a human participants review board as unethical.

It is a prime example of the "wanton depravity" that Shermer insists he would not, but in fact did, perpetrate.

GENERAL DISCUSSION

Most people, most of the time, take for granted that *reality*—the objective world "out there"—is revealed by common sense. This is as true for the general public as it is for most scientists. It certainly seems to be true for the critics discussed before. Common sense presents a reality where objects are obviously separate from one another in space and time, where the world is stable and independent of our attention and intentions, where causality is a strictly mechanistic, deterministic process, and where time is scrupulously unidirectional.

Unfortunately, there is a serious problem with this picture of reality. We know it is wrong. And not just slightly off the beam, but fundamentally wrong. By probing ever deeper into the fabric of reality, physics has revealed that what philosophers call "naïve realism" is based upon a miniscule slice of a much larger and exceedingly peculiar world. Einstein's theories tell us that what were once thought to be the building blocks of reality—space, time, matter, and energy—are not foundational after all. Rather, they are intertwined relationships. Quantum mechanics tells us that objects are not as separate as they appear to be, but entangled beyond the ordinary boundaries of space and time. Even our most cherished assumptions about local reality—that the world exists independently of observation—have been *empirically* falsified (Gröblacher et al., 2007).

This realization has led some physicists to go so far to suggest, in the august pages of *Nature* no less, that the "only reality is mind and observations, but observations are not of things. To see the Universe as it really is, we must abandon our tendency to conceptualize observations as things" (Henry, 2005, p. 29). If all this were not enough to cause us to seriously doubt common sense, then prevailing cosmological theories indicate that our most sophisticated physical theories, which already defy every common sense assumption, are themselves based on a mere 4 percent of the detectable universe (Ellis, 2007). The remaining 96 percent of dark matter and energy remains an enigma.

Exotic physics may seem too far removed from human experience to matter, so consider naïve reality from the neuroscience perspective: Conscious awareness is our only direct link to reality, and awareness is known to be a mere trickle of the torrents of information unconsciously processed by the nervous system and brain. In the process of throttling down this information for the sake of cognitive efficiency, the brain tricks us into perceiving not the world as it is, but as we expect it to be. The lesson is that when it comes to pondering the boundary between objective and subjective realities, and judging what is possible versus not possible, it is essential to cultivate high tolerance for ambiguity and the unexpected. This is a quality that comes naturally for scientific explorers, but it seems to elude those who specialize in criticism. When we probe the enigmatic boundary between mind and matter, phenomena regularly appear that violate common sense. Those phenomena include psi.

Evidence

For over 100 years, numerous methods for testing psi effects have been refined and repeatedly tested. One in particular, the ganzfeld telepathy experiment, has been tempered by four decades of severe criticism into a simple but highly effective laboratory method. Skipping over the specifics of the design, which are described elsewhere (e.g., Radin, 2006, Chapter 6), under the null hypothesis the probability that the receiver will correctly guess the actual target is 1 in 4, for a 25 percent chance hit rate. If the average hit rate obtained over repeated sessions is significantly above 25 percent, this provides evidence for a communications anomaly in accordance with the claim of telepathy.

From 1974 to 2009, three dozen principal investigators representing at least a dozen laboratories in Europe, North and South America, collectively published over 100 articles describing ganzfeld telepathy experiments. Overall they reported an overall hit rate of 32 percent in over 4,700 trials, as compared to the chance expected 25 percent. This hit rate is associated with odds against chance of beyond a quadrillion to one. In other words, whatever is going on in these studies is definitely not due to dumb luck. Is it due to telepathy?

Beginning with Hyman (1985), the accumulated database has been repeatedly reviewed using meta-analytic techniques. This history is reviewed in Storm and Ertel (2001) and Radin (2006). Of the half-dozen published reviews, including two by critics with long histories of skepticism about this phenomenon, all agreed that the effect size was significantly positive. (As mentioned previously, the negative conclusion reached by Milton and Wiseman in 1999 was later found to be incorrect.) In addition, all of the analysts agreed that the results could not be plausibly explained by selective reporting practices, and all but one found that effect sizes did not vary with experimental quality. In the one exception, Hyman (1985) claimed that effect sizes declined with improved experimental quality, implying that apparently positive results were due to design or implementation flaws. But ten independent scientists, including two statisticians and two psychologists not previously involved in the debate, reviewed his argument and not one agreed with his conclusion (reviewed in Radin, 1997, Chapter 6). More recently, a team of avowedly skeptical researchers led by Delgado-Romero and Howard (2005) repeated the ganzfeld experiment and they obtained a significant result. In fact, they observed the same 32 percent hit rate estimated by a grand meta-analysis applied to all ganzfeld sessions.

Meta-analysis of experiments conceptually similar to the ganzfeld test, based on conscious perception of the feeling of being stared at by a distant person, reported by Sheldrake (2003) and others, also show highly significant outcomes (Radin, 2005). In 60 reported experiments comprising a total of 33,357 individual trials, an overall hit rate of 54 percent was obtained where chance expectation was 50 percent. This outcome is associated with $p = 5 \times 10^{-17}$.

If the conscious-report telepathy experiment results are correct, then we should expect to find evidence for unconscious forms of telepathy as well. Experiments investigating such effects using EEG measures were first reported in student-teacher dyads by Tart (1963) and in identical twins by Duane and Behrendt (1965), the latter report published in *Science*. Those articles stimulated ten replications by eight groups around the world. Of the ten, nine reported positive results, including reports by Targ and Puthoff (1974) in *Nature*, Rebert and Turner (1974) in *Behavioral Neuropsychiatry*, and Orme-Johnson et al. (1982) in the *International Journal of Neuroscience*.

In the 1990s, a new series of EEG correlation studies were reported by Grinberg-Zylberbaum et al. (1994) in *Physics Essays*. Those studies stimulated another flurry of successful replications (including Radin, 2004; Standish et al., 2004; and Wackermann et al., 2003). To investigate the source of these EEG correlations, experiments were conducted by Standish et al. (2003) using an fMRI. They found that the visual cortex of the "receiving" person was significantly activated while the distant "sender" viewed a flickering checkerboard pattern. This result was later successfully replicated (Richards et al., 2005).

Besides studies involving telepathic-like correlations in central nervous system measures, some three dozen additional experiments, reported by laboratories in the United States, Germany, and the United Kingdom, have used autonomic measures such as skin conductance and heart rate. Meta-analysis of these studies (Schmidt et al., 2004), published in the *British Journal of Psychology*, concluded that those studies too showed significant, repeatable effects ($p < 0.001$).

Models of Reality

In sum, based on innumerable historical and contemporary anecdotes, scientific experiments were devised to test the scientific plausibility of telepathy. Positive evidence has been repeatedly observed in hundreds of experiments, and publications describing these studies and their meta-analyses have appeared in mainstream, peer-reviewed journals. Based on the preponderance of the empirical evidence accumulated to date, for those who are familiar with the relevant literature the existence of telepathy is a slam dunk. Even some staunch critics of parapsychology, such as Richard Wiseman, now agree that if we were discussing something less controversial, then the existing evidence would easily "prove" the case. Still, critics continue to deny that the evidence is sufficient. Why?

The short answer is that many critics assume that what is possible in human experience must be based on common sense models of reality. From this perspective, telepathy is literally impossible because it violates the tenets of naïve realism. As a result, with no plausible alternatives available, critics are reduced to offering complaints about replication rates despite analyses that objectively counter those complaints, or they suggest that results must be due to selective reporting practices despite counterarguments that show such suggestions are highly implausible. At last resort, the "potential flaw" argument is exploited, but this promissory critique is unfalsifiable and as such it is a polemical rather than a scientific argument.

It is possible to break this impasse? I believe it is. We know that naïve realism is an incorrect ontology, so we should ask whether a more comprehensive understanding of the fabric of reality would provide plausible theoretical support for telepathy. For an adequate ontology, we need a way to get information from point A to B without conventional signaling. This information transfer mechanism should: (a) have a well-accepted theoretical basis and ample empirical support; (b) it should provide interconnections that transcend the classical boundaries of space and time; (c) it should provide information processing algorithms that are infinitely more powerful than any classical computational technique; (d) it should extend into the macroscopic world; and (e) it should involve consciousness as an inextricable component (Rosenblum & Kuttner, 2006).

Until recently, there was no such reality. Indeed, Alcock insists that such a reality is "impossible." And yet, today points (a)–(d) are well-accepted in mainstream physics, primarily in the sub-disciplines of quantum entanglement and quantum information processing. The open question required to connect this "impossible" but demonstrably real ontology with psi is point (e), and whether quantum effects operate in the brain. This is an active debate, with some arguing in the affirmative (Josephson & Pallikari-Viras, 1991; Stapp, 1999), and others in the negative (Smith, 2009). While the debate continues to unfold, it is worth considering that quantum interconnections easily observed at the microscopic scale do not magically vanish in macroscopic systems. They just become more complex. Our present ability to detect connections in macroscopic systems is rapidly advancing, and there is already evidence that quantum effects are found not only in exotic conditions, but in everyday macroscopic systems.

For example, according to Vedral (2008), "Traditionally, entanglement was considered to be a quirk of microscopic objects that defied a common-sense explanation. Now, however, entanglement is recognized to be ubiquitous and robust" (p. 1005). Physicists have observed high quality quantum correlations in diamond that persist on millisecond time scales at room temperature (Neumann et al., 2008), in macroscopic mechanical membranes (Thompson et al., 2008), in photosynthesis (Engel et al., 2007), in electronic circuits (Ansmann et al., 2009), and in avian magnetonavigation (Solov'yov & Schulten, 2009). These developments, all occurring since the turn of the twenty-first century, suggest that quantum processing in the human nervous system is no longer unthinkable. Indeed, given the pace of progress today in quantum biology, it seems inevitable. What is the consequence of this "new" reality for understanding psi?

It means that we need to reframe our understanding of physical objects and what they may be capable of, including the brain. The quantum brain would no longer be exclusively locked inside the skull; parts of it would reside beyond the classical boundaries of space and time. This means that brain processes responsible for ordinary perception, and all the other cognitive processes studied by the neurosciences, may be influenced not only by local sensory information, but by impressions received from what common sense would label "at a distance."

With the brain viewed as a quantum object, people who are asked to keep each other "in mind" would be entangled not just emotionally, but physically. Those brains might "co-process" information regarded as important by both individuals, and as such these psychophysical entanglements might explain the remarkable coincidences reported between separated loved ones and identical twins. For example, Playfair (2003) reports a case (one of many) in which a healthy man suddenly experienced a suffocating pain in his chest while hundreds of miles away, at the same moment, his identical twin was suffering a heart attack. When I give presentations and ask if anyone in the audience personally knows similar stories first-hand, and not as hearsay, invariably a few people will raise their hands.

For the most part, scientists who are not directly involved in quantum physics and its leading-edge applications are not aware that the physics of the twenty-first century *requires* spooky action at a distance. Physics today *is* the radical worldview shift called for by French in this volume. The critic's lament is that for psi to be true, as Alcock wrote, there is something "horribly and fundamentally in error" in physics and in biology and in neuroscience. Critics can rest assured that this fear is unfounded. Physics, biology, and neuroscience are not horribly wrong. They are just evolving into a direction that happens to provide strong support for psi experiences regarded not as unexpected or paranormal, but as expected, normal consequences of residing in a connected fabric of reality.

Conclusion

Whether a plausible explanation for psi eventually includes quantum theory as presently understood, or a more comprehensive future theory that includes quantum mechanics as an approximation of something even stranger (a more likely scenario), then the likelihood that psi exists is systematically improving both empirically and theoretically. I believe that critics' pleas to abandon this line of research are woefully premature, that their concerns about difficulties in replication are overly pessimistic, and their fears about "impossible things" are unfounded.

NOTE

1. In the late 1990s, I was told by a program director at the National Science Foundation (NFS) who was personally very interested in psi that the NSF's public position was, of course, complete openness to all research topics, but in fact it would not consider funding research proposals involving psi.

REFERENCES

Ansmann, M., Wang, H., Bialczak, R. C., Hofheinz, M., Lucero, E., Neeley, M., O'Connell, A. D., et al. (2009). Violation of Bell's inequality in Josephson phase qubits. *Nature*, 461, 504–506.

Bem, D. J., & Honorton, C. (1994). Does psi exist? Replicable evidence for an anomalous process of information transfer. *Psychological Bulletin*, 115, 4–14.

Bierman, D. J. (2001). On the nature of anomalous phenomena: Another reality between the world of subjective consciousness and the objective world of physics?

In P. van Locke (Ed.), *The physical nature of consciousness* (pp. 269–292). New York: Benjamins.

Cerf, C., & Navasky, V. (1998). *The experts speak: The definitive compendium of authoritative misinformation.* New York: Villard/Random House.

Collins, H. M. (1992). *Changing order: Replication and induction in scientific practice* (2nd ed.). Chicago: University of Chicago Press.

Delgado-Romero, E., & Howard, G. (2005). Finding and correcting flawed research literatures. *The Humanistic Psychologist, 33*(4), 293–303.

Duane, T. D., & Behrendt, T. (1965). Extrasensory electroencephalographic induction between identical twins. *Science, 150,* 367.

Ellis, G. F. R. (2007). Issues in the philosophy of cosmology. In J. Butterfield & J. Earman (Eds.), *Handbook of the philosophy of science: Philosophy of physics* (pp. 1183–1285). Amsterdam: Elsevier Press.

Engel G. S., Calhoun, T. R., Read, E. L., Ahn, T. K., Mančal, T., Cheng, Y. C., et al. (2007). Evidence for wavelike energy transfer through quantum coherence in photosynthetic systems. *Nature, 446,* 782–786.

Freedman, M., Jeffers, S., Saeger, K., Binns, M., & Black, S. (2003). Effects of frontal lobe lesions on intentionality and random physical phenomena. *Journal of Scientific Exploration, 17*(4), 651–668.

Grinberg-Zylberbaum, J., Delaflor, M., Attie, L., & Goswami, L. (1994). The Einstein-Podolsky-Rosen paradox in the brain: The transferred potential. *Physics Essays, 7,* 422–428.

Gröblacher, S., Paterek, T., Kaltenbaek, R., Brukner, Č., Żukowski, M., Aspelmeyer, M., et al. (2007). An experimental test of non-local realism. *Nature, 446,* 871–875.

Henry, R. C. (2005). The mental universe. *Nature, 436,* 29.

Hyman, R. (1985). The Ganzfeld psi experiment: A critical appraisal. *Journal of Parapsychology, 49,* 3–49.

Jeffers, S. (2003). Physics and claims for anomalous effects related to consciousness. *Journal of Consciousness Studies, 10,* 135–152.

Jeng, M. (2006). A selected history of expectation bias in physics. *American Journal of Physics, 74,* 578–583.

Josephson, B. D., & Pallikari-Viras, F. (1991). Biological utilization of quantum nonlocality. *Foundations of Physics, 21,* 197–207.

McClenon, J. (1984). *Deviant science: The case of parapsychology.* Philadelphia: University of Pennsylvania Press.

Milton, J., & Wiseman, R. (1999). Does psi exist? Lack of replication of an anomalous process of information transfer. *Psychological Bulletin, 125,* 387–391.

Neumann P., Mizuochi, N., Rempp, F., Hemmer, P., Watanabe, H., Yamasaki, S., et al. (2008). Multipartite entanglement among single spins in diamond, *Science, 320,* 1326–1329.

Orme-Johnson, D. W., Dillbeck, M. C., Wallace, R. K., & Landrith, G. S. (1982). Intersubject EEG coherence: Is consciousness a field? *International Journal of Neuroscience, 16,* 203–209.

Playfair, G. L. (2003). *Twin telepathy: The psychic connection.* London: Vega.

Radin, D. I. (1997). *The conscious universe.* San Francisco: HarperOne.

Radin, D. I. (2004). Event-related electroencephalographic correlations between isolated human subjects. *Journal of Alternative and Complementary Medicine, 10,* 315–323.

Radin, D. I. (2005). The sense of being stared at: A preliminary meta-analysis. *Journal of Consciousness Studies, 12*(6), 95–100.

Radin, D. I. (2006). *Entangled minds*. New York: Simon & Schuster.

Rebert, C. S., & Turner, A. (1974). EEG spectrum analysis techniques applied to the problem of psi phenomena. *Behavioral Neuropsychiatry*, 6, 18–24.

Richards, T. L., Kozak, L., Johnson, L. C., & Standish, L. J. (2005). Replicable functional magnetic resonance imaging evidence of correlated brain signals between physically and sensory isolated subjects. *Journal of Alternative and Complementary Medicine*, 11, 955–963.

Rosenblum, B., & Kuttner, F. (2006). *Quantum enigma*. London: Oxford University Press.

Roy, R., Tiller, W. A., Bell, I., & Hoover, M. R. (2005). The structure of liquid water. Novel insights from materials research: Potential relevance to homeopathy. *Materials Research Innovations*, 9(4), 577–608.

Schmidt, S., Schneider, R., Utts, J., & Walach, H. (2004). Distant intentionality and the feeling of being stared at: Two meta-analyses. *British Journal of Psychology*, 95, 235–247.

Sheldrake, R. (2003). *The sense of being stared at*. New York: Crown.

Smith, C. U. M. (2009). The "hard problem" and the quantum physicists. Part 2: Modern times. *Brain and Cognition*, 71, 54–63.

Solov'yov, I. A., & Schulten, K. (2009). Magnetoreception through cryptochrome may involve superoxide. *Biophysical Journal*, 96(12), 4804–4813.

Standish, L. J., Johnson, L. C., Richards, T., & Kozak, L. (2003). Evidence of correlated functional MRI signals between distant human brains. *Alternative Therapies in Health and Medicine*, 9, 122–128.

Standish, L. J., Kozak, L., Johnson, L. C., & Richards, T. (2004). Electroencephalographic evidence of correlated event-related signals between the brains of spatially and sensory isolated human subjects. *Journal of Alternative and Complementary Medicine*, 10, 307–314.

Stapp, H. (1999). Attention, intention and will in quantum physics. In B. Libet, A. Freeman, & K. Sutherland (Eds.), *The volitional brain* (pp. 143–164). Thorverton, UK: Imprint Academic.

Storm, L., & Ertel, S. (2001). Does psi exist? Comments on Milton and Wiseman's (1999) meta-analysis of Ganzfeld research. *Psychological Bulletin*, 127, 424–433.

Targ, R., & Puthoff, H. (1974). Information transmission under conditions of sensory shielding. *Nature*, 251, 602–607.

Tart, C. T. (1963). Possible physiological correlates of psi cognition. *International Journal of Parapsychology*, 5, 375–386.

Thompson, J. D., Zwickl, B. M., Jayich, A. M., Marquardt, F., Girvin, S. M., & Harris, J. G. E. (2008). Strong dispersive coupling of a high-finesse cavity to a micromechanical membrane, *Nature*, 452, 72–75.

Trushin, M. V. (2004). Light-mediated "conversation" among microorganisms. *Microbiological Research*, 159(1), 1–10.

Vedral, V. (2008). Quantifying entanglement in macroscopic systems. *Nature*, 453, 1004–1007.

Voeikov, V. L., & Belousov, L. V. (2005). From mitogenetic rays to biophotons. In L. V. Belousov, V. L. Voeikov, & V. S. Martynyuk (Eds.), *Biophotonics and coherent systems in biology* (pp. 1–16). New York: Springer.

Vybíral, B., & Voráček, P. (2007). Long term structural effects in water: Autothixotropy of water and its hysteresis. *Homeopathy*, 96(3), 183–188.

Wackermann, J., Seiter, C., Keibel, H., & Walach, H. (2003). Correlations between spatially separated human subjects. *Neuroscience Letters*, 336, 60–64.

"The Nocturnal Visitor" (© Dierdre Luzwick. Used by permission.)

CHAPTER 8

Let's Focus on the Data

James E. Alcock

I am disappointed by the contributions to this volume made by those who advocate for parapsychology, for those authors appear to misunderstand completely why mainstream science continues to be unpersuaded by their claims. Rather than acknowledging the legitimacy of scientists' reservations and addressing them in a reasoned manner, they instead rail at "the unfairness of it all" and at times resort to condescending attributions about those who carry the message. None even considers the possibility that their quest might be in vain, that psi may not actually exist. This is hardly an open-minded attitude. Contrast this with the offerings from the counteradvocates: not one of them, despite their strong reservations at present, absolutely rules out the possibility that psi exists. Neither do they stoop to *ad hominem* attacks, but focus instead on the methodological problems inherent in parapsychological research.

And whether parapsychologists like it or not, it is only the weakness of parapsychological data that keeps parapsychology from scientific acceptance. Bay at the moon if one wants, rail at the critics if one wishes, but it changes nothing. It is not scientific bigotry that is responsible for parapsychology's exclusion, nor is it, as Chris Carter would have us believe, a deep-seated fear of the paranormal. It is the data. Moreover, even if we wanted to do so—and this is certainly not the case— there is nothing that Ray Hyman or Michael Shermer or Christopher French or Richard Wiseman or I could do to keep parapsychology from scientific acceptance if there were solid, replicable data. Science ultimately responds to reliable data. The theory of relativity—which was expressed not in the vague generalities typical of parapsychological theories, but in precise mathematical language—was much maligned at first; it was powerful empirical data that led to its acceptance within mainstream science. Similarly, scientists accept the weirdness of the quantum world, not because it fits well with common experience, for it most certainly does not, but because of reliable data that support its precisely articulated theory.

Carter, in his chapter for this volume, disagrees with my view for he is convinced that parapsychology has already produced strong, replicable data, and that, were it not for pernicious or misguided critics, it would assume its rightful place in the hall of science. He rejects, virtually by fiat, earlier critiques made by Hyman and myself, and suggests that we are reacting in a hysterical manner to protect our "scientific assumptions," which are challenged by putative evidence of psi. Space does not permit a detailed response to his litany of criticisms, which are generally polemical rather than substantial. However, it appears that Carter simply fails to comprehend the nature and the seriousness of the problems that I have outlined. A few examples:

1. He naively views the affiliate status granted to the Parapsychology Association by the American Association for the Advancement of Science in 1969 as countering my statement that parapsychology has been rebuffed by science. However, he is wrong to interpret that gesture, which was brought about by the efforts of then-president Margaret Mead, as an indication that science has accepted the reality of the paranormal. Furthermore, one cannot have it both ways. If parapsychology has not been rebuffed by science as he claims, then surely he has no dispute with the counteradvocates, and there would be no need for this present volume of writings.

2. He totally misunderstands my concern about the negative definition of psi, and quotes Dean Radin's view that psi is positively defined as a means by which information can be gained from a distance without the use of the ordinary senses. This of course means that one must first rule out "the use of the ordinary senses," which is, of course, the very essence of a negative definition.

3. He misunderstands my concerns about the leap from statistical conclusions to attributions of psi. All that statistical testing can tell us is that something is unlikely to have occurred by chance alone. To assume that the cause in a given parapsychological experiment was paranormal is totally arbitrary. The cause of a statistical deviation could be anything: undetected methodological flaws; calculation errors; or even a mischievous Zeus. Suppose my alternate hypothesis were that Zeus from time to time brings about statistical deviations in order to tease researchers: I doubt that anyone would accept a statistical deviation as evidence for the existence of Zeus. The simple finding that chance is an unlikely explanation does not in itself add validity to a paranormal explanation.

4. Again with reference to my criticism of the reliance on a statistical approach, Carter shows more statistical naïveté by referring to Burton

Camp's 1937 statement about the use of statistics in parapsychological research of the day. First of all, Camp referred only to the statistical procedures being used, and this has nothing to do with the interpretation of statistical deviations, which is the basis of my concern. Moreover, it would make no sense to cite Camp even if procedures were the issue: it is akin to saying that Transworld Airlines passed a safety audit back in 1937, and so there is no need to have any concern about their safety procedures today.

5. In response to my statement that paranormal "anomalies" are never observed in modern physical research, he counters with Helmut Schmidt's research. This misses the point completely, for Schmidt's so-called anomalies did not occur in the course of normal physical research. He deliberately set up situations in which he hoped to demonstrate paranormal effects. Moreover, none of his research was without significant methodological flaws or independently replicable (Alcock, 1987).

These are but a few examples of Carter's obvious failure to understand and address my concerns.

Turning to Radin's chapter, he acknowledges that repeatability is the "single most important criterion for distinguishing science from religious faith." He then refers to two classes of repeatability. The first of these corresponds to what is generally meant by "repeatability" within science: the replication of experiments carried out under controlled conditions. However, his second "class" of repeatability is described as "reports of human experience and the ways that people have tried to study them." It is not clear just how that refers in any meaningful sense to the repeatability sought by scientists. In any case, it is this that is the focus of Radin's chapter.

What Radin provides is a light historical narrative; he refers to various historical reports as well as to a various twentieth century studies, and treats each as though it constitutes persuasive evidence of the paranormal. However, the empirical studies that he addresses have all received substantial criticism over the years, and none are accepted—I daresay even by most parapsychologists—as providing the long-sought scientific demonstration of the reality of psi. Then, in an amazing triumph of hope over experience, Radin suggests that in only a few years' time, before 2015, some psi applications and methods may already be in "common use." Such a blinkered view of the state of parapsychology makes critical dialogue impossible.

I need to add a few words about the contributions from the counteradvocates:

Shermer's anecdotal account of his experience as a psychic carries an important lesson for those who are impressed by anecdotal testimony about paranormal events: it is frightfully easy to lead others to believe that one has psychic powers. Had Shermer not made the effort to disabuse them, those who were taken in would no doubt forever remember his "feats" as evidence of psychic phenomena. He makes the important observation that while there may be people out to fool us, we are very capable of fooling ourselves, and this leaves us very vulnerable to deception and error. This is of course why it is so important to treat Radin's historical accounts with great caution: no matter how trustworthy an individual, and notwithstanding his or her scientific credentials, personal experience is often a poor guide to reality, and it is particularly so when dealing with putative paranormal/supernatural phenomena.

French encourages the continuation of parapsychological research, despite its many problems. He provides a good discussion of many of those problems, and he focuses as well on the great divide between advocates and counteradvocates. He hopes for more constructive communication. However, his hopes are not borne out in this volume, in my opinion, for the advocates represented here simply reject the message and revile the messenger.

Hyman addresses the failure of parapsychology to demonstrate a scientific basis for its supposed phenomena despite over a century of dedicated effort. He reminds us of the importance that science places on being able to predict outcomes of experiments, and he points out that parapsychology relies not upon prediction, but post-diction: Rather than successfully predicting what will occur in an experiment, success is claimed through *post hoc* interpretations. And while parapsychologists have increasingly turned to meta-analysis to support the existence of psi, he discusses the serious difficulties that the meta-analytic approach presents. He points out that parapsychological theories do not connect with parapsychological research: they do not establish boundaries as to what is considered evidence for psi, and they are not constrained by the outcomes of psi experiments. Thus, they are not useful scientific theories.

Until advocates of parapsychology can take seriously the concerns of counteradvocates, parapsychology will continue to spin its wheels. However, judging by the contributions of the advocates to this volume, it is much easier to make attributions about the characters of the critics than it is to deal appropriately with the substance of the criticism. If, as I believe likely, there is no psi, then perhaps that is all that is left in defence of their beliefs.

REFERENCE

Alcock, J. E. (1987). A comprehensive review of major empirical studies in parapsychology involving random event generators and remote viewing. In D. Druckman & J. Swets (Eds.), *Enhancing human performance: Issues, theories and techniques* (Vol. 2, pp. 99–102). Washington, DC: National Academy Press.

CHAPTER 9

What's Wrong with Materialism?

Ray Hyman

It is often implied that the research findings within our field constitute a death blow to materialism. I am puzzled by this claim, since I thought that few people were really so unsophisticated as to mistake our concepts for reality.

Martin Johnson (1976)

All the chapters in this book provide much food for thought. Both the critics and the defenders of parapsychological claims raise issues that, given time and relatively unlimited space, I am tempted to discuss. Given that neither my time nor my space is unlimited, I will restrict my comments to some of the provocative opinions contained in Chris Carter's chapter, "Persistent Denial: A Century of Denying the Evidence."

Carter assails the "materialism" of science. His characterization of this materialism is rather simplistic. It is true that scientists work within a materialistic framework. They could not do otherwise and still do science. Science came into being as a way to explain the world in terms of material rather than spiritual or supernatural substances. Materialism provides a working framework for doing science. Spiritual and supernatural explanations of phenomena have been with us since our species began raising questions about our origins and the meaning of life. Such explanations, which attribute happenings to idiosyncratic gods and supernatural forces, do not foster the search for lawful, predictable, and controllable causes. It was the advent of modern science, fuelled by the willingness to search for non-supernatural causes, that enabled, and continues to enable, the explosion of knowledge and technology.

Carter seems to believe that materialism is some sort of rigid straitjacket that prevents scientists from accepting the reality of his brand of supernaturalism. A materialistic framework is necessary to do scientific work. However, people can work as scientists and still privately adhere to a variety of other belief systems. Most of the earlier scientists were devoutly religious. Many prominent scientists today openly profess a deep belief in a religion. So whatever the materialism is that underlies science, it obviously does not preclude individual scientists from holding a variety of non-materialistic beliefs. This typically does not create problems as long as these individuals, qua scientists, operate within a materialistic framework when doing and communicating science.

As some philosophers have noted, the material of science is not well circumscribed and has undergone dramatic changes. A world that consists of radiation, fields, quanta, and curved space was not part of the materialism of early scientists. One could argue that the change in the material worlds implied by general relativity and quantum mechanics constitute as dramatic a departure from the materialism of previous scientific generations as that implied by psychic phenomena.

Although Carter and Dean Radin rant against the materialism of science, this materialism has changed dramatically and presumably will do so in the future. It is not a fixed, immutable belief system. However, and this is what Carter and Radin seem to overlook, the materialistic belief system of science has undergone these dramatic transformations in response to evidence that is rigorous, replicable, and irrefutable. This is how science works. If Carter and his fellow parapsychologists put forth equally rigorous, replicable, and irrefutable evidence for something they call "psi," the scientific community's materialism will change yet again to accommodate this new input.

Carter's mantra, echoing that of many of his fellow parapsychologists, is that, in fact, the parapsychologists have provided just such irreproachable evidence for the reality of psi. They assert that the scientific community has not recognized this because of an inherent bias against paranormal claims. If, as Cater maintains, the scientific community treated parapsychology in the same way it treated other disciplines, it would long ago have accepted the reality of psi. To support this fantasy, Carter implies that skeptics, such as James Alcock and me, have deliberately selected and/or distorted the evidence to maintain their claims that parapsychological evidence does not pass muster. Indeed, he accuses us of deliberately going out our way to demean parapsychology.

Sadly, his chapter is based on misrepresentations of the facts, accusations of biased and irresponsible behavior on the part of critics, and blatant failure to deal with the many legitimate arguments against the validity of the parapsychological claims. Before I explicate these points, I want to make a few comments about Carter's argument that the real issue is that scientists and the critics have a worldview that cannot tolerate the possibility of non-materialistic alternatives (whatever they might be). He focuses on the alleged bias of critics and simply assumes, rather than demonstrates, that the parapsychological evidence is rock solid.

Despite our obvious disagreements, Carter and I have one thing in common. We both use the history of science to illuminate our arguments. However, we differ in our reading of this history (or perhaps on what we read) and the lessons to be drawn. Carter is correct in asserting that scientists are biased against the claims for psi. He errs, however, in assuming that parapsychology is unique in this respect. A central feature of scientific inquiry is that scientists are biased against claims that are inconsistent with the current framework within which they are working. This was true for relativity, quantum mechanics, evolution by natural selection, N-rays, continental drift, and just about every other novel claim that was inconsistent with a current theoretical framework.

In many of these cases, solid, replicable evidence accumulated and the scientific community revised or adjusted its existing theories to accommodate this evidence. In other cases, such as the claims for Martian canals, N-rays, and mitogenetic radiation, the evidence, which at first seemed impressive, became inconsistent. With increasing numbers of failed replications, the claims of an anomaly were dismissed. In this respect, the claims for psi resemble those, say, for N-rays. At first, many successful papers were published on N-rays, especially by eminent French scientists. Other scientists were encouraged to investigate N-rays. As more and more scientists began working on N-rays, more and more reports were published of failed replications. Eventually, the scientific community relegated N-rays to the discard pile. In various domains of parapsychological inquiry a similar pattern is seen. At first there are many papers that claim "statistical significance." Eventually, some of the original investigators along with new ones fail to obtain significant results. This "decline effect" is just one of the ways that inconsistencies plague lines of parapsychological research. Kennedy (2001, 2003) lists several others.

As I mentioned in my chapter, parapsychological claims resemble these other failed claims of anomalies in science in that the proponents of the claim defended the inconsistencies in terms of experimenter effects, non-conducive conditions, and the like. Carter is one of those writers sympathetic to parapsychology, who, along with Radin, argues that "consistent, replicable" evidence for psi exists. This claim, of course, flies in the face of those parapsychologists (as I discussed in my chapter) who argue that not only have parapsychologists failed in their attempts to produce consistent and replicable evidence for psi, but such evidence *in principle* cannot be produced! This is because, in their view, an intrinsic property of psi is that it actively evades scientific scrutiny (Bierman, 2001; Jahn & Dunne, 2008; Kennedy, 2001, 2003; Lucadou, 2001).

I suspect that Carter, like many of his colleagues, uses the term "replicable" in a way quite different from how it is understood in orthodox science. Radin, among others, have maintained that the lack of replication of evidence for psi was more apparent than real. Because of low to moderate effect sizes, most psi experiments lack adequate power to detect a real effect. Indeed, the use of meta-analysis was seen as a way to overcome this defect. However, there now have been a number of failed replications of key parapsychological findings that had sufficient power. The most visible one was the massive attempt to independently replicate the key findings of the Princeton random event generator experiments (Jahn et al., 2000). Such striking failures cannot be brushed aside. As I have pointed out in my chapter and elsewhere, some replications that parapsychologists have claimed as successes were actually failed replications. The claims for success in these cases come about from a very lax standard for "success." Because of the loose ties between theory and data, parapsychologists often are willing to claim as a successful replication any outcome that is "significant," even if the pattern of the outcome contradicts that of the original experiment.

My point is that, yes, scientists are biased against the claims for psi. And this is as it *should* be. Science has been successful just because it has been conservative. It is suspicious of any claims that apparently violate expectations based on the current framework within a given area of inquiry. The claims for an anomaly in the orbit of Uranus, for example, were viewed with suspicion. Even more, the claims that the anomaly was due to a failure of Newton's laws of gravity when applied to outer space were met with disbelief. After all, Newton's mechanics had survived many previous challenges and had provided a host of striking successes. The anomaly was resolved, and resistance to the proposed solution vanished in the face of good and replicable evidence for the existence of the new planet.

Scientists have at least two good reasons for maintaining a bias against claims for psi. Parapsychologists, along with others who have claimed the discovery of an "anomaly," imply that they have uncovered a meaningful discrepancy from what should be expected under an existing scientific framework. Urbain Le Verrier, for example, convincingly demonstrated that the orbit of Uranus departed in a small, but very reliable way from what was predicted under Newtonian mechanics. Le Verrier's exhaustive re-analysis of all the data on the orbit of Uranus convincingly showed that the anomaly was real. He then provided an explanation that could be scientifically verified.

In those cases within science where an anomaly was claimed, the anomaly was depicted as a precisely delineated departure from a given baseline. The baseline in question was always a theoretical expectation within a more or less delimited area of science—planetary astronomy, energy physics, genetic biology, etc. Parapsychology stands out as an exception. Here the claimed "anomaly" is not a well specified departure from a theoretical prediction within a given domain of science. Instead it could be any departure from a generic baseline. The connection between parapsychological theory (which is also amorphous) and specific outcomes in psi research is such that the theory places no constraints on which statistical departures constitute evidence for psi and which do not. The parapsychologists have no disciplined way to even show that the statistical discrepancies in one experiment have any relation to the statistical discrepancies in another. Nor has anyone reported a single case of a discrepancy within regular scientific research that can be attributed to something called "psi" (unless the parapsychologists want to claim that every unexpected glitch in a scientific experiment is due to psi).

Such a lack of constraint between theory and data provide plenty of degrees of freedom to consider any departure from chance as evidence for psi. This helps boost the illusion of many more successful outcomes than actually exist. It also provides justification for scientists to be suspicious of the claims for psi.

The second reason for being dubious is the issue of replicability. Many failed claims in science passed the first test of being based on a clearly defined discrepancy from a theoretical prediction with a given field of science. However, they failed the second test in that the evidence supporting the claimed anomaly became inconsistent and could not be reliably replicated by independent experimenters. Radin and Carter are among those writers who boldly declare that the evidence for psi is strong, lawful, and replicable. What they seem to have in mind is that in many areas of psi research a new experimental design apparently yields several studies that produce statistical significance (regardless of whether the internal patterns of outcomes replicate). As Bierman, Kennedy, and other parapsychologists point out, the problem is that over time the experimental design no longer shows consistent results and, in many cases, no longer can yield significance.

As I keep emphasizing, regular science has a stricter standard for replicability. For one thing, a claimed anomaly, as already discussed, must be a clearly defined pattern of deviation from a theoretical prediction. Clearly, parapsychology cannot meet this standard. Along with this first condition, the clearly defined pattern must be able to be replicated by independent investigators given adequate research design and power. Parapsychology has also failed to meet the second condition. Retrospective demonstrations of statistical significance of combined effect sizes in meta-analyses of past experiments are insufficient. Even if the underlying assumptions of meta-analysis were met—which they decidedly have not been—it is a retrospective procedure. The idea of replicability within science is a predictive one—given adequate conditions and power, can an experimenter obtain the predicted result? Again, the several examples in which this has been attempted in parapsychology have failed.

Consider this sobering fact. Every discipline that claims to be a science can provide hundreds of examples of what Thomas Kuhn called paradigm[1] experiments (Kuhn, 1970). These are experiments that introductory textbooks and laboratories in each discipline can assign to their students with the strong expectation that the students will obtain the predicted results. In psychology, a discipline with which parapsychologists often favorably compare their discipline, introductory students can be assigned hundreds of paradigm experiments in perception, memory, learning, decision making, and the like with full confidence that the students will obtain the expected outcome. Parapsychology stands alone as the only discipline claiming to be a science that has not one such experiment. This fact alone makes it clear that parapsychology is unique in lacking replicability.

Unfortunately, I have to conclude that Carter's chapter comes close to consisting of an *ad hominem* attack against critics of parapsychology. His emphasis is on the alleged worldview that impels the critics to go to any lengths—including deliberate suppression of data. Indeed, there are, and there have been, vocal skeptics who have behaved in ways that might justify some of Carter's concerns. On the other hand it is a logical fallacy to dismiss a person's criticisms on the basis of their alleged motivations and mindsets. Worse, attributing motivations and worldviews to critics on the basis of flimsy gossip makes for misleading and irrelevant arguments.

Because Carter makes James Alcock and me the chief villains in his diatribe, I feel compelled to depart from the stance that I preach to others and try to follow in my own argumentation. I have always argued that the critics should focus on the issues and avoid personalities. My article on "Proper Criticism," which was first published in 1987 and has been subsequently reprinted online, is just one example of my position (Hyman, 1987). I believe that my approximately 100 published critical assessments of parapsychology adequately demonstrate that Carter's repeated attempts to caste me in the role of a bigoted fanatic whose mission is to suppress and destroy parapsychology have no basis. As I will point out, whatever Carter wants to say about Alcock and me, he cannot in good faith accuse us of not having done our homework. I have always carefully examined the best evidence for a parapsychological claim before providing a critique. The reason I chose Alcock for the National Research Council (NRC) Committee was simply because he also is one of the few critics who conscientiously makes sure to examine the best evidence available that supports a parapsychological claim. Ironically, such conscientiousness is glaringly absence in Carter's attacks.

Carter begins his chapter with a quote from John Alexander that states that "Hyman and James Alcock proceeded on an intentional path to discredit the work in parapsychology . . . What we may ask, are they afraid of? Is protecting scientific orthodoxy so vital that they must deny evidence and suppress contrary opinion?" Later in his chapter, Carter provides a lengthy quotation (460 words) from this same source (Alexander, 1989). This quotation gives at best a misleading account of the NRC Committee's treatment of parapsychology. Apparently, Alexander's report is the main source of Carter's account. It seems likely that Carter did not read either the NRC Committee's report on the parapsychological research (Hyman, 1988) or Alcock's commissioned paper (1988). If he had done so he would have realized that much of what he said is simply not true.

John Alexander played a limited role in the Committee's work. In 1985, at the first meeting of the Committee on Techniques to Enhance Human Performance, Lt. General Albert Stubblebine III (retired) and then Lt. Colonel John Alexander briefed the Committee on potential applications and some research on the paranormal in the armed forces. Alexander claimed that he could provide the Committee with evidence, as well as a demonstration, of a parapsychological experiment that could be repeated on demand. He urged the Committee to visit San Diego to witness this demonstration. Alexander had been using Army money to support the research of Cleve Backster. Backster, who is a polygraph expert, had gained public attention in 1966 when he hooked up a polygraph to a philodendron plant and recorded a response that he claimed was similar to that of humans in an emotional state. Backster argued that the plant exhibited this emotional response when brine shrimp were either threatened or killed in an adjoining room. This work instigated a highly controversial movement dealing with "primary perception" in plants (e.g., Backster, 2003).

When the Committee held one of its meetings in San Diego in February, 1986, Alexander arranged for us to spend a day at the Backster Research Foundation. Alexander and Backster informed us that Backster had devised a technique for recording electrical activity in leukocytes taken from a donor's mouth. These leukocytes would subsequently show reactions to the donor's emotional states, even if the donor were separated as much as a mile from the leukocytes. Backster showed us his apparatus and the data he had collected so far. He also attempted to demonstrate the phenomenon with a volunteer from our Committee. Suffice it to say, that neither Backster's data nor the demonstration showed any evidence of a paranormal phenomenon. Not only did the apparatus suffer from inadequate shielding and other defects, but the apparent correlations between emotional states of the donor and the detached leukocytes seemed to be due to statistical artifacts and misinterpretation of the data.

We included a description of the Backster experiment in our report only because Colonel Alexander had insisted that the Committee should investigate it as an example of that elusive quarry—the replicable parapsychological experiment. Unfortunately, it was far from what it purported to be. I believe that most mainstream parapsychologists would not want Backster's work to serve as an exemplar of parapsychological work. Although I did provide a description of Backster's work in our report, we did not base our assessment of parapsychological research in general on his project. And contrary to what our critics such as Carter and Alexander allege, we certainly did not refer "only to those published articles that supported [our] position and ignored material that did not..." I consider this accusation to be highly offensive. Throughout my professional career I have always preached, as well as practiced, that one should always evaluate an argument in the light of the best evidence in its support (known as the principle of charity in philosophy). In addition to my paper on "Proper Criticism," mentioned before, the reader might want to read my article for psychologists on how to critique a published article (Hyman, 1995). My publications both on parapsychology and other matters, I believe, contradict the image of me that Carter is trying to promote.

Parapsychologists were understandably disappointed, and—to put it mildly—upset by the Committee report. They complained that the report was biased because it did not contain the input of a parapsychologist. They even managed to enlist U.S. Senator Claiborne Pell in their attack on the Committee's activities. Along the way, many distortions and misrepresentations about how and what we did, especially with respect to the activities of the Subcommittee on Parapsychology which I chaired, have taken on the status of an urban legend. As a result, it is little wonder that Carter has obtained a distorted image of the why, what, and how of our project. He might have presented a more accurate picture by reading the relevant report and supporting papers rather than relying upon secondary and untrustworthy sources.

It may help to consider the context in which the Subcommittee on Parapsychology was created. The Committee on Enhancing Human Performance (CEHP) consisted of 14 members who first met in June 1985. The Committee was created in response to a request by the Army Research Institute (ARI). ARI was interested in assessing the potential value of a number of borderline and controversial techniques that had been offered to the Army and other governmental institutions as ways to enhance human performance. These included guided imagery, mental rehearsal, biofeedback, Hemi-Sync technology, stress management techniques, Neurolinguisitic Programming, and others. Just prior to the formation of CEHP, ARI, which supplied the financial support for the Committee's work, had commissioned the parapsychologist, John Palmer, to perform a comprehensive review of the current status of parapsychology. Palmer prepared a 240-page report (Palmer, 1985). His evaluation focused on eight major research areas over the previous 20 years. The areas included: the Maimonides Medical Center's dream experiments, remote viewing, the ganzfeld research, random event generator (REG) research, the Delmore experiments, correlational studies (attempting to find psychological correlates of psi), the psi-mediated instrumental response, and metal bending. Palmer's report is thorough and he conscientiously spelled out the weaknesses as well as the strengths of the research into each of these areas. He concluded that the data cannot support the existence of paranormal phenomena (because of lack of an adequate theory of the paranormal) but, even with all the flaws and inconsistencies, he still felt that, overall, something beyond flaws and chance was occurring.

When the Committee was formed, ARI provided me with a copy of Palmer's report and asked us to provide a second opinion. They expressly asked us to focus upon the remote viewing and random event generator research. With the exception of the ganzfeld research, they had little interest in the other areas covered in the report. Because they already had input from a competent parapsychologist, they wanted the second opinion to be from a non-parapsychologist. I commissioned Alcock to supply this second opinion knowing that he was already very familiar with much of this research and that he would provide a thorough assessment of the research. I would then ask experts sympathetic to parapsychology to read Alcock's report (1988) carefully. Alcock's report was at least as comprehensive as that of Palmer and, surprisingly, he and Palmer agreed on many of the weaknesses of the individual studies. The major disagreement was that Palmer was willing to argue that something is going on despite these weaknesses whereas Alcock argued that these weaknesses were too widespread and serious to justify any conclusions about psi or an anomaly.

Both Palmer and Alcock should be commended for such a detailed and comprehensive evaluation of the literature in the fields of remote viewing and REG research. Regardless of one's position on psi, both deserve to have their arguments taken seriously. If one is going to dismiss Alcock's conclusions, the responsible and ethical way is to consider his detailed arguments (ideally, along with those of Palmer) and provide reasoned rebuttals to these arguments. I believe it is irresponsible to ignore Alcock's detailed reasons and simply dismiss his position as that of fanatic naysayer.

So, despite Alexander's and Carter's claims that we deliberately selected the worst examples of parapsychological research, all the research studies evaluated in the CEHP report were chosen for us by Palmer and Alexander with an assist from ARI. Of course, Carter's statement that we restricted our evaluation to the ganzfeld studies is also false. I believe Alcock's (1988) discussion of this matter in his commissioned paper is worth quoting:

> In an area as controversial as that of parapsychology, there is often disagreement as to what evidence or which research reports really reflect the mainstream of the domain. Critics are sometimes accused of holding up poorer examples of parapsychological research as though they were representative of the best the area has to offer. In order to avoid the possibility of such charges, and in order as well to make the reviewing task more straightforward and manageable, this present review is limited to those research papers already selected for review by a leading parapsychologist, John Palmer (1985). His paper evaluates eight areas of parapsychology, including the two areas which this review addresses. Since he has already selected the studies which provide the best case for remote viewing and for mental influence on random event generators (and the present reviewer agrees with his delineation in this regard), there should be no apprehension about whether or not the studies reviewed herein reflect the bias of a skeptical reviewer. (I have added a few more recent papers by the same authors that Palmer chose; I am sure that these would have been included in Palmer's review had they been available at the time. Their inclusion in no way changes the outcome of my evaluation). (pp. 15–16)

While I find myself in this unaccustomed role of defending myself against unfounded accusations, I will briefly comment on other allegations that appear to me to be erroneous or unfounded. Carter characterizes *The Skeptical Inquirer* as a propaganda organ to discredit parapsychology. I have been the Committee for Skeptical Inquiry's Chairman of the Parapsychology Subcommittee since the founding of CSI (formerly CSICOP). I also have been on the editorial board of *The Skeptical Inquirer* from its inception. In these roles I have always made a strict distinction between parapsychological versus other paranormal claims. The former are based on scientific procedures whereas the others are not. CSI's position, as far as I am concerned, is that we have no quarrel with parapsychology. Our concern is with questionable and bizarre claims that are not supported by sufficient evidence.

Probably it has not happened as often as it should, but throughout the years parapsychologists and members of CSI have worked together on some projects. Despite possible differences, there are many issues on which we agree. Before his unfortunate death, Robert Morris and some skeptics, including myself, agreed to work together on research projects of mutual interest.

I am not sure what point Carter is trying to make about the ganzfeld debate between Charles Honorton and me and the events leading up to our joint communiqué. The March 1985 issue of the *Journal of Parapsychology* was devoted to my detailed critique of the original ganzfeld data base and Honorton's detailed response (Honorton, 1985; Hyman, 1985). This original data base, as supplied to me by Honorton, consisted of 42 separate experiments (by Honorton's count). Subsequent arguments over interpretations of this database have focused on the subset of 28 experiments that Honorton included in his meta-analysis. He excluded 14 studies because they used a dependent variable other than direct hits. This was done because it simplified the combining of the studies in his meta-analysis. Unfortunately, this resulted in a non-trivial inflation of the overall effect size and significance because the 14 excluded studies happened to have a significantly lower average effect size. For my meta-analysis, I used a subset of 36 of the studies. My overall analysis, however, used all 42 studies. Some of the discrepancies between my meta-analysis and Honorton's were partly a matter of the fact that I included more of the studies in my analysis. This made a difference both in the overall effect size and the power to detect correlations between effect size and flaws.

Because Carter refers several times to historical occurrences of parapsychological debates in which I was directly involved, I will try to correct several of the misrepresentations that he repeats. Because each of the events was complex and multi-faceted, I cannot provide a complete account in this paper. But I will try to supply enough to correct some of the distortions in his portrayals.

Around 1980, I received requests to provide a critical overview of parapsychological research from two separate sources. I decided that it would be impossible to survey the entire field of parapsychology. Nor would a random sample provide a fair basis for an assessment. The typical experiment in most domains of research is likely to be mediocre. Any field should be evaluated by its best products. My goal was to find the best experimental program in parapsychology for evaluation. To this end, I communicated with several parapsychologists and asked them to nominate the most promising line of research in contemporary parapsychology. The ganzfeld experiments were the overwhelming favorite. I contacted Honorton and asked him to indicate where I could find reports on ganzfeld experiments.

Honorton expressed delight that I was interested in doing such an evaluation and offered to supply me with a copy of every report—published or unpublished— that he could find. Eventually, in 1982, he sent me a box containing around 600 pages of reports. Several of the reports contained more than one experiment. By Honorton's count, the entire data base consisted of 42 experiments included in 34 separate reports. Many of these experiments had been conducted by some of the major parapsychologists. Because of this and because these were presented to me as an example of the best that parapsychology had to offer, I was shocked by how many flaws I detected in the database. These were not subtle or esoteric flaws. Instead, they involved failure to include the safeguards that any competent parapsychologist would demand of a good experiment. I tried to limit my flaw assignments to simple dichotomies that required a minimum of subjective judgment. For example, did the experimenter use a single target in such a way that there was a possibility that the sender could deliberately or inadvertently convey the correct target to the subject? Were the appropriate statistical tests used? And, if so, were they used correctly (with the correct degrees of freedom, etc.)? If several different dependent variables and various tests were used, were the significance levels adjusted accordingly? Were appropriate randomization procedures used both during the sending and judging phases? Were reasonable security precautions put into play?

Although Honorton and I differed on our assignment of flaws to the studies, even by Honorton's standards the database had too many problems to allow for any conclusions about a true ganzfeld psi effect. In our debate (Honorton, 1985; Hyman, 1985), Honorton challenged my flaw assignments. He accepted all my assignments of statistical improprieties, yet ignored taking these statistical defects into account in his own assessment of the effects of flaws upon outcome. His challenges were mostly to my assignment of procedural flaws. In a couple of instances he turned out be correct (partly because he had access to additional information that was not contained in the report I was given). In the other cases, his objections were that I had assigned a flaw to say my Feedback category rather to my Security Category. In his coding of flaws, he used trichotomous ordering of each flaw category (instead of my simple dichotomies) and he simply did not include in his analysis several of my procedural flaws. This approach made it seem as if we differed much more on our flaw assignments than was the fact. In my rebuttal to Honorton's response (which never got published; see the following for the reasons), I transformed Honorton's flaw assignments into dichotomies that most resembled the ones I used.

The point of this procedure was to show that though Honorton ignored several of my flaw assignments and disagreed with me on some specific ones, even by his more lenient assessment, the database was clearly riddled with too many weaknesses. This procedure allowed me to extract five flaw categories (compared with the 12 that I used) from Honorton's assignments. These corresponded to my categories of ST (single target), R (randomization), FB (feedback), DOC (documentation), and STAT (statistics). Not a single study in Honorton's meta-analysis is methodologically adequate on all five of these categories. The percentages of studies that exhibit each flaw in Honorton's meta-analytic sample are: R (71%), ST (64%), FB (36%), DOC (25%), and STAT (21%). The situation is even worse when we consider my ratings on 12 flaws. So even though the debate makes it seem as if Honorton and I differed greatly on how many flaws existed in this data base, both of us found substantial drawbacks in this data base. I am sure this is one of the reasons why Honorton agreed with me that this database was inadequate for drawing conclusions about the existence of psi.

Ultimately, Honorton and I spent five years on this project. We exchanged communications, mostly respectful, but occasionally acrimonious. Much of our interchange involved the issue of flaws. Honorton never disputed the existence of flaws, but did challenge me on the assignment of some flaws. The biggest difference between us on this issue was that Honorton was not concerned about the existence of flaws but rather about the possible correlation of flaws with effect size and/or significance. Honorton was keen to show that there was no correlation between flaws and effect size. He argued that unless a critic could demonstrate that an alleged flaw affected the outcome of an experiment than, in effect, the critic had no right to call it a flaw. I, on the other hand, was more concerned about the existence of the flaws, regardless of whether their existence correlated with outcomes. The scientific community will not consider seriously a claim, especially a controversial one that is based upon a database that is riddled with flaws.

The debate was scheduled to continue. The *Journal of Parapsychology* had agreed to devote another issue to a second round in the debate. I submitted a detailed, and somewhat spirited, rebuttal (62 pages in length) to Honorton's response to my first critique. The *Journal of Parapsychology* gave Honorton a copy of my rebuttal and gave him a few months to prepare his defense. This was the situation when I met Honorton at the Parapsychological Association meetings at Sonoma State University in August, 1986. Honorton, Marcello Truzzi, and I sat down to lunch and discussed our mutual differences. Honorton informed me that he had read my rebuttal and felt hurt by what he considered my overly aggressive attack on his arguments. I, in turn, expressed surprise because, in my opinion, I was simply responding in kind to what I considered his false accusations in his response to my initial critique. As the conversation continued, I realized that we actually agreed about a number of issues regarding the evidential value of the original ganzfeld database.

I was surprised to learn, for example, that Honorton actually agreed with me that the original ganzfeld database had too many problems to count as a definitive demonstration of psi. He agreed with me that only if the experiments could be replicated with new studies that were free of the problems that the plagued the original database, could the parapsychologists argue that they had scientifically established an anomaly. I offered to recall my latest rebuttal. Instead, I suggested that he and I might collaborate on a paper that highlighted our agreements rather than our disagreements—which were becoming more and more esoteric for our potential readers. Honorton immediately accepted the offer and the rest is history.

As a result of the debate between Honorton and me, the quality of ganzfeld psi experiments has improved greatly. Along with this improved quality, the average effect sizes have also declined, although many parapsychologists would argue that there is no causal relationship between the increased quality and the declining effect size. Before trying to defend the original ganzfeld psi experiments as examples of good experimentation, I strongly urge Carter and other writers sympathetic to parapsychology to obtain the original reports and carefully examine them for procedural and statistical quality. Admittedly, this will take persistence and time. However, I cannot believe that anyone who has taken the trouble to carefully assess the original database will want to defend these experiments as having been well conducted.

With hindsight, I now believe that Honorton and I both spent an excessive amount of time in focusing on minutia such as the assignment of flaws. Such quibbling over minutia occupied much of our time over a period of five years. Only Honorton and I were privy to the details of the many fine points about statistics, procedures, flaws, and various other methodological trivia that dominated our debate. What frustrated me was the realization that only Honorton and I had mastered the details of this database in such a way that we understood each other's arguments. After the 1985 publication of the debate, many parapsychologists were treating Honorton as a hero for successfully vanquishing Hyman. At the same time, the critics were proclaiming how I had shown that the best evidence that parapsychology had to offer was built on a house of cards. Neither Honorton's supporters nor mine had the necessary grasp of the details to independently judge which one of us was right. This applies not only to the general population of parapsycholgical supporters and detractors, but also to the array of major commentators who weighed in on one side or the other.

Even worse, our debate over the possible role of flaws as causes of the effects overshadowed two very important issues regarding the ganzfeld database. I have already discussed one issue which is simply the unexpected number of procedural and statistical flaws in what was supposed the best evidence for psi. Even more important is the fact that this database within itself showed that the ganzfeld experiments cannot easily be replicated, even by some of the best parapsychologists in the world. Almost lost in the tortured details of my analysis of flaws and other weaknesses of the database are my findings of experimenter effects. Both effect size and significance of outcome were highly dependent on individual experimenters and/or laboratories in this database. I reported an analysis of variance on the relationship between investigator and effect size that was statistically significant. The levels consisted of the seven investigators who had contributed two or more studies to the database. An additional level consisted of the pooled results from the eight investigators who had contributed only one study to the database. For this analysis I used my meta-analytic sample of 36 studies rather than Honorton's sample of 28 (the results were the same for both samples, but significance levels were obviously higher for the larger sample). For the overall database the average effect size corresponded to a hit rate of 35 percent compared with the chance level of 25 percent (which is approximately the same hit rate reported by Honorton and subsequent parapsychologists for this database). Just about all of this effect size was due to four experimenters who had contributed 50 percent of the studies to the database. These four experimenters reported results whose average effect size corresponded to a direct hit rate of 44 percent. The remaining studies yielded an average effect size that corresponded to a hit rate of 26 percent. So a group of investigators accounting for half of this database failed to replicate the significant effect obtained by the four successful ones.

The failure of parapsychologists to take this into account has had several misleading consequences. The original database has been, and still is, treated by parapsychologists as a homogeneous data base with an effect size corresponding a hit rate of 35 percent. The automated ganzfeld experiments were hailed by everyone (with, of course the exception of me) as a successful replication of the original ganzfeld database because the overall effect size in both groups were approximately the same. This claim was badly mistaken on several grounds. The original database clearly violated the meta-analytic requirements of homogeneity. The overall direct hit rate was a meaningless composite of two subgroups: one with a hit rate of 44 percent and the other with a hit rate at the chance level. The composite hit rate is arbitrary for another reason: it could have been much higher or much lower depending upon the proportion of studies contributed by each investigator. These mistakes are compounded by comparing the artificial hit rate of 35 percent in the original database with the similar sized hit rate in the autoganzfeld experiments. The significance of the overall hit rate for the autoganzfeld is due entirely to the dynamic targets; the static targets, which were the type used in the original database, yielded a hit rate at the chance level. This is another reason why the autoganzfeld experiments should be considered a failure to replicate the original database.

Because of the heterogeneity of the original database, including the fact that it contains at least two groups of inconsistent outcomes, obviously any meta-analyses on this group dealing with a composite effect size and related issues is illegitimate. This applies to my own meta-analysis as well as those of Honorton, and to that provided by Monica Harris and Robert Rosenthal. Even if such meta-analyses could be justified, they would be incapable of answering the important question: can parapsychologists find a way to achieve significant and consistent effect sizes with well designed experiments?

As I indicated, I now believe both my original critique of the ganzfeld experiments, as well as my unpublished follow-up, were misguided. At most it should have been sufficient for me to call attention to the surprising number of procedural and statistical defects in the database. In addition, I should have made it clear that the striking experimenter effects in the database indicated a failure to replicate. Beyond that, I should have restricted my argument to saying that it is up to the parapsychologists to demonstrate they can find a way to produce successful and consistent replications with data of higher quality.

By devoting my efforts and time towards defending my assignment of flaws and showing how they could have accounted for the effects, I allowed the parapsychologists to switch the burden of proof from their side to my side. It was now up to me to prove that the flaws made a difference. This is impossible to do on the basis of a single database. The arguments raised by what I now realize are at best, a side issue, deflected the controversy from the issues that really mattered. The joint communiqué by Honorton and me, as I see it, was simply an attempt to belatedly restore some balance to the matter.

I will curb my temptation to respond to other comments and accusations in Carter's lengthy chapter. For example, he quotes a story by Gary Schwartz which is supposed to illustrate my "irrational attitude" towards parapsychology. I have just deleted three pages that I wrote about this because I do not think it is worthwhile to take up the reader's time about this silly anecdote. Schwartz has distorted and embellished a story that I told, one which has nothing to do with my attitudes towards parapsychology or anything else. But I give him high marks for creativity in finding a way to make something out of nothing.

CONCLUSIONS

Carter's premises are: (1) the evidence in support of psi is scientifically sound; (2) the scientific community as well as parapsychologists critics are imbued with a materialistic worldview that precludes the possibility of paranormal phenomena; (3) the grip of this mindset is so strong that it produces irrational fear of the possibilities of non-materialistic processes; (4) it even leads to active attempts to suppress parapsychological evidence; and (5) that, were it not for premises 2–4, the reality of psi would have long ago been accepted by mainstream science and society.

If the first premise were true, then, perhaps, Carter might be justified in looking for non-rational reasons for the failure to accept parapsychological claims. However, Carter's argument seems more like begging the question. Because he assumes that the first premise is correct, he believes the others to be true. However, his argument faces problems. It is not just critics who point to the lack of consistency in parapsychological research. Throughout the history of psychical research and parapsychology, many prominent parapsychologists have bemoaned the elusiveness of evidence for psi.

I began this commentary with a quotation from Martin Johnson. Although I consider Martin to be a good friend, we have only met on two occasions. On both occasions he befriended me and saved me from a potentially uncomfortable experience. I remember a conversation we had the first time we met in 1979. He told me that, as a teenager growing up in Sweden, he had experiences that he was convinced were paranormal. Later, he received training in general science and astronomy. His scientific background made him realize that, although he personally believed in the existence of paranormal phenomena, the existing data were insufficient to justify such a belief. He became a parapsychologist because of his personal beliefs. As a scientist, however, he realizes he has no right to argue for the reality of psi until the evidence meets scientific standards.

I believe it is worthwhile to end this commentary by providing a larger sample of Johnson's (1976) words from which I quoted at the beginning:

> I must confess that I have some difficulties understanding the logic of some parapsychologists when they proclaim the standpoint that findings within our field have wide-ranging consequences for science in general, and especially for our world picture. It is often implied that the research findings within our field constitute a death blow to materialism. I am puzzled by this claim, since I thought that few people were really so unsophisticated as to mistake our concepts for reality. I am, of course, just as puzzled by the attempt to unify science and religion based on parapsychological findings . . . It is hard to deny, however, that the motivation behind parapsychological research has, from the very beginning, been religious rather than purely scientific. I would not like to go so far as to say that parapsychology will not perhaps provide us with knowledge relevant to the understanding of some religious phenomena, but I believe that we should not make extravagant and, as I see it, unwarranted claims about the wide-ranging consequences of our scattered, undigested, indeed rather 'soft' facts, if we can speak at all about facts within our field. I firmly believe that wide-ranging interpretations based on such scanty data tend to give us, and with some justification, a bad reputation among our colleagues within the more established fields of science. (pp. 139–140)

NOTE

1. Thomas Kuhn admitted that he had used the notion of "paradigm" in several different senses. His preferred usage was the sense in which I am following here.

REFERENCES

Alcock, J. E. (1988). A comprehensive review of major empirical studies in parapsychology involving random event generators and remote viewing. In D. Druckman & J. A. Swets (Eds.), *Enhancing human performance: Issues, theories, and techniques, background papers* (pp. 602–719). Washington, DC: National Academy Press.

Alexander, J. A. (1989). Enhancing human performance: A challenge to the report. *New Realities, 9*(4), 10–15, 52–53.

Backster, C. (2003). *Primary perception: Biocommunication with plants, living foods, and human cells.* Anza, CA: White Rose Millennium Press.

Bierman, D. J. (2001). On the nature of anomalous phenomena: Another reality between the world of subjective consciousness and the objective world of physics? In P. van Locke (Ed.), *The physical nature of consciousness* (pp. 269–292). New York: Benjamins.

Honorton, C. (1985). Meta-analysis of psi ganzfeld research: A response to Hyman. *Journal of Parapsychology, 49,* 51–91.

Hyman, R. (1985). The ganzfeld psi experiment: A critical appraisal. *Journal of Parapsychology, 49,* 3–49.

Hyman, R. (1987, May). Proper criticism. *Skeptical Briefs, 3,* 4–5.

Hyman, R. (1988). Paranormal phenomena. In D. Druckman & J. A. Swets (Eds.), *Enhancing human performance: Issues, theories, and techniques* (pp. 169–208). Washington, DC: National Academy Press.

Hyman, R. (1995). How to critique a published article. *Psychological Bulletin, 118,* 178–182.

Jahn, R. G., & Dunne, B. J. (2008). Change the rules! *Journal of Scientific Exploration, 22,* 193–213.

Jahn, R., Dunne, B., Brandish, G., Dobyns, Y., Lettierie, A., Nelson, R., et al. (2000). Mind-machine interaction consortium: PortREG replication experiments. *Journal of Scientific Exploration, 14,* 499–555.

Johnson, M. (1976). Parapsychology and education. B. Shapin & L. Colby (Eds.), *Education in parapsychology* (pp. 130–215). New York: Parapsychology Foundation.

Kennedy, J. E. (2001). Why is psi so elusive? A review and proposed model. *Journal of Parapsychology, 65,* 219–246.

Kennedy, J. E. (2003). The capricious, actively evasive, unsustainable nature of psi: A summary and hypotheses. *Journal of Parapsychology, 67,* 53–74.

Kuhn, T. S. (1970). Reflections on my critics. In I. Lakatos & A. Musgrave (Eds.), *Criticism and the growth of knowledge* (pp. 231–278). London: Cambridge University Press.

Lucadou, W. V. (2001). Hans in luck: The currency of evidence in parapsychology. *Journal of Parapsychology, 65,* 3–16.

Palmer, J. (1985). *An evaluative report on the current status of parapsychology.* (Prepared under contract number DAJA 45-84-M-0405). Alexandria, VA: United States Army Research Institute for the Behavioral and Social Sciences.

CHAPTER 10

Missing the Point?

Christopher C. French

As I stated in my chapter for this collection, these days I view myself as a "moderate skeptic" when it comes to the paranormal. I was intrigued as to whether reading the other contributions to this volume would shift my position towards the more skeptical end of the belief spectrum or move me further towards the belief end. In fact, I have found myself even less convinced regarding the reality of psi. Some might argue that this was inevitable given my starting position but I welcome this opportunity to present some of my reasons for this shift. In my view, the contributions from the advocates in this volume often simply miss the point when it comes to debating the reality of psi and fail to address the very real and important objections that have been raised by the counteradvocates. Due to space limitations, I will limit my comments to those relating to the advocates' chapters.

Dean Radin provides a brief and extremely selective historical overview of parapsychology. For example, he completely fails to mention that two of the three Fox sisters publicly confessed that their alleged communications with the spirit world were fraudulent. Similarly, the fact that Sir William Crookes was convinced that Florence Cook had genuine mediumistic powers despite the fact that she was caught red-handed engaged in acts of trickery both before and after his investigations is not referred to in Radin's piece. He lists many eminent names from the history of science who were convinced that psi was real but this, in and of itself, can never settle the dispute over whether psi is or is not real. It would be a trivially easy (but pointless) task to assemble an equally long list of names of eminent scientists who did not or do not believe in the paranormal—indeed, for me, the evidence shows that eminence in science correlates with greater skepticism. But, once again, this is irrelevant to the central issue. It is notable that many of the eminent scientists who have spoken out in favor of the existence of psi, both past and present, were making pronouncements outside of their own areas of expertise. Most of them have never actually directly engaged in testing paranormal claims (in contrast to most of the counteradvocates featured in this collection). At least Radin is willing to present us with a falsifiable hypothesis concerning the immediate future of psi research. I will be glad (although admittedly slightly embarrassed) to publicly acknowledge the existence of psi if a single demonstrable and unambiguous application of psi to the fields of electronics, biochemistry, or biology has appeared by 2015 (or indeed if it turns out that China or Russia already have such applications).

Chris Carter's chapter also misses the point in some major ways. As it happens, I would agree with him that there is prejudice within mainstream science against parapsychology. A small minority of vocal critics of parapsychology express strong opposition to any kind of paranormal claim purely on the basis that they "know" that such claims cannot be true without any need to actually examine the evidence (although this cannot be said of the counteradvocates contributing to this volume). The fact that such prejudice exists, however, does not demonstrate that psi exists.

I disagree strongly with Carter on two of his major points. The first is his assertion that counteradvocates are motivated by fear of the paranormal. Such assertions, as in this case, usually rest upon unfalsifiable psychoanalytic foundations and are supported by very little in the way real evidence. As this fear is *unconscious*, this claim is almost by definition untestable and therefore pseudoscientific. In terms of conscious attitudes, the evidence tends to undermine the assertion insofar as many counteradvocates, including myself, used to be "believers."

The second assertion with which I would disagree is Carter's insistence that the debate is not about the evidence. Much as he might like it not to be so, the debate is, in fact, centrally focused upon the evidence—and in particular the failure of parapsychology to produce a single robust and replicable psi effect to the satisfaction of the wider scientific community. He seems to be arguing that a few vocal skeptics can have such a huge effect upon this wider community that real effects supported by strong evidence are simply ignored or even actively denied. Scientists are, by nature, curious and open-minded and there is no doubt at all that the conventional scientific worldview as exemplified by modern physics is one in which notions far stranger than telepathy are accepted without any qualms. Is it really conceivable that in such a context all of these curious and open-minded scientists would hesitate for even an instant to investigate psi if the evidence was really that strong? The truth is that most mainstream scientists do not view parapsychological hypotheses as likely to be fruitful topics for investigation—but a single powerful and robust demonstration of a psi effect would probably change that situation very quickly. After all, physicists were not slow in attempting to replicate cold fusion despite their skepticism about the results reported by Stanley Pons and Martin Fleischmann in 1989.

Carter attempts to explain the high level of skepticism regarding psi among psychologists in terms of psychologists retaining an outmoded view of metaphysics. No systematic evidence is presented in support of this assertion and no attempt is made to explain why it should be the case that psychologists, alone amongst the sciences, should behave in this way. His assertion that physicists are more open to investigating psi than psychologists does not ring true in terms of the parapsychologists I know, most of whom of were trained initially as psychologists. I do accept that here I am relying purely upon my subjective impressions and not on a systematic objective survey and may therefore be mistaken (just as Carter may be mistaken).

There are, of course, a couple of far more obvious reasons why psychologists might be more skeptical of the paranormal than scientists generally. First, they are familiar with the cognitive biases that might lead individuals to believe that they had personally experienced a paranormal event when in fact the experience could adequately be explained in psychological terms. Secondly, they are used to dealing with messy, real-life data and are probably more aware of the biases that can creep into the evaluation of data collected in scientific investigations. As Rupert Sheldrake's analysis has shown, natural scientists typically do not see the need to employ double-blind methodologies. The outcomes of experiments in the natural sciences are typically far more predictable (and replicable) than those in the social sciences (including both psychology and parapsychology). It is very likely that psychologists are more aware of the psychological factors that can affect the evaluation of data than scientists generally. Classic cases of pathological science, such as the alleged "discovery" of canals on Mars, N-rays, polywater, cold fusion, and so on are all testament to the fact that dozens of papers can appear in the scientific literature attesting to the reality of phenomena, which turn out to be entirely illusory. It is well worth bearing such episodes in mind when evaluating parapsychology. The reason such claims were ultimately rejected by the wider scientific community was due to the fact that the evidence put forward in support of them was simply too weak. Other propositions, such as the claim that meteorites were stones that fell from the sky and that the continents were originally joined together in a single land mass, were originally rejected by the wider scientific community but ultimately accepted because the evidence in favor of them accumulated and got stronger. That is the only way forward for parapsychology. Contrary to Carter's mantra, the skeptical position focuses on evidence. Anything else is missing the point.

"Magdalene" (© Dierdre Luzwick. Used by permission.)

CHAPTER 11

The Devil Is in the Details

Michael Shermer

The contributions by James Alcock, Ray Hyman, and Christopher C. French, in this volume are so comprehensive and conclusive that I have little to add in the way of skeptical commentary, with one exception. In reading Dean Radin's "A Brief History of Science and Psychic Phenomena," one is struck by the sheer force of chronological enumeration of the numerous experiments, studies, institutes, organizations, and research programs purporting to prove the existence of psi. The devil is in the details, however, which when examined prove otherwise—that psi is a chimera. Radin's brief mention of the U.S. government's Stargate program is emblematic.

In 1970 the C.I.A. began a systematic program in the study of remote viewing and other forms of ESP and psi. This was the age of paranormal proliferation. When I was a graduate student in experimental psychology during this time I saw on television the Israeli "psychic" Uri Geller bend cutlery and reproduce drawings using, so he said, psychic powers alone. For awhile I kept an open mind to the possibility that such phenomena could be real, until I saw James "the Amazing" Randi on Johnny Carson's *Tonight Show*, where Randi used magic tricks to replicate Geller's effects. (As Randi once remarked, "If Geller is bending spoons with psychic power he's doing it the hard way.") Randi bent spoons, duplicated drawings, levitated tables, and even performed a psychic surgery. When asked about Geller's ability to pass the tests of professional scientists,

An earlier version of this chapter was published in eSkeptic, April 26, 2005.

Randi explained that scientists are not trained to detect trickery and intentional deception, the very art of magic.

I always assumed, however, that the paranormal was the province of the cultural fringes. Then, in 1995, just as *Skeptic* magazine really started to take off in popularity and began consuming most of my waking hours, the story broke that for the previous quarter century the Central Intelligence Agency (CIA) in conjunction with the U.S. Army had invested $20 million in a highly secret psychic spy program called Stargate (also Grill Flame and Scanate). Stargate was a Cold War project intended to close the "psi gap" (the psychic equivalent of the missile gap) between the United States and Soviet Union. The Soviets were training psychic spies, so we would as well. The story of Stargate was recently featured in a film based on the book *The Men Who Stare at Goats*, by British investigative journalist Jon Ronson (2004). This is a Looking Glass-like story of what the CIA—operating through something called Psychological Operations (PsyOps)—was researching: invisibility, levitation, telekinesis, walking through walls, and even killing goats just by staring at them (the ultimate goal was killing enemy soldiers telepathically). In one project, psychic spies attempted to use "remote viewing" to identify the location of missile silos, submarines, POWs, and MIAs from a small room in a run-down Maryland building. If these skills could be honed and combined, it was believed, perhaps military officials could zap remotely viewed enemy missiles in their silos.

Initially, the Stargate story received broad media attention—including a special investigation by ABC's *Nightline*—and made minor celebrities out of a few of the psychic spies, such as Ed Dames and Joe McMoneagle. As regular guests on Art Bell's pro-paranormal radio talk show Coast-to-Coast, the former spies spun tales that, had they not been documented elsewhere, would have seemed like the ramblings of paranoid delusionists. For example, Ronson connects some of the bizarre torture techniques used on prisoners at Guantanamo Bay, Cuba, and Iraq's Abu Ghraib prison, with similar techniques employed during the FBI siege of the Branch Davidians in Waco, Texas. FBI agents blasted the Branch Davidians all night with such obnoxious sounds as screaming rabbits, crying seagulls, dentist drills, and (I'm not making this up) Nancy Sinatra's song "These Boots Are Made for Walking." The U.S. military employed the same technique on Iraqi prisoners of war, replacing Sinatra's ballad with the theme song from the PBS children's television series Barney and Friends—a tune many parents concur does become torturous with repetition.

One of Ronson's sources, none other than Uri Geller, led him to one Major General Albert Stubblebine III, who directed the psychic spy network from his office in Arlington, Virginia. Stubblebine thought that with enough practice he could learn to walk through walls, a belief encouraged by Lt. Col. Jim Channon, a Vietnam vet whose post-war experiences at such new age Mecca's as the Esalen Institute in Big Sur, California, led him to found the "first earth battalion" of "warrior monks" and "Jedi knights." These warriors, according to Channon, would transform the nature of war by entering hostile lands with "sparkly eyes," marching to the mantra of "aum," and presenting the enemy with "automatic hugs" (all brilliantly exhibited by George Clooney's character in the film version of *The Men Who Stare at Goats*). Disillusioned by the ugly carnage of modern war, Channon envisioned a battalion armory of machines that would produce "discordant sounds" (Nancy and Barney?) and "psycho-electric" guns that would shoot "positive energy" at enemy soldiers.

As entertaining as all this is, can anyone actually levitate, turn invisible, walk through walls, or remote view a hidden object? No. Under controlled conditions remote viewers have never succeeded in finding a hidden target with greater accuracy than random guessing. The occasional successes you hear about are due either to chance or suspect experimental conditions, such as when the person who subjectively assesses whether the remote viewer's narrative description seems to match the target already knows the target location and its characteristics. When both the experimenter and the remote viewer are blinded to the target, my analysis of the literature indicates that psychic powers vanish.

Herein lies an important lesson that I have learned in many years of paranormal investigations: What people remember rarely corresponds to what actually happened. Case in point: A man named Guy Savelli told Ronson that he had seen soldiers kill goats by staring at them, and that he himself had done so as well. But as the details of the story unfold we discover that Savelli is recalling, years later, what he remembers about a particular "experiment" with 30 numbered goats. Savelli randomly chose goat number 16 and gave it his best death stare. But he couldn't concentrate that day, so he quit the experiment, only to be told later that goat number 17 had subsequently died. End of story. No autopsy or explanation of the cause of death. No information about how much time had elapsed between the staring episode and death; the conditions of the room into which the 30 goats had been placed (temperature, humidity, ventilation, etc.), how long the goats were in the room, and so forth. When asked for corroborating evidence of this extraordinary claim, Savelli triumphantly produced a videotape of another experiment where someone else supposedly stopped the heart of a goat. But the tape showed only a goat whose heart rate dropped from 65 to 55 beats per minute. That was the extent of the empirical evidence of goat killing, and as someone who has spent decades in the same fruitless pursuit of phantom goats, I conclude that the evidence for the paranormal in general doesn't get much better than this. They shoot horses, don't they?

REFERENCE

Ronson, J. (2004). *The men who stare at goats*. London: Picador/Pan Macmillan.

"The Watchman" (© Dierdre Luzwick. Used by permission.)

CHAPTER 12

Still in Denial: A Reply to the Critics

Chris Carter

> It seems to me that we have no right, from a physical standpoint, to deny a priori the possibility of telepathy. For that sort of denial the foundations of our science are too unsure and too incomplete.
> Albert Einstein by M. Gardner, 1989, pp. 156–157

In this commentary, I will respond to the chapters written for this book by Ray Hyman, Michael Shermer, and James Alcock.

REPEATABILITY DENIED: HOW RAY HYMAN CONTINUES TO DENY THE FACTS

In his chapter "Unrepeatability: Parapsychology's Achilles Heel," Ray Hyman continues to insist that the ganzfeld database lacks adequate replication. In the draft of his chapter submitted to this book,[1] he wrote:

> A successful replication is one that achieves essentially the same result that was *predicted* on the basis of a previously conducted experiment. The parapsychologists who try to justify the replicability of psi results with meta-analysis are using a *retrospective* notion. They are arguing for successful replication if a set of already completed experiments show evidence of similar effect sizes whose combined average is significantly different from chance. Replicability implies the ability to predict successfully from the

results of a meta-analysis to a new set of independent data. This is where parapsychological evidence falls woefully short.

And later in the same chapter he added:

> Consider the parapsychological claims that the autoganzfeld experiments successfully replicated the original ganzfeld data base (Bem & Honorton 1994). [But] . . . autoganzfeld experiments *failed to replicate* the original ganzfeld data base. In the original data base the average effect size was derived from studies that all used static targets. The autoganzfeld experiments used both static and dynamic (action video clips) targets. Only the dynamic targets produced a significant effect. The results on the static targets were consistent with chance and differed significantly from the results on the static targets in the original data base.

The truth of the matter seems closer to the opposite of what Hyman tells us. The original ganzfeld experiments used quasi-dynamic targets (View Master "slide" reels) in addition to completely static targets. Studies using the View Master reels produced significantly higher hit rates than did studies using single-image targets (50% versus 34%). Meta-analysis of the original data led to the prediction that dynamic targets would show greater results than static targets. This prediction was in fact strongly corroborated, as Bem and Honorton (1994) reported:

> Dynamic versus static targets. The success of [these studies] raises the question of whether dynamic targets are, in general, more effective than static targets. This possibility was also suggested by earlier meta-analysis, which revealed that studies using multiple-image targets (View Master stereoscopic slide reels) obtained significantly higher hit rates than did studies using single-image targets. By adding motion and sound, the video clips might be thought of as high-tech versions of the View Master reels. The 10 autoganzfeld studies that randomly sampled from both dynamic and static target pools yielded 164 sessions with dynamic targets and 165 sessions with static targets. As predicted, sessions using dynamic targets yielded significantly more hits that did sessions using static targets (37 percent vs. 27 percent, p < .04). (p. 12)

As Hyman observed, "replicability implies the ability to predict successfully from the results of a meta-analysis to a new set of independent data." And because of these results, virtually all ganzfeld studies ever since have used only dynamic targets.

Bem and Honorton (1994) reported several other successful predictions, but the most striking was the relationship between psi performance and artistic ability. In a session with 20 undergraduates from the Julliard School of Performing Arts, the students achieved a hit rate of 50 percent, one of the highest hit rates ever reported for a single sample (Schlitz & Honorton, 1992).

Have the Ganzfeld Results Been Corroborated by Other Investigators?

In their joint communiqué Hyman and Honorton (1986) wrote: "We agree that the final verdict awaits the outcome of future experiments conducted by a broader range of investigators and according to more stringent standards" (p. 351). The autoganzfeld experiments certainly met the "more stringent standards" requirement. The results were statistically significant and consistent with those in the earlier database. Also, since *all studies* completed were included, there was no "file-drawer" problem: that is, no unreported data were filed in a drawer and ignored. In addition, there were reliable relationships between conceptually relevant variables and psi performance, relationships that also replicate previous findings. Hyman (1991) commented on these studies:

> Honorton's experiments have produced intriguing results. If ... independent laboratories can produce similar results with the same relationships and with the same attention to rigorous methodology, then parapsychology may indeed have finally captured its elusive quarry. (p. 392)

But as Hyman's remark implies, Honorton's autoganzfeld experiments did not satisfy the requirement that replications be conducted by "a broader range of investigators." Since then, what have other investigators found? Table 12.1 provides the answer.

The first line shows the results of the initial autoganzfeld replications at Honorton's laboratory. The others show the results of eight independent replications.

Table 12.1
Standard Ganzfeld Replications (1991–2003)

Laboratory	Sessions	Hit Rate[a] (%)
PRL, Princeton, NJ, USA	354	34
University of Amsterdam, Netherlands	76	38
University of Edinburgh, Scotland	97	33
Institute for Parapsychology, NC, USA	100	33
University of Edinburgh, Scotland	151	27
University of Amsterdam, Netherlands	64	30
University of Edinburgh, Scotland[b]	128	47
University of Gothenburg, Sweden	150	36
University of Gothenburg, Sweden	74	32
Totals	1,194	34.4

[a]Expected chance hit rate is 25%.
[b]Artistically gifted sample.

Strangely, in his draft chapter Hyman mentioned only one of these replication studies:

> Instead of conducting meta-analyses on already completed experiments on the ganzfeld, for example, the parapsychologists might have tried to directly replicate the autoganzfeld experiments with a study created for the stated purpose of replication. The study would be designed specifically for this purpose and would have adequate power. In fact, such studies have been carried out. An example would be Broughton's attempt to deliberately replicate the autoganzfeld results with enough subjects to insure adequate power. This replication failed. *From a scientific viewpoint this replication attempt is much more meaningful than the retrospective combining of already completed (and clearly heterogeneous) experiments.* (emphasis added)

But is this replication attempt really "much more meaningful from a scientific viewpoint" than the combined results in a meta-analysis? If the true hit rate were 33 percent with 25 percent expected by chance alone, then the probability that a sample size of 151 will *fail* to yield results significant at the 5 percent level is 28 percent. In other words, Broughton's failure to replicate with a sample that small is even less remarkable than flipping a coin twice and getting *heads* both times.

As an example of a replication study, Hyman could just have easily mentioned Kathy Dalton's (1997) study using creative individuals, which achieved a hit rate of 47 percent. The odds-against-chance of this result is over 140 million to one. This closely replicated the autoganzfeld results mentioned before (Schlitz & Honorton, 1992), which found a 50 percent hit rate for students from the Juilliard School. It also closely matched results from a study using primarily musicians (Morris, Cunningham, McAlpine, & Taylor, 1993), which found a 41 percent hit rate.

A Decline Effect?

It is sometimes alleged that psi effects exhibit a decline effect over time, raising the suspicion that as controls are tightened, effects disappear. Hyman wrote that "the parapsychological domains in which meta-analyses have been conducted are all subject to the decline effect." But the replication studies in Table 12.1 are listed in chronological order, and no decline effect is evident.

However, not all experiments are designed as *replications*: some are meant to break new ground. As parapsychologists have become satisfied that previous findings have been replicated, it is to be expected that they will increasingly attempt to discover new relationships. Some of course will fail to find new relationships. But it is not valid to treat such *exploratory* studies as replications, and thereby argue that effects are declining.

In their joint communiqué Hyman and Honorton (1986) had asked future ganzfeld investigators, as part of their "more stringent standards," to clearly document the status of the experiment: that is, whether it is meant to merely *confirm* previous findings or to *explore* novel conditions (p. 361).

In a debate over this issue with Richard Wiseman, Bem, Palmer, and Broughton (2001) wrote:

> Many psi researchers believe that the reliability of the basic procedure is sufficiently well established to warrant using it as a tool for the further exploration of psi. Thus, rather than continuing to conduct exact replications, they have been modifying the procedure and extending it into unknown territory. Not unexpectedly, such deviations from exact replication are at increased risk for failure. For example, rather than using visual stimuli, [another investigator] modified the Ganzfeld procedure to test whether senders could communicate musical targets to receivers. They could not. When such studies are thrown into an undifferentiated meta-analysis, the overall effect size is thereby reduced, and perversely, the Ganzfeld procedure becomes a victim of its own success. (p. 208)

Bem, Palmer, and Broughton (2001) set out to test their hypothesis that the decline in average scoring was due to the studies that were meant to be exploratory rather than confirmatory. Three independent raters, unaware of each study outcome, were asked to rate the degree to which each of the recent studies deviated from the standard ganzfeld protocol. The database was then reexamined to test the hypothesis that hit rates were positively correlated with the degree to which the experimental procedures adhered to the standard protocol.

The raters assigned a rank to each of the 40 studies, and the ranks were then averaged for each study. The ranking ranged from "1" to "7" with a rank of "7" indicating the highest degree of adherence to standard protocol as described in two articles written by Honorton in the early 1990s.

As hypothesized, hit rates were significantly correlated with the degree to which the experimental procedures adhered to the standard protocol. If we consider only those replication studies ranked "6" and above, 21 studies (more than half the sample) achieved an overall hit rate of 33 percent, almost identical to that of the earlier studies.

There is little point in continuing with more replication studies: Hyman and others with a prior commitment to contrary views will never change their publicly stated opinions, no matter how many replication studies are performed. Real progress can only be made if investigators are willing to explore new frontiers.

Table 12.2 summarizes all reported ganzfeld experiments performed over nearly three decades.

These figures should make the conclusion clear: the earlier results have been replicated by a variety of researchers in different laboratories in different cultures, with similar hit rates. Hyman (1996) wrote: "The case for psychic functioning seems better than it has ever been. . . . I also have to admit that I do not have a ready explanation for these observed effects" (p. 43). It seems clear that Hyman and the other counteradvocates have lost the ganzfeld debate.

Table 12.2
All Ganzfeld Studies (1974–1999)

Source	Years	Hit Rate (%)
Original 28 ganzfeld	1974–1981	35
11 autoganzfeld	1983–1989	34
Standard replications (rated 6+)	1991–1999	33
Standard replications (rated > 4)	1991–1999	31
Non-standard studies (rated < 4)	1991–1999	24
All 40 studies:	1991–1999	30.1

Meta-Analysis of the Ganzfeld

However, instead of debating the merits of individual studies, what does the data considered *as a whole* tell us? Meta-analysis is designed specifically to answer this question, and Radin (2006) has performed it on all ganzfeld experiments (confirmatory and exploratory) undertaken over a 30-year period. He wrote:

> From 1974 through 2004 a total of 88 Ganzfeld experiments reporting 1,008 hits in 3,145 trials were conducted. The combined hit rate was 32 percent as compared to the chance-expected 25 percent. This 7 percent above-chance effect is associated with odds against chance of 29 quintillion to 1. (p. 120)

Could the results be due to a file-drawer problem of unreported failures? Radin (2006) answered:

> If we insisted that there *had* to be a selective reporting problem, even though there's no evidence of one, then a conservative estimate of the number of studies needed to nullify the observed results is 2,002. That's a ratio of 23 file drawer studies to each known study, which means that each of the 30 known investigators would have had to conduct but not report 67 additional studies. Because the average Ganzfeld study had 36 trials, these 2,002 "missing" studies would have required 72,072 additional sessions (36 × 2002). To generate this many sessions would mean continually running Ganzfeld sessions 24 hours a day, 7 days a week, for 36 years, and for not a single one of those sessions to see the light of day. (p. 121)

SHERMER IS PSYCHIC FOR A DAY

Michael Shermer, editor of *Skeptic* magazine, told us in his contribution to this volume how he managed to successfully simulate several psychic readings on a TV show with little preparation. To his credit, he did tell us that, "This was meant to be a demonstration of how psychic claimants attempt to do readings, not a scientific 'experiment' with controlled conditions."

In his "Disclosure" at the end, he asserted an article of his faith: "I do not believe that precognition, telepathy, clairvoyance, or any of the other forms of alleged psychic manifestation have any factual basis." He did not give us any reason for his belief, except that his success at fooling people shows, "just how vulnerable people are to these very effective nostrums." Of course, the fact that we can fool some people with simulated psi does not imply the real phenomenon does not exist.

Relevant here is the set of experiments performed by Gary Schwartz at the University of Arizona. Schwartz has presented evidence for the survival hypothesis that included single-blind and double-blind studies of mediums. He maintained that conventional counter-explanations—such as fraud, cold reading, wishful thinking, or experimenter bias—were ruled out by the experimental designs. Communications via human mediums were rated for accuracy on a scale from −3 to +3, with −3 indicating a total miss, and +3 indicating a definite hit. Schwartz reported that counting only the +3 scores as hits, the average accuracy across all mediums and sittings was 83 percent, as against 36 percent in control conditions involving random guessing (Schwartz & Simon, 2002).

Shermer and Hyman have argued that mentalists (magicians that specialize in simulating psi effects) could in principle replicate Schwartz's results with mediums (Schwartz, personal communication, Sept. 2009). In response, Schwartz challenged Shermer, Hyman, and the mentalists involved to replicate what the mediums have done under the same tightly controlled conditions. So far, Shermer, Hyman, and several of the mentalists have simply refused to take up his challenge, and three of the mentalists involved have admitted to Schwartz that their tricks would not work under the same controlled conditions (Schwartz, personal communication, December, 2008). To put it bluntly, Shermer and Hyman should either put up or shut up.

ATTRIBUTIONS ABOUT POSSIBLE THINGS

James Alcock's essay in this volume titled "Attributions About Impossible Things" is nearly identical to his earlier essay "The Parapsychologists' Lament." Since I have already responded in my chapter for this volume to most of the points he raises in both these essays, I will confine my remarks here to the two central points that he elaborates upon in his second essay. These two points are: (1) "the failure of parapsychology to gain admission into mainstream science," and (2) "the incompatibility of parapsychological claims with modern scientific theory."

We should not be surprised that Alcock provided no evidence at all in support of these claims; as such evidence does not exist. Indeed, I will show instead that the evidence clearly refutes both of these claims.

In response to his claim that parapsychology is not accepted by mainstream science, I noted earlier that parapsychology has been an affiliate of the American Association for the Advancement of Science (AAAS) since 1969. In contrast, *not one* of the so-called skeptical organizations—including the one Alcock belongs to—is affiliated with the AAAS.

As Radin (1997) has pointed out:

In the 1990s alone, seminars on psi research were part of the regular programs at the annual conferences of the American Association for the Advancement of Science, the American Psychological Association, and the American Statistical Association. Invited lectures on the status of psi research were presented for diplomats at the United Nations, for academics at Harvard University, and for scientists at Bell Laboratories. (p. 3)

These facts clearly demonstrate that parapsychology has not met with, as Alcock puts it, "failure to gain admission into mainstream science."

Yet Alcock vehemently insists that "*the mainstream scientific community continues to reject or simply ignore their claims and their evidence*", and writes of "*the continuing rejection of parapsychology and its data by most scientists*" (emphasis added). Alcock does not provide any supporting documentation for these repeated claims, nor could he. They are, I suspect, nothing more than rhetorical claims designed to persuade the reader of the falsehood that most scientists have carefully examined the evidence and have rejected it for good reason.

In fact, surveys consistently show that a large proportion of scientists accept the possibility that telepathy exists. Two surveys of over 500 scientists in one case and over 1,000 in another both found that the majority of respondents considered ESP "an established fact" or "a likely possibility": 56 percent in one and 67 percent in the other (Evans, 1973; Wagner & Monet, 1979). In the former study only 3 percent of natural scientists considered ESP "an impossibility" compared to 34 percent of psychologists. (As is the case with most counteradvocates of parapsychology, Alcock is a psychologist.)

So, not much can be said for "the failure of parapsychology to gain admission into mainstream science." What about his second central point, "the incompatibility of parapsychological claims with modern scientific theory?"

At several points in the draft copy of the essay he submitted for this book, Alcock strongly stated this claim in various forms. In his very first paragraph he argued that if extrasensory perception were demonstrated to be real, then "the laws of physics as we know them will have been shown to be terribly wrong in some very important respects." Later, he added:

Parapsychology by its very nature stands in contradiction to basic principles in mainstream science. There is nothing in physics or neurology that would allow for processes such as extrasensory perception or psychokinesis or other putative paranormal phenomena. This is unlike any area in normal science: biochemical knowledge does not violate the basic principles of physics.

Once again, Alcock does not provide any supporting evidence for these repeated claims, nor could he. As we have seen, surveys have shown that the vast majority of natural scientists (those in the fields of physics, chemistry, and biology) reject the idea that psi phenomena are somehow impossible. Furthermore, a number of leading physicists such as Henry Margenau, David Bohm, Brian Josephson, and Olivier Costa de Beauregard have repeatedly pointed out that nothing in quantum mechanics forbids psi phenomena. Costa de Beauregard (1975) even maintains that the theory of quantum physics virtually *demands* that psi phenomena exist. And Evan Harris Walker (1979, 1984) has developed a theoretical model of psi based upon the orthodox von Neumann formulation of quantum mechanics.

In chapters 9 through 12 of my book, *Parapsychology and the Skeptics* (Carter, 2007), I discuss in detail the full compatibility of modern physics with the existence of psi phenomena. Limitations of space do not allow me to present the full arguments here; but suffice to say that objections that psi phenomena would violate the basic principles of physics are based upon the principles of classical physics, which have been known to be grossly and fundamentally incorrect for almost a century. Alcock needs to heed the words of his fellow psychologist and past president of both the American Psychological Association and the American Society for Psychical Research, Gardner Murphy (1969), who urged psychologists to become better acquainted with the findings of modern physics.

NOTE

1. All of the quotes from Ray Hyman, Michael Shermer, and James Alcock are taken from draft chapters they submitted for this book, except where otherwise indicated.

REFERENCES

Bem, D. J., & Honorton, C. (1994). Does psi exist? Replicable evidence for an anomalous process of information transfer. *Psychological Bulletin, 115,* 4–18.

Bem, D. J., Palmer, J., & Broughton, R. S. (2001). Updating the ganzfeld database: A victim of its own success? *Journal of Parapsychology, 65*(3), 207–218.

Carter, C. (2007). *Parapsychology and the skeptics.* Pittsburgh, PA: Sterling House.

Costa de Beauregard, O. (1975). Quantum paradoxes and Aristotle's twofold information concept. In L. Oteri (Ed.), *Quantum physics and parapsychology* (pp. 91–102). New York: Parapsychology Foundation.

Dalton, K. (1997). Exploring the links: Creativity and psi in the ganzfeld. In *Proceedings of Presented Papers of the Parapsychological Association 40th Annual Convention* (p. 119–134). Durham, NC: Parapsychological Association.

Evans, C. (1973, January). Parapsychology—what the questionnaire revealed. *New Scientist,* 25, p. 209.

Gardner, M. (1989). *Science: Good, bad, and bogus* (pp. 156–157). Buffalo, NY: Prometheus Books.

Hyman, R. (1991). Comment. *Statistical Science*, 6, 389–392.

Hyman, R. (1996). Evaluation of a program on anomalous mental phenomena. *Journal of Scientific Exploration*, 10 (1), 31–58.

Hyman, R., & Honorton, C. (1986). A joint communiqué. The psi ganzfeld controversy. *Journal of Parapsychology*, 50, 351–364.

Morris, R. L., Cunningham, S., McAlpine, S., & Taylor, R. (1993). Toward replication and extension of autoganzfeld results. In *The Parapsychological Association 36th Annual Convention: Proceedings of presented papers* (pp. 177–191). Durham, NC: Parapsychological Association.

Murphy, G. (1969). Psychology in the year 2000. *American Psychologist*, 24, 523–530.

Radin, D. (1997). *The conscious universe: The scientific truth of psychic phenomena.* San Francisco: HarperCollins.

Radin, D. (2006). *Entangled minds.* New York: Paraview/Pocket.

Schlitz, M. J., & Honorton, C. (1992). Ganzfeld psi performance within an artistically gifted population. *Journal of the American Society for Psychical Research*, 86, 83–98.

Schwartz, G., & Simon, W. (2002). *The afterlife experiments: Breakthrough scientific evidence of live after death.* New York: Atria Books.

Wagner, M., & Monet, M. (1979). Attitudes of college professors toward extra-sensory perception. *Zetetic Scholar*, 5, 7–16.

Walker, E. H. (1979). The quantum theory of psi phenomena. *Psychoenergetic Systems*, 3, 259–299.

Walker, E. H. (1984). A review of criticisms of the quantum mechanical theory of psi phenomena. *Journal of Parapsychology*, 48, 277–332.

PART THREE

Epilogues

"Secret Snow" (© Dierdre Luzwick. Used by permission.)

Heads I Win, Tails You Lose: How Some Parapsychologists Nullify Null Results and What to Do about It

Richard S. Wiseman

This collection of essays makes me very concerned. I worry because after over one hundred years of parapsychological research there exists no real consensus on the most fundamental question facing the field—does psi exist? Worse still, time is running out. Mainstream science is now progressing at a tremendous pace and resources for fringe areas are becoming increasingly scarce. Indeed, I believe that if parapsychology continues on its current trajectory, university-based psi research has only another few years to run. Samuel Johnson once famously remarked that, "... when a man knows he is to be hanged in a fortnight, it concentrates his mind wonderfully." Similarly, I hope that the sense of urgency created by the possible demise of the field will encourage those who truly care about the psi question to concentrate their attention on the key issues at hand.

One thing seems obvious. If researchers continue to adopt the strategies that have led them to this unimpressive state of affairs, there is every reason to be pessimistic about obtaining closure on the psi question in the limited time remaining. As the old adage goes, "Do what you've always done and you'll get what you've always got." Given that this is the case, what is the best way forward?

Debates about the existence of psychic ability usually have focused on those parapsychological studies that have yielded positive results, and involved

A version of this essay appeared in *Skeptical Inquirer*, 34(1), 2010.

advocates and counteradvocates arguing about whether such findings can be accounted for by "normal" explanations. More often than not this has involved skeptics pointing out possible methodological and statistical shortcomings, proponents arguing against the likelihood of such scenarios, and both sides eventually agreeing that the best way to settle the issue would be to attempt to replicate the alleged psi effect under more rigorous conditions. Although such debates are vitally important for identifying and minimising possible flaws in experimental design, I do not think that they alone will lead to consensus on the psi question.

After spending more than 15 years working in parapsychology, I believe that there is a second equally important issue to be discussed: the way in which researchers deal with null findings. Throughout the history of the field, parapsychologists have tended to adopt a "heads I win, tails you lose" approach to their findings, viewing positive results as supportive of the psi hypothesis whilst ensuring that null results do not count as evidence against it. The first section of this paper looks at the way in which this win-win principle has resulted in the evolution of different paradigms within parapsychology, with null results causing researchers to alter the type of alleged psychic ability they are looking for rather than reject the psi hypothesis. The second section examines how the principle operates in modern day parapsychology, focusing on how it prevents closure on the psi question, and making recommendations for how such problems can be overcome in the future.

NULLIFYING NULL RESULTS BY SHIFTING PARADIGMS

Around the turn of the 20th century a small band of pioneering researchers initiated the first program of systematic scientific research into the possible existence of psychic ability. They assumed, quite reasonably, that if psi did exist it would probably be most apparent in those claiming to possess significant psychic abilities. Unfortunately, their investigations into the best-known claimant mediums and psychic claimants of the day quickly revealed that many of these alleged abilities were actually the result of either fraud or self-delusion. It is easy to imagine how this catalogue of null findings might have caused the majority of these researchers to conclude that psychic ability did not exist and move on to investigating other topics. This was not, however, the case. Rather than abandoning the psi hypothesis, they simply concluded that working with mediums and psychics was not the best way forward, and went in search of a very different kind of psychic star.

In the early 1930s, biologist-turned-parapsychologist Joseph Banks Rhine initiated this new era in parapsychology, searching for people who did not claim to possess extraordinary psychic ability but nevertheless consistently obtained high scores in controlled tests of extrasensory perception. A few years later Rhine published his seminal text, *Extrasensory Perception*, announcing that he had discovered a handful of these psychically talented individuals. Unfortunately, replicating Rhine's work proved highly problematic, with researchers struggling to find individuals who could reliably produce above-chance scoring (for an excellent description of this period, see Pratt, 1975).

Once again, it would be easy to imagine how these null findings would cause the parapsychological community to abandon their quest. In practice parapsychological researchers simply changed tack a second time, jettisoning the "psychic star" model and instead suggesting that such abilities are relatively subtle, unreliable, and distributed throughout the population. This emotionally appealing idea currently forms the dominant paradigm within the field.

In short, throughout history, parapsychologists have reacted to null findings by altering the type of alleged psychic ability that they are looking for, rather than reject the psi hypothesis. This has resulted in the evolution of different paradigms within parapsychology, with the latest incarnation of their efforts being cantered around the notion that such abilities are relatively subtle and unreliable, yet are distributed throughout the population.

HEADS I WIN, TAILS YOU LOSE: THE ROLE OF NULL RESULTS IN MODERN-DAY PARAPSYCHOLOGY

In theory, the "everyone's a little bit psychic" paradigm is fine. Instead of trawling the population for high scorers, parapsychologists have people take part in various psi tests, pool their results, and hope for significant and replicable effects. Unfortunately, in practice it hasn't turned out to be quite so simple. After over six decades of experimentation in this paradigm, researchers have failed to reach a consensus about the existence of psi. Although a minority of parapsychologists argue that the evidence is overwhelming, most parapsychological researchers believe that it simply isn't possible to answer the question with any certainty one way or the other. This lack of closure is due, in part, to the way in which null results are viewed at four key stages of the research process.

Stage 1: Cherry-Picking New Procedures

Parapsychologists frequently create and test new experimental procedures in an attempt to produce laboratory evidence for psi. These studies are most often carried out both by professional parapsychologists as exploratory investigations and by students as project work. Because there are no agreed-upon theoretical constraints surrounding psi, it is possible to form a convincing-sounding argument to justify almost any new procedure. For example, researchers with psychoanalytic leanings might think that psychic experiences involve the unconscious, and so argue that psi is especially likely to emerge during dreaming. Alternatively, psi can be viewed as an evolutionary survival mechanism that will operate best when people feel under some kind of threat, such as when they are placed in a room with a large spider. There again, one could adopt a neuropsychological stance, and argue that psychic ability is associated with right hemisphere functioning and thus should be enhanced after listening to relaxing music.

Most of these studies yield non-significant results and are either never published, or make it into a journal or conference proceedings but are quietly forgotten. Rather than being seen as evidence against the existence of psychic ability, such null findings are usually attributed to the experiment being carried out under non psi-conducive conditions. The pervasiveness of this practise is usually quickly revealed when chatting to those engaged in parapsychological research. Ask them what they are up to, and they will often describe an experiment involving some kind of new procedure, e.g., "I am looking to see if psi effects are especially strong among groups of professional artists at a New Age retreat" or "I am looking at whether astute waiters score especially well on tests involving the remote detection of staring," or "I am looking at whether people arriving late at a train station are especially likely to find that their train has been delayed." During my time in the field I have heard talk of large numbers of such studies, but only seen a minority make it into print or be presented at a conference. Of course, it could be that the researchers did not actually get around to running the various studies. However, I suspect that in many cases the early results were not promising and thus the study was abandoned, or that the study was completed but did not yield significant results and so remains tucked away at the back of a file drawer. Interestingly, ask researchers engaged in these tests what they will conclude if the study yields null results and they rarely mention disconfirmation of the psi hypothesis but instead explain that this would suggest that the new procedure is not psi-conducive. Pursue the point by asking them how many null findings would convince them that psi does not exist and the silence is usually deafening.

Once in a while one of these studies produces significant results. The evidential status of these positive findings is impossible to judge because all too often they have emerged from a mass of non-significant studies. Nevertheless they are more likely than non-significant studies to be presented at a conference or published in a journal, usually viewed as tentative evidence for psi, and act as a catalyst for further work.

To my knowledge, only one paper has revealed an insight into the potential scale of this problem. Watt (2006) summarized all of the psi-related final year undergraduate projects that had been supervised by staff at Edinburgh University's Koestler Parapsychology Unit between 1987 and 2007. Watt tracked down 38 projects, 27 of which predicted overall significant performance on a psi task. The work examined a range of new and established procedures, including, for example, dowsing for a hidden penny, the psychokinetic control of a visual display of a balloon being driven by a fan onto spikes, presentiment of photographs depicting emotional facial expressions, detecting the emotional state of a sender in a telepathy experiment, ganzfeld studies, and card guessing. Interestingly, Watt's paper also demonstrated a reporting bias. Only 7 of the 38 studies had made it into the public domain, being presented as papers at conferences held by the Parapsychological Association. All of these papers had predicted overall significant performance on the psi task. There was a strong tendency for researchers to make public those studies that had obtained positive findings, with just over 70%

(5 out of 7) of the studies presented at conference showing an overall significant result, versus just 15% (3 out of 20) of those that remained unreported.

Watt's analysis, although informative, underestimates the total number of psi-related studies undertaken at Edinburgh University because it did not include projects undertaken by students prior to their final year, experiments run by post-graduate students and staff, or any work conducted before 1987. Multiply these figures by the number of researchers who have conducted and supervised psi research across the world over the last 60 years or so, and the scale of the issue becomes apparent.

This process is the "heads I win, tails you lose" principle in action, with researchers trying a large number of new procedures, only to ignore the sizable catalogue of null findings and view the few positive results as being suggestive of psi.

Stage 2: Attempted Replications of "Successful" Procedures

Any procedure that seems to yield significant psi effects usually results in additional follow-up studies that utilize that procedure. Although these additional studies occasionally take the form of strict replications, it is more usual for them to involve some form of variation (e.g., Braud, Smith, Andrew, & Willis, 1976). These changes may be made for practical reasons or to explore the conditions that may influence the alleged effect. For example, if the original study into precognitive dreaming involved monitoring participants' REM state and waking them whenever they had a dream, a follow-up study might involve giving them a good night's sleep and asking them to recall all of their dreams in the morning. Likewise, if the original study into the evolutionary roots of psi made participants feel anxious by placing them in a room with a large live spider, a follow-up experiment might involve showing them photographs of the aforementioned creepy-crawlies. Similarly, if the original work into hemispheric processing involved participants listening to live music, a follow-up study might play them pre-recorded tracks.

If these follow-up studies obtain significant results, and do not appear to be due to any methodological or statistical problems, then the findings are seen as evidence for psi. However, any failure to replicate the original effect is often explained away in various ways.

They can, for example, be attributed to the procedural modifications rather than to the non-existence of psi. Again, because there are no theoretical constraints surrounding psi, it is easy to produce convincing sounding arguments to explain how any changes might have produced null effects. For example, researchers may argue that people's dream recall in the morning is less accurate than immediately after REM, that seeing a photograph of a spider does not produce the same level of anxiety as the real thing, or that pre-recorded music lacks the psi-conducive impact of a live performance. Perhaps the most far-reaching version of this "get out of a null effect free" card involves an appeal to the "experimenter effect," (e.g., Roll & Williams, 2010) wherein any negative findings are attributed to the psi inhibitory nature of the researchers running the study (e.g., Van de Castle, 1989).

In addition to explaining away null findings via allegedly failed procedural modifications, some researchers also adopt an "any anomaly will do" attitude, and data-mine in an attempt to produce some kind of psi-related result. Suddenly the emphasis is shifted away from a main effect and toward, for example, gender differences, or those who had vivid dreams versus those who did not, or those who gave especially high anxiety ratings to the photographs of the spiders, or those who reported finding the recorded music particularly enjoyable. Although such *post hoc* data mining might help guide future work, it has little, if any, evidential value. Nevertheless, researchers often present it as tentative evidence in support of the psi hypothesis.

Once again, this entire process represents the "heads I win, tails you lose" principle. Successful replications are seen as evidence of psi while null results are attributed to the non psi-conducive conditions under which the replication was carried out, with many researchers then quickly scurrying around to find *post hoc* effects.

Stage 3: Meta-Analyses and Retrospective Data Selection

After several studies have been conducted using a new procedure, researchers usually carry out some form of meta-analytic review of the work (e.g., Watt, 1994). If the combined outcome of the studies is significant, and does not appear to be due to any methodological or statistical problems, then the research is viewed as evidence for psi. However, if the cumulative effect is non-significant, researchers often attribute this null effect to the "non psi-conducive" procedural variations described in the preceding section.

Perhaps more importantly, the procedurally heterogeneous collection of studies usually presents researchers with an opportunity to "explain away" overall null effects by retrospectively identifying a sub-set of studies that used a certain procedure. Although such *post hoc* data mining has little evidential value, researchers often offer it as tentative evidence in support of the psi hypothesis.

A striking illustration of this occurred in the late 1990s during a meta-analytic debate surrounding the ganzfeld psi studies. In 1999 Julie Milton and I published a meta-analysis of all ganzfeld studies that were begun after 1987 and published by the beginning of 1997, and noted that the cumulative effect was both small and non-significant (Milton & Wiseman, 1999). Some researchers criticized this analysis, noting that we had included all of the ganzfeld studies conducted during this period, and that we should have instead focused on those that had employed a "standard" procedure developed by parapsychologist Charles Honorton and his colleagues during a seminal set of ganzfeld studies conducted at the Psychophysical Research Laboratory (PRL) in the late 1980s. The difficulties with this approach were revealed when researchers were unable to settle on what would constitute a "standard" set of procedures (Schmeidler & Edge, 1999). Eventually, Bem, Palmer, and Broughton (2001) set out to tackle this issue experimentally, asking several people to rate the degree to which the studies in our analysis had employed Honorton's "standard" ganzfeld procedure and then correlating their ratings against the effect size of each study. Rather than provide their own description of this "standard" procedure, Bem, Palmer, and Broughton had the raters read relevant sections in two previous papers describing the PRL studies. However, they also added a series of additional conditions, informing their raters, for example:

> You should treat as standard the use of artistic or creative subject samples (as one of the most successful components of the PRL experiments used such a sample) or subjects having had previous psi experiences or having practised a mental discipline such as meditation (as such subjects were shown to be the best scorers in the PRL experiments). (p. 210)

The addition of participant selection as an allegedly "standard" condition was not mentioned in the "method" section of either of the papers describing the PRL work. Once again, it's the "heads I win, tails you lose" principle.

Stage 4: Decline Effects and Repeating History

The alleged psi effects associated with a certain procedure frequently have a curious habit of fading over the course of repeated experimentation. Critics have argued that this is due to the researchers identifying and minimizing potential methodological and statistical flaws over time (e.g., Alcock, 2003, 2010). However, some parapsychologists have come up with creative ways of avoiding this potential threat, arguing that such decline effects are either an inherent property of psi or that psychic ability really does exist but is inversely related to the level of experimental controls employed in a study (see Kennedy, 2003, for a review of this approach). This may represent the next paradigm shift in parapsychology. If this proves to be the case it will be yet another (and possibly final) instance of parapsychologists changing their model of psi in the face of null findings, moving from the current "everyone has it to a small amount" paradigm to an unfalsifiable, and some would say bizarre, psi as an "all-knowing but elusive force."

Regardless, the decrease in alleged psi often causes researchers to abandon ship in search of a new procedure, placing them back to square one and ready to repeat history. This is not a new observation, with commentators remarking on this pattern throughout the history of the field. For example, writing over three decades ago, the parapsychologist Joseph Gaither Pratt (1978) noted:

> One could almost pick a date at random since 1882 and find in the literature that someone somewhere had recently obtained results described in terms implying that others should be able to confirm the findings. . . . One after another, however, the specific ways of working used in these initially successful psi projects have fallen out of favor and faded from the research scene—except for the latest investigations which, one may reasonably suppose, have not yet had enough time to falter and fade away as others before them have done. (p. 129)

This constant "ship jumping" is one of the defining features of psi research, with new paradigms emerging every decade or so. Take, for example, the different trends in ESP research that have emerged over the years. Initial work, conducted between the early 1930s and late 1950s primarily involved card guessing experiments, in which people were asked to guess the identity of specially printed playing cards carrying one of five simple symbols (e.g., Rhine, 1948). By the mid-1960s researchers had realized that such studies were problematic to replicate and so turned their attention to the possibility of participants predicting the outcome of targets selected by machines (e.g., Forwald, 1969), and to dream telepathy (e.g., White, Krippner, & Ullman, 1968). In the mid 1970s and early 1980s the ganzfeld experiments and remote viewing took over as dominant paradigms (e.g., Honorton, 1977; Targ & Morris, 1982). In 1987, a major review of the area by parapsychologists K. Ramakrishna Rao and John Palmer argued that two sets of ESP studies provided the best evidence for the replicability of psi: the ganzfeld experiments and the differential ESP effect (wherein participants apparently score above chance in one condition of an experiment and below chance in another). More recently researchers have shifted their attention to alleged presentiment effects, wherein participants appear to be responding to stimuli before they are presented (e.g., Radin, 1997). It seems likely that the next new procedure is likely to adopt a neuropsychological perspective, perhaps focusing on EEG measurements or functional MRI scans as people complete psi tasks (e.g., Don & Moura, 2000; Moulton & Kosslyn, 2008).

CONCLUSION

And so it goes on: around and around in circles, with researchers cherry-picking new procedures from a mass of chance results, varying any allegedly "successful" procedures and then blaming these variations for any lack of replication, searching for pockets of *post hoc* significance whenever a meta-analysis produces a null result, explaining away decline effects as an inherent property of psi, and finally jumping into bed with the next new promising procedure. This giddy process results in an ambiguous data set that, just like the classic optical illusion of the old hag and attractive young woman, never contains enough information to allow closure in one direction or the other.

The good news is that the framework outlined above presents a way to move forward and rapidly reach closure on the issue. To achieve this, researchers should change the way in which they view null findings. They might stop trying numerous new procedures and cherry-picking those that seem to work, and instead identify one or two that have already yielded the most promising results. They could stop varying these procedures, and instead have a series of labs carry out strict replications that are both methodologically sound and incorporate the most psi-conducive conditions possible. They could avoid the haunting spectre of retrospective meta-analysis by pre-registering the key details involved in each of the studies. And finally, they might agree to stop jumping ship, and instead have the courage to accept the null hypothesis if the selected front-runners do not produce evidence of a significant and replicable effect.

My hope is that such a process will stop researchers from finding themselves forever perched on the fence parroting the hackneyed "there is enough evidence to justify further work, but not enough to conclude one way or the other" position. They will instead put their feet on the ground and be the generation of experimenters that were brave enough to give it their best shot. Finally, they will be the ones to discover whether psi actually exists.

REFERENCES

Alcock, J. E. (2003). Give the null hypothesis a chance: Reasons to remain doubtful about the existence of psi. In J. Alcock, J. Burns, & A. Freeman (Eds.), *Psi wars: Getting to grips with the paranormal* (pp. 29–50). Charlottesville, VA: Imprint Academic.

Alcock, J. E. (2010). The parapsychologist's lament. In S. Krippner & H. L. Friedman (Eds.), *Mysterious minds: The neurobiology of psychics, mediums, and other extraordinary people* (pp. 35–43). Santa Barbara, CA: Praeger.

Bem, D. J., Palmer, J., & Broughton, R. S. (2001). Updating the Ganzfeld database: A victim of its own success? *Journal of Parapsychology, 65,* 207–218.

Braud, W. G., Smith, G., Andrew, K., & Willis, W. (1976). Psychokinetic influences on random number generators during evocation of "analytic" vs. "nonanalytic" modes of information processing. In J. D. Morris, W. G. Roll, & R. L. Morris (Eds.), *Research in Parapsychology 1975* (pp. 85–88). Metuchen, NJ: Scarecrow Press.

Don, N. E., & Moura, G. (2000). Trance surgery in Brazil. *Alternative Therapies in Health and Medicine, 6*(4), 39–48.

Forwald, H. (1969). *Mind, matter, and gravitation: A theoretical and experimental study.* New York: Parapsychological Foundation.

Honorton, C. (1977). Psi and internal attention states. In B. B. Wolman (Ed.), *Handbook of parapsychology* (pp. 435–472). New York: Van Nostrand Reinhold.

Kennedy, J. E. (2003). The capricious, actively evasive, unsustainable nature of psi: A summary and hypotheses. *Journal of Parapsychology, 67,* 53–74.

Milton, J., & Wiseman, R. (1999). Does psi exist? Lack of replication of an anomalous process of information transfer. *Psychological Bulletin, 125,* 387–391.

Moulton, S. T., & Kosslyn, S. M. (2008). Using neuroimaging to resolve the psi debate. *Journal of Cognitive Neuroscience, 20,* 180–192.

Pratt, J. G. (1975). Outstanding subjects in ESP. *Journal of the American Society for Psychical Research, 69,* 151–160.

Pratt, J. G. (1978). Prologue to a debate: Some assumptions relevant to research in parapsychology. *Journal of the American Society for Psychical Research, 72,* 127–139.

Radin, D. I. (1997). Unconscious perception of future emotions: An experiment in presentiment. *Journal of Scientific Exploration, 11,* 163–180.

Rao, K. R., & Palmer, J. R. (1987). The anomaly called psi: Recent research and criticism. *Behavioral and Brain Sciences, 10,* 539–551.

Rhine, J. B. (1948). Conditions favoring success in psi tests. *Journal of Parapsychology, 12,* 58–75.

Roll, W. G., & Williams, B. J. (2010). Quantum theory, neurobiology, and parapsychology. In S. Krippner & H. L. Friedman (Eds.),*Mysterious minds: The neurobiology of psychics, mediums, and other extraordinary people* (pp. 1–33). Santa Barbara, CA: Praeger.

Schmeidler, G. R., & Edge, H. (1999). Should ganzfeld research continue to be crucial in the search for a replicable psi effect? Part II. Edited ganzfeld debate. *Journal of Parapsychology, 63,* 335–388.

Targ, R., & Morris, R. L. (1982). Note on a reanalysis of the UCSB remote-viewing experiments. *Journal of Parapsychology 46,* 47–50.

Van de Castle, R. L. (1989). ESP in dreams: Comments on a replication "failure" by the "failing" subject. In M. Ullman & S. Krippner with A. Vaughan, *Dream telepathy: Experiments in nocturnal ESP* (pp. 209–216). Jefferson, NC: McFarland.

Watt, C. A. (1994). Meta-analysis of DMT-ESP students and an experimental investigation of perceptual defense/vigilance and extrasensory perception. In E.W. Cook & D.L. Delanoy (Eds.), *Research in Parapsychology 1991* (pp. 64–68). Metuchen, NJ: Scarecrow Press.

Watt, C. A. (2006). Research assistants or budding scientists? A review of 96 undergraduate student projects at the Koestler Parapsychology Unit. *Journal of Parapsychology, 70,* 335–356.

White, R. A., Krippner, S., & Ullman, M. (1968). Experimentally-induced telepathic dreams with EEG-REM monitoring: Some manifest content variables related to psi operation. In H. Bender (Ed.), *Papers Presented for the Eleventh Annual Convention of the Parapsychological Association* (pp. 431–433). Freiburg, West Germany: Institute fur Grenzgebiete der Psychologie [Institute for the Study of Borderline Areas of Psychology].

The Antique Roadshow: How Denier Movements Critique Evolution, Climate Change, and Nonlocal Consciousness

Stephan A. Schwartz

In our culture right now we have several "denier" movements actively engaged in trying to impede the free development of science: the Creationists (e.g., Hornyanszky & Tasi, 2002), the climate change deniers (e.g., Lomborg, 2008), and the consciousness-deniers who cannot, or will not, consider consciousness as anything other than materialistic processes. For all their lack of substance, these movements represent powerful forces in the culture, producing substantial detrimental effects.

Creationism, on its face, seems medieval and absurd. However, the Pew Research Center for the People and the Press (2008), just one of several organizations tracking the Creationist issue for many years, reports that 55 percent of Americans believe the world was created within the last 10,000 years with all the species pretty much as they are today. As appalling as that is, I want to point out in the context of this essay it is getting worse. Creationists are winning the hearts and minds of the American public. Consider, Epilogue Table 2.1, a 2005 poll by the Harris organization.

Epilogue Table 2.1
"Do You Believe Apes and Man Have a Common Ancestry or Not?"

Base: All Adults		
	July 1996	June 2005
	%	%
Yes, apes and man do have a common ancestry.	51	46
No, apes and man do not have a common ancestry.	43	47
Not sure/Decline to answer	05	07

Note: Percentages may not add up exactly to 100% due to rounding. (Harris, 2005, online)

Climate change deniers have seriously impeded the development of rational policies to deal with what the best scientific research tells us is happening with our climate, a distortion that may prove to have fatal consequences.

Consciousness-deniers are materialists who conceive of all aspects of consciousness as entirely a construct of physiological processes, in spite of hundreds of studies demonstrating this conclusion is not justified. This, just as Creationists in the face of hundreds of studies, demand that evolution be considered no more than an unproven theory, or that climate deniers see extreme snow storms as proof that climate change is a fallacy. As a result of these denier efforts, research in all three areas has been made more difficult, and this has had both unfortunate scientific and social implications.

The denier disruptions created in evolutionary and climate research are well-known. The impact of consciousness-deniers is less known or understood. But here is one consideration: progress in understanding the nature of consciousness, particularly that aspect, the nonlocal that has not been explained by physiology, but is addressed by nonlocality and quantum processes, has a very direct social consequence. The nonlocal aspect of consciousness may very well account for the insight of genius, for religious epiphany, as well as for psychic experiences. In an age when the acquisition and analysis of information as well as the fostering of innovation that produces breakthroughs will be critical determinants of societal success, learning how individuals make intuitive leaps that change the game is no small matter. More profoundly these studies, the collective product of multiple disciplines, are beginning to describe how consciousness and matter interact. Collectively they are defining a new paradigm.

The three denier movements—Creationists, climate change deniers, and consciousness-deniers—all share certain commonalities. Deniers from all these movements make a point of defining themselves as skeptics, so we should begin by noting that "skeptic" comes from the Greek root *skepsis* meaning "inquiry and doubt." Yet any objective analysis of these movements makes it clear that their hallmarks include a lack of interest in further inquiry, and an absence of doubt concerning their own positions. So if deniers are not skeptics what are they?

I believe these movements represent classic examples of defense positions concerning a cherished paradigm slowly moving into crisis, just as described by the physicist and philosopher of science Thomas Kuhn (1962). With Creationists it is the inerrancy of the Bible and the presentation in Genesis of the creation of the world. For climate change deniers it is the conviction that human intervention is not the source of massive climate change. For consciousness-deniers it is a materialistic perspective.

In this essay, I draw comparisons amongst the denier movements and particularly focus on the consciousness-deniers, because their attacks and the disruptive friction they produce have a particularly deleterious effect on many of the lines of research covered in these pages.

If one follows the threads of consciousness-denier criticism over the past century it is notable that while, in the early years, attacks mostly centered on methodology, after an exchange between psychologist Ray Hyman and statistician Jessica Utts that line of criticism largely ceased (Hyman, 1995; Utts, 1995). Why did this happen? In 1995 the U.S. Congress commissioned the American Institutes for Research (AIR), a Washington, DC based not-for-profit think tank with a long history of work in human performance and close government ties, to assess the reality of remote viewing in research the U.S. government had previously funded (Utts, 1995). Remote viewing is a protocol for obtaining objectively verifiable information that can only be obtained through accessing nonlocal awareness, that aspect of consciousness presumptively outside of conventional conceptualizations of space/time.

To make the assessment, AIR selected the nationally recognized statistics professor Jessica Utts of the University of California - Davis, and the well-known skeptic Ray Hyman, a psychology professor on the faculty of the University of Oregon and a fellow of the Committee for the Scientific Investigation of Claims of the Paranormal (now the Committee for Skeptical Inquiry). Both had previously written on this topic and were notably sophisticated in the issues involved. Utts (1991) had already addressed the question that Congress was asking in a paper published in the journal *Statistical Science*.

Hyman and Utts were each asked by AIR to produce an independent report by a fixed date (Utts, 1995). Utts complied, and submitted her report by the deadline. Hyman did not. As a result he was able to see her report before writing his own, and the approach he chose to take, when he did write, was largely a commentary on her analysis. To compensate for this inequity, AIR allowed Utts to write a response that was incorporated into the final document submitted to Congress (Utts, 1995). It is in this unplanned form of exchange that the essence of the two positions is revealed. Utts' initial statement is remarkable for its clarity. She wrote:

> Using the standards applied to any other area of science, it is concluded that psychic functioning has been well established. The statistical results of the studies examined are far beyond what is expected by chance. Arguments that these results could be due to methodological flaws in the experiments are soundly refuted. Effects of similar magnitude have been replicated at a number of laboratories across the world. Such consistency cannot be readily explained by claims of flaws or fraud. The magnitude of psychic functioning

exhibited appears to be in the range between what social scientists call a small and medium effect. That means that it is reliable enough to be replicated in properly conducted experiments, with sufficient trials to achieve the long-run statistical results needed for replicability. (Utts, 1995, Chap. 3, p. 23)

In responding to Utts' report, Hyman (1995) wrote:

I want to state that we agree on many [other] points. We both agree that the experiments [being assessed] were free of the methodological weaknesses that plagued the early . . . research. We also agree that the . . . experiments appear to be free of the more obvious and better known flaws that can invalidate the results of parapsychological investigations. We agree that the effect sizes reported . . . are too large and consistent to be dismissed as statistical flukes. (Hyman, 1995, Chap. 3, p. 63)

This is important because what Hyman is conceding is that the way in which the kinds of laboratory experiments described in the AIR report had been conducted, and the way in which they were analyzed, is no longer a matter for dispute. In other words, nonlocal perception cannot be explained away as some artifact resulting from how the data were collected, or evaluated.

Nor is this research vulnerable to criticisms based on blindness and randomness. In my own opinion, no other field of science is so obsessed with the gold standard issues of blindness and randomness.

English biologist Rupert Sheldrake (1999) conducted a survey of leading journals published between October 1996 and April 1998. The papers these journals had published were broken into three categories: "(1) Not applicable: papers that did not involve experimental investigations, for example theoretical or review articles; (2) Blind or double-blind methodologies used; and, (3) Blind or double-blind methodologies not used" (Sheldrake, 1999, p. 90). The reader may find the results surprising. As can be seen in Epilogue Table 2.2, parapsychology overwhelmingly utilizes this third protocol more than does any other discipline.

Five years later Caroline Watt and Marleen Nagtegaal (2004), working at University of Edinburgh, restudied the use of the double-blind protocol in the various disciplines of science and reported that in the ensuing years little had changed.

With the Utts/Hyman (Hyman, 1995; Utts, 1995) exchange, the work by Sheldrake (1999), and Watt and Nagtegaal (2004) on record, the deniers have been denied the line of attack that parapsychological methods are typically faulty.

Their focus now is centered, as the denier commentaries in this book illustrate, on replication rates—it works but not as well as we demand it should—and the fact that a single paradigm-achieving theory has not emerged. To anyone familiar with Thomas Kuhn (1962), of course, consciousness research is evolving just as it should, and, equally predictably, the deniers are mounting increasingly implausible paradigm defenses just as Kuhn's model predicts.

What the deniers do not acknowledge is that paradigms do change, and that it is theories, and the experiments that test them, that create paradigms. Further, no

Epilogue Table 2.2
Blind Methodologies Used by Various Disciplines

Area of Science	Number of Papers	Number with Blind Methodologies Not Used Percent of Total (0.00%)
Physical Science	237	00
Biological Science	914	07 (0.8%)
Medical Science	227	55 (24.2%)
Psychology and animal behavior	143	07 (4.9%)
Parapsychology	27	23 (85.2%)

Source: "Numbers of papers reviewed, and the number involving blind or double-blind methodologies in a range of scientific journals. Only papers reporting experimental results were included in this survey; theoretical papers and review articles were excluded. All publications appeared in 1996–98 unless otherwise indicated" (Sheldrake, 1999, p. 90).

one discipline can create a new paradigm; only many disciplines reaching a consensus can do that. This is the process now going on and, in this context consciousness researchers such as parapsychologists are simply early-adapters. Science, in its many manifestations, is finally grappling seriously with consciousness and nonlocality, but the deniers will not join this quest.

How ironic it is then that Kuhn (1962), whose mind conceived of the paradigm concept in science—and paradigm is the core of all denier arguments—fully, if somewhat uncomfortably, recognized the nonlocal aspect of consciousness. In his classic book, *The Structure of Scientific Revolutions*, he wrote:

No ordinary sense of the term "interpretation" fits these flashes of intuition through which a new paradigm is born. Though such intuitions depend upon the experience, both anomalous and congruent, gained with the old paradigm, they are not logically or piecemeal linked to particular items of that experience as an interpretation would be. (pp. 122–123)

Comparing this with the statements made by "singular people" upon whom history confers the title genius, prophet, or seer, reveals that Kuhn (1962) echoed their words almost exactly. As Albert Einstein (1931) explained it, "I believe in intuition and inspiration; I feel certain I am right while not knowing the reason" (p. 97). Einstein's assistant Banesh Hoffman, himself a major physicist, observed, "When excited discussions failed to break the deadlock [of a problem], Einstein would quietly say in his quaint English, 'I will have a little tink' " (as cited in Infeld & Isacsson, 2007, para. 1). As Hoffman and Leopold Infeld, Einstein's other major assistant (also a renowned physicist), looked on in silence, Einstein would pace the room, coiling and uncoiling his signature hair around a finger as he walked, his sockless ankles winking into view as his pants flapped. "There was a dreamy faraway, yet inward look on his face," (as cited in

Infeld & Isacsson, 2007, para. 1). Hoffman recalled, but "no sign of stress. No outward indication of intense concentration" (as cited in Infeld & Isacsson, 2007, para. 1). Neither assistant felt he could say a word. After a few minutes, Einstein would suddenly come back to ordinary consciousness, "a smile on his face and an answer to the problem on his lips." Hoffman noted that the ideas "seemed to come from left field, to be quite extraordinary" (as cited in Infeld & Isaacson, 2007, para. 1).

Johannes Brahms described his own moments of creative breakthroughs this way:

> In this exalted state I see clearly what is obscure in my ordinary moods; then I feel capable of drawing inspiration from above as Beethoven did. ... Those vibrations assume the form of distinct mental images. ... Straightaway the ideas flow in upon me ... and not only do I see distinct themes in the mind's eye, but they are clothed in the right forms, harmonies, and orchestration. Measure by measure the finished product is revealed to me when I am in those rare inspired moods. (as cited in Abell, 1964, pp. 19–21)

Wolfgang Amadeus Mozart and Aaron Copland also seem to have had similar experiences (in Abell, 1964). In Mozart's case the connection was so clear and strong the pages of his compositions show few alterations; they appear to be finished transcriptions.

Remote viewers say of their experiences: "I kind of space out," or "It's sort of like focusing my mind at some middle distance" (Schwartz, 2007, p. 34). They describe the moment itself by saying, "It came in a flash," or, "It was like a hologram. ... Images are all there ... as if it were a hologram hanging in my mind" (Schwartz, 2007, p. 34).

Henri Poincaré described his work on a mathematical problem in the same vein: "One day, as I was crossing the street, the solution of the difficulty which had brought me to a standstill came to me all at once" (Goldenberg, Levav, Mazursky, & Solomon, 2009, p. 3).

Consider also one of history's most renowned psychics, Edgar Cayce, describing what he was doing. Speaking from his self-induced trance, in 1923, in response to a question about the process and source of his nonlocal ability:

> The information as given or obtained from this body is gathered from the sources from which the suggestion may derive its information. In this state the conscious mind becomes subjugated to the subconscious, superconscious or soul mind; and may and does communicate with like minds, and the subconscious or soul force becomes universal. From any subconscious mind information may be obtained, either from this plane or from the impressions as left by the individuals that have gone on before, as we see a mirror reflecting direct that which is before it. ... Through the forces of the soul, through the mind of others as presented, or that have gone on before; through the

subjugation of the physical forces in this manner, the body obtains the information. (Cayce, 1923, reading number 3744–3)

How is it that the great geniuses of history in both science and the arts, as well as ordinary remote viewers, and one of history's great clairvoyants all have reported similar experiences in the process of attaining insight—and yet consciousness-deniers feel this is not a fruitful area for serious scientific inquiry? Inasmuch as our history is largely defined by the breakthroughs resulting from such insights, surely understanding the processes involved should be of primary importance.

Because they are not data based, all three denier movements have a certain antique quality about them. Each speaks about the field it attempts to debunk from a position far behind the cutting edge of the science being attacked. This antique roadshow is a sure sign that denier arguments are based on attitude not data. Deniers all display what can only be called willful ignorance. In the case of the Creationists this is easy to see, since, to maintain their position, they have to discard geology, paleontology, anthropology, chemistry, astro-physics, astronomy, and the rest of modern science, except perhaps for medicine.

Climate change deniers simply will not deal with the mass of data collected showing not only that climate change is real, but that human activity not natural cycles is the dynamic driving it. This creates severe political problems for democracies where forcing endless debate becomes a weapon. Nobel laureate economist Paul Krugman (2009) has described the denier's behavior in the debate leading up to the passage by the U.S. Congress of the Waxman-Markey climate-change bill:

If you watched the debate . . . you didn't see people who've thought hard about a crucial issue, and are trying to do the right thing. What you saw, instead, were people who show no sign of being interested in the truth. They don't like the political and policy implications of climate change, so they've decided not to believe in it—and they'll grab any argument, no matter how disreputable, that feeds their denial. (p. A21)

Notably, corporations who live in the continuing glare of profit and loss, in its way a more stringent standard even than scientific protocol, have no time for such unworldly bias. As I write this essay in January 2010, at the United Nations Investor Summit on Climate Risk, 450 of the world's largest investors have issued a statement calling on the United States and other governments to "act now to catalyze development of a low-carbon economy and to attract the vast amount of private capital necessary for such transformation" (Environmental News Service Web site, 2010, para.1).

The United States, European, and Australian investor groups, who together represent $13 trillion in assets, have called for "a price on carbon emissions" and "well-designed carbon markets" to provide "a cost-effective way of achieving emissions reductions" (Environmental News Service Web site, 2010, para. 2).

In consciousness-deniers, willful ignorance can similarly be seen. They speak about a parapsychology that has not existed in decades, if it ever did and, even more revealingly, they ignore all the other areas of research where work is going on that is essentially parapsychological by another name. Therapeutic intention research such as immunologist Leonard Leibovici's (2001) study on remote retro-active intercessory prayer, or the near-death experience studies of cardiologist Pim van Lommel and his associates (2001, 2006) are two examples. One wonders if these studies are even known to the denier community. This is not really a rhetorical question. At a conference in Vancouver, British Columbia, when asked directly in open session whether he was familiar with the remote viewing literature, I recall well-known denier psychologist Richard Wiseman recognizing he was about to be asked a specific question about this line of research, confessing he had not read it, and did not know where it was to be found (Personal communication, Meeting of the Minds on Anomalous Cognition Conference, 2007).

The denier commentaries do not seem to apprehend that some of the largest, most important, and best-funded research studies on consciousness and nonlocality have been carried out in disciplines other than parapsychology—Leibovici (2001) and van Lommel et al. (2001, 2006) being only two examples. Let me cite a few lines of inquiry to give a sense of how far behind the times the consciousness-denier community actually is. And let me point out that all of this could be discovered in half an hour by a college sophomore searching a freely available recognized index such as *PubMed*.

First I will cite a paper by three leading physicists who have explored the issue of consciousness in the context of physics. Because of its unequivocal clarity I quote the entire statement:

> Neuropsychological research on the neural basis of behavior generally posits that brain mechanisms will ultimately suffice to explain all psychologically described phenomena. This assumption stems from the idea that the brain is made up entirely of material particles and fields, and that all causal mechanisms relevant to neuroscience can therefore be formulated solely in terms of properties of these elements. Thus, terms having intrinsic mentalistic and/or experiential content (e.g., "feeling," "knowing" and "effort") are not included as primary causal factors. *This theoretical restriction is motivated primarily by ideas about the natural world that have been known to be fundamentally incorrect for more than three-quarters of a century* [emphasis added]. Contemporary basic physical theory differs profoundly from classic physics on the important matter of how the consciousness of human agents enters into the structure of empirical phenomena. The new principles contradict the older idea that local mechanical processes alone can account for the structure of all observed empirical data. Contemporary physical theory brings directly and irreducibly into the overall causal structure certain psychologically described choices made by human agents about how they will act. This key development in basic physical theory is applicable to neuroscience, and it provides neuroscientists and psychologists with an alternative conceptual framework for describing neural processes. Indeed, owing to certain structural features of ion channels critical to synaptic function, contemporary physical theory

must in principle be used when analyzing human brain dynamics. The new framework, unlike its classic-physics-based predecessor, is erected directly upon, and is compatible with, the prevailing principles of physics. It is able to represent more adequately than classic concepts the neuroplastic mechanisms relevant to the growing number of empirical studies of the capacity of directed attention and mental effort to systematically alter brain function. (Schwartz, Stapp, & Beauregard, 2005, p. 1)

Second, let me cite a report by Frecska and Luna (2006) of the National Institute for Psychiatry and Neurology in Budapest, in which they present a neuro-ontological interpretation of spiritual experiences:

The prevailing neuroscientific paradigm considers information processing within the central nervous system as occurring through hierarchically organized and interconnected neural networks. The hierarchy of neural networks doesn't end at the neuroaxonal level; it incorporates subcellular mechanisms as well. When the size of the hierarchical components reaches the nanometer range and the number of elements exceeds that of the neuro-axonal system, an interface emerges for a possible transition between neuro-chemical and quantum physical events. "Signal nonlocality," accessed by means of quantum entanglement is an essential feature of the quantum physical domain. The presented interface may imply that some manifestations of altered states of consciousness, unconscious/conscious shifts have quantum origin with significant psychosomatic implications. (p. 143)

Nowhere in any of the denier commentaries is there any recognition of this work. Clearly there is a whole world beyond arguing whether nonlocality is real or a statistical artifact or a magic trick. But one would not know it from reading contemporary parapsychological criticism, just as one would know nothing of modern paleontology by reading a Creationist tract, or fully comprehend the acidification of the world's oceans by reading climate change denier literature.

Another hallmark of denier criticism is that nothing ever really changes and, depending on the audience, issues long settled will emerge from their crypts to distort and confuse once again. Remember the exchange between Hyman (1995) and Utts (1995)? Well, here is an example of what I mean. Almost five years after his exchange with Jessica Utts, Professor Hyman, in July 2002, was interviewed by a reporter from the *Austin American-Statesman*. Hyman is reported as saying: "The issue is, what kind of evidence do they have? I didn't see any science at all, any evidence they got anything right other than pure guesswork" (Leblanc, 2002, online). Even if remote viewing worked, Hyman stated, it would be too erratic to rely on. "People who believe it admit that only 15 percent of what remote viewers tell you is true, which means 85 percent is wrong," he remarked, although he did not mention the origin of this statistic, and it directly contradicts the published research. He concluded, "You don't know which is which, so it's of no practical use." If remote viewing could be demonstrated, "It would overturn almost everything we know in science" (Leblanc, 2002, online).

How does one reconcile Hyman's words in 1995 with his interview in 2002? The answer, of course, is one cannot. It is worth noting that the "15 percent of what remote viewers tell you is true" (Leblanc, 2002, online) is fanciful, and could not produce the statistical outcomes that are part of the published AIR record. Moreover it directly contradicts what has been reported in the peer-reviewed literature for almost four decades. I will cite here only one such report showing what the most casual research in the peer-reviewed remote viewing literature will quickly yield. In their initial 1976 paper on their research at SRI International, physicists Harold Puthoff and Russell Targ reported: "Using Edington's method for combining the probabilities from independent experiments, the probability of observing these six experimental outcomes by chance alone is 7.8×10^{-9}, one-tailed" (Puthoff & Targ, 1976, online). When one sees comments such as Hyman's it becomes clear that to deniers a preconceived conclusion is far more important than actual data. As George Orwell (1962) wrote in his novel 1984, "And if the facts say otherwise, then the facts must be altered. Thus history is continuously rewritten" (p. 213).

This leads to a final point, a very sad one that only rarely turns up in the scholarly community, where a conscious and purposeful commitment to integrity is a basic part of science. There is a propensity in denier movements, all of whose members ostensibly ground their arguments in science, to behave in ways that are demonstrably unscientific and even, on occasion, of dubious ethicality.

In climate change, where there are vast sums at risk, the frauds are biggest and most complex, carefully filtered through a network of denier institutes and think tanks. One brief account will serve as representative. Mitchell Anderson, a Vancouver-based researcher and writer and former staff scientist at the Sierra Legal Defense Fund, describes the back-story behind the climate denier Skeptic's Handbook. This manual was compiled by the Heartland Institute, created and funded by oil interests including $676,000 from ExxonMobil (Anderson, 2009). In a typical denier move to manipulate media and policy, they sent 150,000 copies of the Handbook across the U.S. including 850 journalists, 26,000 schools, and 19,000 "leaders and politicians." The Handbook coaches "skeptics" to keep from being pinned down by the evidence demonstrating climate change (Anderson, 2009, no page number designated).

Anderson (2009) noted:

It is also interesting that this latest product of the denial machine is washing over the nation less than a month after the U.S. government released their Climate Change Literacy brochure—cosigned by 13 federal agencies and 24 educational and scientific partners. Membership in the supposed climate change conspiracy now includes what deniers term "eco-freaks" as the U.S. Department of Defense, the U.S. Department of the Interior and the U.S. Forest Service. (Online, no page specified)

Exactly these same techniques of widespread distribution of false or highly distorted information are employed by the other denier movements. Creationists, using the political power they wield, in 2006 pressured the Bush Administration to direct the Grand Canyon National Park that it was not to provide an official estimate of the geologic age of the canyon. "In order to avoid offending religious fundamentalists, our National Park Service is under orders to suspend its belief in geology" (Public Employees for Environmental Responsibility Web site, 2006, online), said Public Employees for Environmental Responsibility Executive Director Jeff Ruch. "It is disconcerting that the official position of a national park as to the geologic age of the Grand Canyon is 'no comment' " (Public Employees for Environmental Responsibility Web site, 2006, online).

Consciousness-deniers similarly maintain an active media influencing program. Because it is both representative and reveals a state of mind, I want to draw attention to one particular example, drawing on the published words of a few of the principal players, a nationally prominent astronomer and two highly regarded professors of psychology and sociology, all of whom became so appalled by what they saw that they not only resigned, they put their views quite deliberately on record in the public press.

Since this story is an integral part of the founding of the Committee for the Scientific Investigation of Claims of the Paranormal (CSICOP) now the Committee for Scientific Inquiry (CSI), and still the principal consciousness-denier group in the United States, it is instructive to consider it. In my opinion, it is probably the clearest story in the record illustrating the difference between deniers and genuine skeptics.

The story has an almost Greek tragedy mytho-poetic quality, in which a group of scientists, some quite prominent in their fields, are presented with the most fundamental choice a scientist can face: Do I go with the data, or with my prejudice? Some rose to the challenge, some did not. It is a complex, cautionary tale that I will go into only to the point of illustrating the relevant denier skeptic issues. However, I strongly encourage any reader interested in better understanding the psychology of denier movements to go to the Web sites cited, where references to the original papers are located, and to pursue what is to be found there.

In brief, here is the story: In 1975 astronomer Dennis Rawlins, already famous for debunking the claims of polar explorers Richard Byrd and Robert Peary and demonstrating that Roald Amundsen was the first man to reach either pole, decided to join a team headed by philosopher Paul Kurtz (the founder of CSICOP) to launch a frontal attack against presumptive "planetary influences" on human behavior reported by the French investigators Michel and his wife (at the time) and research partner Francoise Gauquelin. Earlier, *The Humanist* had published a paper that included an attack on the Gauquelins. It was a curious attack; the Gauquelins had their own reservations about astrology; indeed, they would go on to dismiss, on the basis of their research data, many claims of Western astrology. Ironically, Michel Gauquelin (1979), a psychologist and statistician, later wrote a book debunking traditional Western astrology's planetary effects that was published by

Prometheus Books, which was founded by Kurtz. Gauquelin (1978) also was to write an article critical of astrology for *The Humanist*, a magazine edited by Kurtz. Even so, exactly because they were rigorous scientists, the Gauquelins reported identifying small but statistically significant relationships between some planetary positions at the time of the birth and later outstanding performance, most notably the position of Mars in a natal chart and later athletic prowess (Gauquelin, 1973, 1975; Gauquelin & Gauquelin, 1970–1972). It was not a huge effect but, to many CSICOP members, these reports were intolerable.

The Humanist group focused their attack on the Gauquelins' statistics (Rawlins, 1981) but it soon became clear that Michel Gauquelin was the better statistician and the denier case collapsed. Undeterred, the group went on for round two, which involved an attempted Committee-sponsored replication of the "Mars effect" and a dispute over the interpretation of the data. Rawlins describes what happened next as a comedy of incompetence, bombast, and a commitment to denialism so power-ful it overturned good sense and ethics, until the deniers were thoroughly tarred by Rawlins (among others) for their unscientific disdain for experimental evidence and integrity.

After furious public exchanges, Rawlins, a skeptic but not a denier, publicly resigned from the group. Shortly thereafter, he put the entire sorry tale in the record via a paper entitled, *sTar baby*, a play on Joel Chandler Harris' late nine-teenth century Uncle Remus stories, where Br'er Rabbit, the Loki-like adventurer around whom many of the stories are built, attacks a tar baby and, each time he hits it he becomes more and more mired in the tar (Rawlins, 1981). Rawlins would not be alone and his was followed by the resignations of several other mem-bers of the Committee. These resignations illustrate the difference between skep-tics and deniers.

The person who saw this distinction most clearly was the sociologist Marcello Truzzi (e.g., 1997), who acted on his beliefs by first resigning from the committee and, then, publishing a new journal *The Zetetic Scholar* (Zetetic from the Greek *zētētikos*, from *zēteō* to seek to proceed by inquiry) in which he decried what he called "pseudo-skepticism." Truzzi (1982) wrote,

> The current evidence strongly indicates that (a) a Mars Correlation was validly found by the Gauquelins, (b) a correlation was found in several replications by the Gauquelins using different samples, (c) a similar cor-relation was found in replications conducted by Kurtz-Zelen-Abell (KZA) [in the CSICOP-sponsored research study]. In regard to (a) and (b) the key question concerns the validity of the Gauquelins' data. It has repeatedly been incorrectly stated that there is no way to check this data. Not only have the Gauquelins published all their data (so computa-tions can easily be checked), they have kept all original records from the birth registries, and these have been made available to any serious researchers. In fact, the Gauquelins have urged critics to check this data. (p. 76)

Truzzi's reasons for resigning from the Committee state clearly the problem with denier movements. He recalled:

> Originally I was invited to be a co-chairman of CSICOP by Paul Kurtz. I helped to write the bylaws and edited their journal. I found myself attacked by the Committee members and board, who considered me to be too soft on the paranormalists. My position was not to treat protoscientists as adversaries, but to look to the best of them and ask them for their best scientific evidence. I found that the Committee was much more interested in attacking the most publicly visible claimants such *as The National Enquirer*. The major interest of the Committee was not inquiry but to serve as an advocacy body, a public relations group for scientific orthodoxy. The Committee has made many mistakes. My main objection to the Committee, and the reason I chose to leave it, was that it was taking the public position that it represented the scientific community, serving as gatekeepers on maverick claims, whereas I felt they were simply unqualified to act as judge and jury when they were simply lawyers. (Truzzi, 1989, online)

New Zealand psychologist Richard Kammann, the third person to resign, would write in his exegetic essay of the whole Gauquelin affair, "When the whole record is examined over five years, there is almost no instance in which merit wins out over self-serving bias" (Kammann, 1982, online). The one clear exception was providing Rawlins a carte blanche space in the CSICOP publication, *The Skeptical Inquirer*, and even this was undermined by a flurry of simultaneous misstatements (Rawlings, 1981–1982, 1982, pp. 29–30). Kammann (1982) wrote:

> The bottom line is that an apology is owed the Gauquelins for the mistreatment of their data, and the aspersions cast on their authenticity. I don't wish to convey that I'm a believer, because I also have skeptical reservations about the Mars effect. What makes this claim suspect is the scientific perversity of the proposition that the location of Mars in the sky at the time a person is born has some effect on that person's athletic performance 30 or 40 years later. (p. 56)

More than a decade later Suitbert Ertel, a German researcher of the next generation, uninvolved with the bitter fight that had gone before, meticulously went back through this entire chapter of denierism (including a subsequent denier round in Paris, France) and confirmed by a variety of statistical analyses, both Kammann's and Truzzi's assessments (Ertel, 1998/1999). Perhaps even more important was the graceless acknowledgement of Paul Kurtz who had begun it all: "It is time, to submit, to move to other more productive topics" (Kurtz, Nienhuys, & Sandhu, 1997, p. 38).

Unfortunately, this controversy is not an isolated event. The "sTarbaby incident" has been followed by numerous subsequent incidents of alleged falsification and distortion amongst consciousness-deniers. Both Rupert Sheldrake and Jim Lippard have been subjected to denier attacks and have created Web sites listing the relevant documents and transcripts of these and other such events. The reader is invited to go through these archives and reach his or her own conclusions (Lippard, 2009; Sheldrake, n.d.).

The controversies involving the three denier movements might superficially appear to be "inside baseball" arguments of interest only to the various research communities. However, stop and think about this for a moment: The truth about our species and our planet, the processes of our planet's climate, and the nature of our consciousness, are the essence of our search to understand who we are, and what it means to be a human being. These three denier movements all, in one way or another, impede the quest for this knowledge. Like pranksters putting up false direction signs, they waste precious resources and time. Worse, they poison the atmosphere of the inquiries. They serve not truth but bias.

REFERENCES

Abell, A. M. (1964). Talks with the great composers. Garmisch, Germany: G. E. Schroeder-Verlag.

Anderson, M. (2009, March 30). The Heartland Institute's skeptic handbook—Get out the shovel [web log message]. Retrieved from http://desmogblog.com/heartland-institute-skeptics-handbook-get-out-shovel

Cayce, E. (1923, October 9). Reading 3744-3, at the Phillips Hotel, Dayton, Ohio. Virginia Beach, VA: Archives, Association for Research and Enlightenment.

Einstein, A. (1931). Cosmic religion: With other opinions and aphorisms. New York: Covici-Friede.

Environmental News Service. (2010). Investors representing $13 trillion call for climate action now. Retrieved January 14, 2010 from http://www.ens-newswire.com/ens/jan2010/2010-01-14-01.html

Ertel, S. (1998/1999). Is there no Mars effect? The CFEPP's verdict scrutinized with the assistance of six independent researchers. Correlation, 17(2), 4–23.

Frecska, E., & Luna, L. E. (2006). Neuro-ontological interpretation of spiritual experiences. Neuropsychopharmacologia Hungarica (Hungary), 8(3), 143–153.

Gauquelin, M. (1973). The cosmic clocks. New York: Paladin.

Gauquelin, M. (1975, October). Spheres of influence. Psychology Today (London), pp. 21–27.

Gauquelin, M. (1978). The influence of planets on human beings: Fact versus fiction. The Humanist, 36, 29–30.

Gauquelin, M. (1979). Dreams and illusions of astrology. Amherst, NY: Prometheus.

Gauquelin, M., & Gauquelin, F. (1970–1972). Birth and planetary data gathered since 1949 (2 vols.). Paris: Laboratoire d'etude des Relations entre Rythmes Cosmiques et Psychophysiologiques.

Goldenberg, J., Levav, A., Mazursky, D., & Solomon, S. (2009). Cracking the ad code. New York: Cambridge University Press.

Harris Poll website. (2005, July 6). Nearly two-thirds of U.S. adults believe human beings were created by God [Harris Poll #52]. Retrieved from http://www.harrisinteractive.com/harris_poll/index.asp?PID=581

Hornyanszky, B., & Tasi, I. (2002). Nature's IQ: Extraordinary animal behavior that defies evolution. Badger, CA: Torchlight.

Hyman, R. (1995). Evaluation of program on "anomalous mental phenomena." In M. D. Mumford, A. M. Rose, & D. A. Goslin (Eds.), *An evaluation of remote viewing: Research and applications* (pp. 62–96). Washington, DC: The American Institutes for Research (AIR). Retrieved from www.lfr.org/LFR/csl/library/AirReport.pdf

Infeld, L., & Isaacson, W. (2007). Introduction. *Einstein: The evolution of physics* (pp. xi–xii). New York: Touchstone.

Kammann, R. (1982). The true disbelievers: Mars effect drives skeptics to irrationality. *Zetetic Scholar, 10*, 50–65. Available online at:http://www.discord.org/~lippard/kammann.html

Krugman, P. (2009, June 29). Betraying the planet. *The New York Times*, p. A–21 Retrieved from http://www.nytimes.com/2009/06/29/opinion/29krugman.html?_r=1

Kuhn, T. (1962). *Structure of scientific revolutions*. Chicago: University of Chicago Press.

Kurtz, P., Nienhuys, J. W., & Sandhu, R. (1997). Is the "Mars effect" genuine? *Journal of Scientific Exploration, 11*, 38.

Leblanc, P. (2002, July 14). Interview with Ray Hyman. *Austin American Statesman*. http://nl .newsbank.com/nl-search/we/Archives?p_product=AASB&p_theme=aasb&p_action =search&p_maxdocs=200&s_hidethis=no&p_field_label-0=Author&p_text_label-0 =leblanc&p_field_label-1=title&p_bool_label-1=AND&s_dispstring=hyman%20 AND%20byline(leblanc)%20AND%20date(all)&p_field_advanced-0=&p_text _advanced-0=(hyman)&p_perpage=10&p_sort=YMD_date:D&xcal_useweights=no

Leibovici, L. (2001). Effects of remote, retroactive intercessory prayer on outcomes in patients with bloodstream infection: Randomized controlled trial. *British Medical Journal, 323*, 1450–1451.

Lippard, J. (2009, August 6). Skeptics and the "Mars Effect": A chronology of events and publications. Retrieved from http://www.discord.org/~lippard/mars-effect-chron.rtf

Lomborg B. (2008). *Cool it: The skeptical environmentalist's guide to global warming*. New York: Vintage Books.

Meeting of the Minds on Anomalous Cognition Conference. (2007). Vancouver, British Columbia, July, 14–16, 2007.

Orwell, G. (1962). *1984*. New York: New American Library.

Pew Research Center for the People and the Press. (2008). *Religion: A strength and weakness for both parties*. Retrieved from http://www.people-press.org/reports/display.php3?ReportID=254

Public Employees for Environmental Responsibility. (2006). *How old is the Grand Canyon? Park service ordered by Bush administration to cater to Creationists*. Retrieved from http://www.peer.org/news/news_id.php?row_id=801

Puthoff, H. E., & Targ, R. A. (1976). A perceptual channel for information transfer over kilometer distances: Historical perspectives and recent research. *Proceedings of the IEEE, 64*, 329–354. Available online at: http://www.espresearch.com/espgeneral/IEEE-329B.shtml

Rawlins, D. (1981). Starbaby fate: Remus extremus. *Skeptical Inquirer, 34*(10), 67–98.

Rawlins, D. (1981–1982). Remus extremus. *Skeptical Inquirer, 6*(2), 58–63.

Rawlins, D. (1982, October). sTarbaby. *Fate*, pp. 1–32.

Schwartz, S. A. (2007). *Opening to the infinite: The art and science of non-local awareness*. Buda, TX, Nemoseen.

Schwartz, J. M., Stapp, H. P., & Beauregard, M. (2005). Quantum physics in neuroscience and psychology: A neurophysical model of mind-brain interaction. *Philosophical Transactions of the Royal Society of Biological Sciences, 360*(1458), 1309–1327.

Sheldrake, R. (1999). How widely is blind assessment used in scientific research? *Alternative Therapies, 5*(3), 88–91.

Sheldrake, R. (n.d). *Skeptical investigations.* Retrieved January 14, 2010 from http://www.skepticalinvestigations.org/New/index.html

Truzzi, M. (1982). Editorial. *Zetetic Scholar, 10,* 76.

Truzzi, M. (1989). Colloquium presented by Marcello Truzzi, Ph.D., Professor of Sociology at Eastern Michigan University at Ypsilanti, Michigan, and Director, Center for Scientific Anomalies Research, Ann Arbor, MI. Available at http://www.fiu.edu/~mizrachs/truzzi.html

Truzzi, M. (1997). Reflections on the sociology and social psychology of conjurors and their relations with psychical research. In S. Krippner (Ed.), *Advances in parapsychological research* (Vol. 8, pp. 221–281). Jefferson, NC: McFarland.

Utts, J. (1991). Replication and meta-analysis in parapsychology. *Statistical Science, 6,* 363–403.

Utts, J. (1995). An assessment of the evidence for psychic functioning. In M. D. Mumford, A. M. Rose, & D. A. Goslin (Eds.), *An evaluation of remote viewing: Research and applications* (pp. 23–51). Washington, DC: The American Institutes for Research (AIR). Retrieved from www.lfr.org/LFR/csl/library/AirReport.pdf

van Lommel, P. (2006). Near-death experiences, consciousness and the brain. *World Futures, 62,* 134–151.

van Lommel, P., van Wees, R., Meyers, V., & Elfferich, I. (2001). Near-death experience survivors of cardiac arrest: A prospective study in the Netherlands. *The Lancet, 358,* 2039–2045.

Watt, C., & Nagtegaal, M. (2004). Reporting of blind methods: An interdisciplinary survey. *Journal of the Society for Psychical Research, 68,* 105–114.

Is It Time for a Détente?

Harris L. Friedman and Stanley Krippner

We, Stanley Krippner (SK) and Harris Friedman (HF), as co-editors, have approached this book with different initial vantages. SK has long been a parapsychological researcher and advocate, whereas HF has only dabbled in a few parapsychological investigations and, until recently, has never published in the parapsychological literature. We start with a few words from each of us regarding our respective positions.

KRIPPNER'S STATEMENT

I have had personal experience with counteradvocates and their criticisms, some of which were justified and some of which were off-the-wall. Between 1966 and 1972, the psychiatrist Montague Ullman and I studied presumptively anomalous dreams collected in a laboratory setting (e.g., 1970). The literature is filled with anecdotal reports of dreams about future occurrences, dreams about distant happenings, and dreams that seemed to correspond with other people's cognitions or behaviors. Most of these reports are highly emotional in nature, many of them referring to accidents, illness, or death. However, associations between the dream and the actual phenomenon may be due to chance, to misinterpreted remarks, unconscious cueing, falsified memory, or deliberate prevarication.

To reproduce the real-life circumstances of a putative precognitive, clairvoyant, or telepathic dream under controlled conditions was not a simple task. Instead of a dreamer who spontaneous reported an unusual dream, we used a research participant who was primed to dream about a distant or future incident. Instead of using a happenstance from daily life, we used a randomly selected print of a celebrated work of art, one containing an emotional component. When our volunteer participants would arrive at our laboratory, in Brooklyn's Maimonides Medical Center, he or she would be greeted by several staff members, two of whom would later monitor the participant's brain waves and eye movements during sleep. Once the participant had retired in a soundproofed room, with electrodes glued to his or her head, die were tossed. The resulting number directed a staff member to a series of digits in a random number table; these digits were added and the resulting numeral would direct the staff member to an envelope containing the art print that would be that night's "target." For telepathic dream studies, the staff member who had spent time establishing rapport with the participant was dubbed the "agent" and went to a distant room before opening the envelope. The agent would spend most of the night focusing on the art print, writing down his or her associations to it, and attempting to "transmit" its contents to the sleeping participant. In turn, the participant would be oriented to "reach out" and "incorporate" elements of the art print into his or her dreams. For clairvoyant dream studies, there was no agent; the envelope remained sealed. For precognitive dream studies, the envelope was not selected until the participant had awakened the next morning.

Once the participant had retired, two staff members took turns observing the electroencephalographic record, awakening the participants after a period of rapid eye movements had been observed. The staff member used a microphone to ask, "Please tell me your dream or anything that was going through your mind when you were awakened," and the participant's response was tape-recorded and later transcribed. Additional questions were asked to obtain as complete a record as possible and then the staff member would state, "Please go back to sleep." A minimum of three dream reports was required for that night to be used for data analysis. At the end of the night a staff member would awaken the participant and request associations to the dream reports. The staff member (unaware of the actual target) would then present copies of all of the art prints in the "pool" from which the target had been selected. The participant would rank order these art prints in terms of their resemblance to his or her reported dreams. In most instances, the participant was not told the identity of the correct target until the entire series of experiments had been completed. Our rationale was that a participant could inadvertently meet a future participant, discuss the procedure, and disclose the correct target. As a result, the participant would not select that target during the matching procedure, knowing it had already been used on a different night.

For all three types of our studies, the tape recordings of the participants' dream reports were sent to a transcriber who was unaware of the target's identity. The transcripts were sent to three judges who matched each potential target against each night of dreams. Sometimes there were ten potential targets and ten experimental sessions. Statistical evaluations determined whether the judges' correct matches received higher scores for correspondences than the incorrect matches. The average (or mean) of the judges' scores were used as data, as were the participants' matches themselves.

For example, one night the research participant was a male psychoanalyst and the target was a print of Edgar Degas' "School of Ballet," which depicts a dance class in progress. The psychoanalyst reported dreams about "being in a class," "a class made up of maybe half a dozen people . . . , like a school," and "there was one little girl that was trying to dance with me." Both the participant and the judges gave a high matching score to this night of dreaming regarding the target (Krippner, 1991, p. 35).

At various times over the years, five magicians were invited to visit our laboratory. One of them served as a research participant and was unable to identify the target either by slight-of-hand or by discerning cues that would have provided information as to the identity of the art print. There was a consensus that fraud could not have been committed by the participants. For them, the most likely fraudulent scenario would have been for someone to alter the transcripts before sending them to the judges, for someone to alter the judges' data before sending them to the statisticians, or for the statisticians to provide spurious results. Because a variety of staff members were in charge of the experimental series over the years, a conspiracy would have had to be hypothesized. The magicians told us that the simplest way to explain out data through fraud would have been to implicate the statisticians; however, we used a variety of statisticians over the years, not all of whom were advocates of the psi hypothesis.

A distinguished Yale University psychologist, Irvin Child (1985), re-analyzed all of the Maimonides data and published his findings in *American Psychologist*, the flagship journal of the American Psychological Association. The overall results were highly significant, from a statistical point of view, even though some experiments yielded chance results. Child noted that some of the earlier studies were flawed because the judges' scores were not independent of each other; when we corrected this flaw, the results actually improved, contrary to the claim of many counteradvocates that the tighter the controls, the less robust are the results. The significance level of these studies was less than 0.000002; in other words there was less than one chance in several thousand that these results were due to coincidence.

Over the years, there have been several attempts to replicate our studies, Sherwood and Roe (2003) made comparisons across the post-Maimonides studies, converting the statistical test results to their common effect size measure. Many of these studies did not use independent blind judges, but instead employed participant and experimenter/sender judging. However, as with the Maimonides studies, many of the post-Maimonides studies employed combined/consensus judging procedures and data from these judgments were used to calculate the effect size whenever possible. Of the 21 studies for which effect sizes could be calculated, 14 gave rise to positive effect sizes, indicating that the targets were identified more often than mean chance expectation, whereas 6 gave negative effect sizes, indicating that the targets were identified less often than mean chance expectation; this shift towards positive effect sizes is suggestive but not statistically significant. Despite having unequal numbers of studies for comparison, it seems clear that those experiments testing for precognition were the least successful; those testing for telepathy were more successful but more variable in outcome; and clairvoyance studies were most successful collectively.

Several attempts at replication were made while our laboratory was still functioning (Ullman & Krippner, 2002). One of these was executed by the distinguished dream theorist and researcher, Calvin Hall (1967), who obtained statistically significant results but observed that there was no dependable "marker" for dreams that would tend to confirm the psi hypothesis. Michael Persinger, a neuroscientist, and I attempted to find such a marker by selecting the first night that each of the Maimonides research participants had visited the laboratory. Persinger matched each of those nights with the Earth's standard geomagnetic measurements, discovering that the participants' "accuracy" was significantly better during calm nights with little sunspot activity and few electrical storms than during "stormy" nights marked by high geomagnetic activity (Persinger & Krippner, 1989). We repeated this analysis with the participants who had spent more nights at the Maimonides laboratory than anyone else, the psychoanalyst whose dreams of Degas' "School of the Ballet" were previously discussed (Krippner & Persinger, 1996). The results were similar, again attaining statistical significance, helping to open up a new avenue of parapsychological research that focused on the neurobiology of psychic claimants (e.g., Krippner & Friedman, 2010). Persinger and I observed that activity in the brain's temporal lobe exists in equilibrium with the Earth's geomagnetic condition. We suggested that when there is a sudden decrease in geomagnetic activity, there may well be an enhancement of processes facilitating non-local phenomena.

Several counteradvocates have criticized our experiments, some with justification and some having made erroneous assumptions. One of the justified criticisms was made by Neher (1980) who correctly noted, "A . . . series of studies of great interest are the dream-telepathy tests done at the Maimonides Medical Center in New York, in which, it is claimed, dreams are influenced telepathically. However, some other investigators have failed to obtain similar results. One unsuccessful replication used a subject who was 'successful' in the Maimonides studies; another was conducted by the Maimonides investigators themselves" (p. 145).

However, an erroneous assumption was made by Clemmer (1986) who maintained that "cues in the transcripts" presented to the judges might have resulted in our positive results since a participant might mention a previous target, hence giving the judges a cue that would help them rule out that target for consideration (pp. 1173–1174). Theoretically, Clemmer makes a useful point, but he assumed that participants received feedback each morning. As was mentioned before, this was rarely the case. In one instance, a participant in an eight-night series did receive feedback, but a different target pool was used every night. In two precognition studies, the target was selected *after* the night's dream reports had been collected and there was an experiential component to the art print (e.g., an art print of Vincent Van Gogh's "Corridor of the St. Paul Hospital" was accompanied by music from the soundtrack of the film "Spellbound," by hysterical laughter, and by having the participant treated as if he were a mental patient—being given a "medicinal pill" and having his skin daubed with a piece of cotton dipped in acetone). In these studies, the transcripts were examined for any mention of pre-vious sessions; only two indirect citations were found and these were deleted before the transcripts were sent to the judges. Clemmer's failure to determine if his assumptions were well-founded displays his knee-jerk reaction to our work rather than any weakness in our experimental protocol.

Another unfounded assumption was made by Romm (1977) who also com-mented on the same precognition study. In this instance, the art print portrayed an Alaskan Eskimo and the participant was escorted into a room draped with white, to resemble snow, where an ice cube was dropped down his back. The par-ticipant had a dream in which the color white played a prominent part, but Romm observed that such words as "miserable," "wet," or "icy" would have been better matches. If E. G. Romm had taken the trouble to read our article, she would have observed that the word "ice" was actually used in a dream report. The participant stated, "I was just standing in a room, surrounded by white. . . . Predominant colors were pale and ice blues and whites" (Krippner, Honorton, & Ullman, 1972, p. 20) Furthermore, it is clear from Romm's critique that she assumed this was a telepathy study rather than a precognition study because she used the word "sender" to refer to the participant.

Yet another incorrect assumption was made by Hansel (1980) who claimed that our precautions against sensory leakage were inadequate. He correctly stated that agents in our studies were encouraged to write down their associations to the target. But he incorrectly stated that an experimenter was with the agents when they wrote down these associations as well as when they opened the envelope containing the art print. Hence, Hansel concluded that this interaction could have been the source of sensory clues given the participants when they evaluated correspondences to each of the possible target pictures (pp. 246, 253). This error was pointed out by several writers (e.g., Child, 1985; Akers, 1984) but he repeated the same claim in a 1985 article (Hansel, 1985, p. 114). Some people never seem to learn.

The grand prize for erroneous assumptions goes to Zusne and Jones (1982) who claimed that: (1) the art print was chosen randomly by an experimenter, placed in an envelope, and given to an agent; (2) the judges knew the identity of the target while evaluating the correspondences; (3) the participants were "primed" before they fell asleep so they could better incorporate the target picture in their dreams (pp. 259–262). As an example of this "priming," Zusne and Jones used the Van Gogh painting previously described, stating that the participant was "shown paint-ings done by mental patients," addressed as "Mr. Van Gogh," and treated as a hos-pital inmate while listening to appropriate music and laughter (pp. 260–261). Zusne and Jones completely missed the point that this was a precognitive dream experiment, and that the participant was put through these experiences after his dream reports had already been collected.

A constructive criticism was offered by Alcock (1981) who called for "a con-trol group, for which no sender or no target was used, would appear essential. . . . One could alternatively, 'send' when the subject was not in the dream state, and compare success' in this case with success in the dream state trials" (p. 163). Child (1985) responded to this proposal by noting that "within-subject control can, where feasible, be much more efficient and pertinent than a separate control group (p. 1220)." As for Alcock's other suggestion, Child added,

> His second statement suggests a type of experiment that is probably impossible (because in satisfactory form it seems to require the subject to dream whether awake or asleep and not to know whether he or she was awake or asleep). This second kind of experiment, moreover, has special pertinence only to a comparison between dreaming and waking, not to the question of whether ESP was manifested in dreaming. (p. 1226)

Even so, Ullman and I took Alcock at his word and randomly assigned dreams reports from one eight-night study to target pictures from a different eight-night study. We felt that this met the request for a control group, in Alcock's words, for which "no sender or no target was used." A judge made 64 comparisons of target/transcript correspondences; even though the results from each eight-night study had been statistically significant, favoring the psi hypothesis, the cross-matching results were at chance. More important, however, is the fact that an internal control was built into each of the separate series by having every dream report evaluated against each target and potential target.

A final example of a counteradvocate's comments came from Hyman (1986) who remarked that "many of the parapsychologists have been well trained in one of the sciences.... They ... know how to produce appropriately controlled and analyzed experiments. A fair and honest review of their reports indicates that they are more sophisticated and 'scientific' than many of their critics give them credit for" (p. 62). Hyman concluded, "Something peculiar is going on. But I do not think it has anything to do with PK or ESP. Rather, I think it will turn out that there are subtle and previously unknown ways that humans, no matter how sincere and dedicated, can become convinced of things that are not so" (p. 62). I would agree that "something peculiar is going on" and would remind Hyman and the other counteradvocates that the Parapsychological Association (1989), in a report for which I was the primary author, stated that "a commitment to the study of psi phenomena does not require assuming the reality of 'non-ordinary' factors of processes. Regardless of what form the final explanations may take, however, the study of these phenomena is likely to expand our understanding of the processes often referred to as 'consciousness' and 'mind' and the nature of disciplined inquiry" (p. 395).

FRIEDMAN'S STATEMENT

In contrast to the wealth of experience in parapsychology shared by SK in his comments, I see myself as staunchly agnostic toward psi and have only participated in a few studies in the area, none of which have been published. However, I have been profoundly interested in spiritual and transpersonal issues and, undeniably, these topics overlap with psi in many ways (e.g., all religions refer in some fashion to events that could be seen as psi, although they are often conceptualized as divine exceptions to the natural order, i.e., "miracles") or are an intrinsic part of the worldview of certain traditions and are not categorized as anything extraordinary (e.g., the "siddhis" or powers that Indic traditions take for granted as being part of higher spiritual development). Although I have been agnostic regarding whether psi experiences are real in any veridical way, I have not wavered in respecting the diversity of psi experiences reported in many cultures and populations. However, I have frequently challenged what I have called the romanticism in many New Age and similar interpretations of the meaning of these phenomena. For example, I recently wrote critically on the martial art of Aikido, which has often been elevated with claims of commonly occurring psi events (e.g., extraordinary powers being gained by advanced practitioners; Friedman, 2005). In that paper, I wrote that I had a modicum of first-hand knowledge about this art (i.e., having personally studied it for close to 40 years and now holding the relatively high rank of 3rd degree black belt), yet I never personally observed anything that I felt needed to be labeled as psi. Accomplished Aikido practitioners can demonstrate impressive skills that to outsiders may appear anomalous, even "magical," but, as an insider, I know how these feats are made possible through ordinary, but skilled, physical and psychological processes. With that said, I cannot say for sure that some Aikido practitioners might not employ extraordinary abilities falling within the realm of psychic phenomena, just because I know of ways to accomplish these feats by less extraordinary means. At the same time that I have objected to romanticizing Aikido and reifying other practices (e.g., astrology), I have also decried "scientism" (i.e., an overly rigid view of science that disallows fair examination of unusual phenomena and stands in stark contrast to the open inquiry encouraged by science; Friedman, 2002). In this sense, as I observe the disparate positions between the advocates and counteradvocates in this book, I see a sincere struggle between worldviews and difficulties in maintaining a scientific balance that is both open-minded, but not so open-minded that "one's brains fall out."

In this regard, I will share one limited experience in parapsychological research in which I found strong evidence for telepathy in a study of U.S. preteens (Friedman, 2010). If I had found a similarly strong result within a mainstream research area, I would have unhesitatingly published it. However, because of various factors (e.g., my then mentor warning me that publishing this investigation could be a career ender for me as a budding academic), this study was relegated to the file drawer. In this sense, parapsychology is undoubtedly embedded within a matrix of political and economic consideration, as is all of science.

OUR TAKE ON THE DISCUSSIONS

We find two major strands of argument being played out in this book. The first is a matter of philosophical ontology and the second of epistemology, namely what are the underlying assumptions about reality and methods used to know reality, respectively, that seem to differentiate advocates from counteradvocates.

Counteradvocates seem to adhere to an ontological position that current models of reality disallow the very existence of psychic phenomena, whereas advocates seem to prefer an ontological position that embraces emerging models of reality, such as those based on quantum notions (e.g., "entanglement" or "spooky action at a distance"). Is one of these positions stronger? We are reminded of a famous quip, "I think it is safe to say that no one understands quantum mechanics" (Feynman, 1967, p. 129), which is as true today as it was when first written. In this regard, it may be difficult to decide which worldview may be more applicable to the possibility or impossibility of psi phenomena, since the application of quantum physics may be a dicey affair. But we largely agree with Penrose (1986) who discussed quantum theory as having,

> two powerful bodies of fact in its favor, and only one thing against it. First, in its favor are all the marvelous agreements that the theory has had with every experimental result to date. Second, it is a theory of astonishing and profound mathematical beauty. The one argument that can be said against it is that it makes absolutely no sense! (p. 129)

If the counteradvocates are rejecting psi evidence based on the assertion that it makes no sense, then likewise the amazing array of modern advancements based on quantum approaches would similarly require rejection, yet our world is undeniably (and increasingly) composed of such innovations. We can only conclude that any *a priori* rejection of psi based on a restriction of what science allows is overly rigid, since science is constantly evolving.

Regarding the issue of methodology, it is amazing in itself that advocates and counteradvocates, both credible on their own terms, can look at the same data and draw vastly different conclusions. Putting aside concerns expressed about dishonesty and conspiracy (while not denying that this may have occurred on either or both sides of the controversy), we know full well from social psychology that such disagreements occur frequently in science—especially when there is ample room for ambiguity (e.g., in meta-analyses in which the rules for including and excluding data are equivocal and there are no singular statistical or other approaches used to evaluate any compilation of findings). So we grant the possibility that people with different worldviews could look at the same data and interpret them in widely divergent ways.

We want to focus on one issue that has been discussed extensively by many of our contributors, namely that of replicability of findings. Indeed for science to be radically open as it should be, lest it become merely another authoritarian proclamation of the "truth," all findings should be replicable by skeptics and never need be accepted on faith. In parapsychology, the replicability rate of studies has been especially suspect with the advocates correctly claiming that hardly any other field of science puts such a premium on openly publishing replication failures, while the counteradvocates stress the low rate of replicability in discrediting the field. This aspect of the controversy becomes more clouded when counteradvocates insist that there is an alleged file-drawer problem in which nonsignificant findings are buried, presumably biasing the literature in support of the existence of psi, although the statistical likelihood that many unpublished studies being filed away is miniscule (see Dean Radin, this volume). The recent report of one of our experiences (i.e., HF's, earlier in this chapter) with having to suppress findings provides a salient counter-example to this alleged source of bias, as does some examples discussed by Chris Carter (previously in this volume). One additional response offered by the advocates is that the expectations regarding the issue of replicability for parapsychology is held too strictly in comparison to standards in other fields, such as mainstream psychology, which decidedly have similar replicability problems. However, it seems that this issue could be used to defend the legitimacy of parapsychology or, alternatively, to level further questioning of the legitimacy of many of the findings widely accepted within mainstream psychology. Consequently, the issue of replicability looms large in all the so-called human sciences.

So how do we, as editors, make sense of this array of ideas, including various claims and counterclaims? The opinion of one of us (SK) on this issue has been and continues to be more favorable to an interpretation of the data as supporting the advocate position. The other one of us (HF) retains his agnosticism regarding whether the data are sufficiently convincing to support the existence of psi. What we do agree upon fully, however, is that this is an important debate that has tremendous bearing on many areas of our lives. We hope readers will thoughtfully consider the different views expressed by us and our contributors, forgive any excessive zeal expressed that may seem unduly accusatory or blaming, and draw their own conclusions, after seeing both sides presented, regarding this fascinating topic.

After reading the various chapters we received, we suspect it may be too early for a synthesis; more realistically we may call for a détente. If this is a timely suggestion, we would call for a more open balance between what is considered possible, whether actually real or not, and what the evidence may show. We also think that the issues studied by parapsychology should not be shunted to the side as irrelevant to our daily lives because, if valid, these would be central, possibly revolutionary, to all aspects of the human condition. As science advances, undoubtedly new techniques to study psi phenomena will emerge, such as the neurobiological advances now being used to peer inside the brains of those reporting extraordinary experiences (see Krippner & Friedman, 2010). Last, parapsychology has led the way in many areas of conducting research, such as heightening our awareness of expectancy effects in all work with humans. The increased realization of the complexity inherent in making sense of data pertaining to psi, which hopefully this book elucidates, can similarly be generalized to other areas of knowledge, which may be better scrutinized with the acumen gained through evaluating parapsychological data. Much that we take for granted as valid can likely better be viewed through such a more focused lens.

REFERENCES

Akers, C. (1984). Methodological criticisms of parapsychology. In S. Krippner (Ed.), *Advances in parapsychological research* (vol. 4, pp. 112–164). Jefferson, NC: McFarland Publishers.

Alcock, J. E. (1981). *Parapsychology: Science or magic? A psychological perspective.* New York: Pergamon Press.

Child, I. L. (1985). Psychology and anomalous observations: The question of ESP in dreams. *American Psychologist, 40,* 1219–1230.

Clemmer, E. J. (1986). Not so anomalous observations question ESP in dreams. *American Psychologist, 41,* 1173–1174.

Feynman, R. (1967). *The character of physical law.* Cambridge, MA: MIT Press.

Friedman, H. (2002). Transpersonal psychology as a scientific field. *International Journal of Transpersonal Studies, 21,* 175–187.

Friedman, H. (2005). Problems of romanticism in transpersonal psychology: A case study of Aikido. *The Humanistic Psychologist, 33,* 3–24.

Friedman, H. (2010). Parapsychology studies. *EXPLORE: The Journal of Science and Healing, 6*(3), 129–130.

Hall, C. S. (1967). Experiments with telepathically-influenced dreams. *Zeitschrift fur Parapsychologie und Grenzgebiete der Psychologie, 10,* 18–47. (in German)

Hansel, C. E. M. (1980). *ESP and parapsychology: A critical re-evaluation.* Buffalo, NY: Prometheus Books.

Hansel, C. E. M. (1985). The search for a demonstration of ESP. In P. Kurtz (Ed.), *A skeptic's handbook of parapsychology* (pp. 97–127). Buffalo, NY: Prometheus Books.

Hyman, R. (1986). Maimonides dream-telepathy experiments. *Skeptical Inquirer, 11*(1), 91–92.

Krippner, S. (1991). Experimental approach to the anomalous dream. In J. Gackenbach & A. A. Sheikh (Eds.), *Dream images: A call to mental arms* (pp. 31–54). Amityville, NY: Baywood.

Krippner, S., & Friedman, H. (Eds.). (2010). *Mysterious minds: The neurobiology of psychics, mediums, and other remarkable people.* Santa Barbara, CA: Praeger.

Krippner, S., Honorton, C., & Ullman, M. (1972). A second precognitive dream study with Malcolm Bessent. *Journal of the American Society for Psychical Research, 66,* 269–279.

Krippner, S., & Persinger, M. A. (1996). Evidence for enhanced congruence between dreams and distant target material during periods of decreased geomagnetic activity. *Journal of Scientific Exploration, 64,* 109–118.

Neher, A. (1980). *The psychology of transcendence.* Englewood Cliffs, NJ: Prentice-Hall.

Parapsychological Association. (1989). Terms and methods in parapsychological research. *Journal of Humanistic Psychology, 29,* 394–399.

Penrose, R. (1986). Gravity and state vector reductions. In R. Penrose & C. Isham (Eds.), *Quantum concepts in space and time.* Oxford, UK: Clarendon.

Persinger, M. A., & Krippner, S. (1989). Dream ESP experiments and geomagnetic activity. *Journal of the American Society for Psychical Research, 83,* 101–116.

Romm, E. G. (1977). When you give a closet occultist a Ph.D., what kind of research can you expect? *The Humanist, 37*(3), 12–15.

Sherwood, S. J., & Roe, C. A. (2003). A review of dream ESP studies conducted since the Maimonides dream ESP programme. *Journal of Consciousness Studies, 10,* 85–109.

Ullman, M., & Krippner, S. (1970). An experimental approach to dreams and telepathy: II. A report of three studies. *American Journal of Psychiatry, 126,* 1282–1289.

Ullman, M., & Krippner, S., & Vaughan, A. (2002). *Dream telepathy: Experiments in nocturnal extrasensory perception* (3rd ed.). Charlottesville, VA: Hampton Roads.

Zusne, L., & Jones, W. H. (1982). *Anomalistic psychology: A study of extraordinary phenomena of behavior and experience.* Hillsdale, NJ: Lawrence Erlbaum.

PART FOUR

Postscripts

"Tyger" (© Dierdre Luzwick. Used by permission.)

Explaining and Unexplaining: Parapsychology's Key Question

Damien Broderick

The entertaining polymath Isaac Asimov once drew a distinction between genuine paradigm changing theories and sloppy-minded crackpot silliness. Fruitful new ideas not only explain and even predict the previously unexpected, he pointed out; they also refuse to *unexplain* what is already known. If we find a tree split in half, we can explain it with a flying elephant that set down briefly in the upper branches. "Unfortunately, in the process, it *unexplains* everything you previously knew about elephants. So, in seeking an explanation for some phenomenon you should be careful that, in doing so, you don't *unexplain* everything else" (as cited in Williams, 1992, p. 11).

The key question about psi is whether it is more akin to an invisible flying elephant or to the radioactivity that solved Lord Kelvin's bafflement over the immense outpouring of the sun's light despite our star's great age. Models of nuclear reactions did more than explain such puzzles; they opened up fresh avenues of investigation, new and sometimes terrifying technologies—and did so without *unexplaining* anything already considered well-established.

That is not quite true, though. Powerful, evidence-supported theories of species evolution by natural selection and solar nuclear dynamics certainly unexplained, with a tremendous echoing clang, the simple scriptural doctrines of a recent divine creation; so much the worse for fundamentalism (except in certain benighted parts of the world). The mysteries were explained, not "explained away." Can the puzzling data accumulated by parapsychologists also be explained—either by demonstrating that they are just ordinary phenomena willfully misunderstood by ardent believers, or by providing, or appropriating, a commanding new theory that explains these oddities without unexplaining everything else science has established—in its always provisional way?

These alternatives are just the end points on a scale, of course; other possibilities include accumulating many instances where alleged psychic effects are demonstrably due to fraud, wishful thinking, or the random conjunctions of a complex world. Or by showing sufficiently that such explanations cannot suffice, even though no satisfactory model yet exists to accommodate the anomalies. Michael Shermer's chapter is a somewhat creepy account of willfully deceiving gullible people is a conspicuously weak instance of the former approach. It reminds us, though we hardly need the reminder, that many people have an urgent wish to gain comfort or insight into the pain of their lives, and that unscrupulous or self-deceiving "psychics" prey on their vulnerability. This gets us nowhere unless Shermer can use his quick-study cold reading skills to emulate, let's say, the prowess of the best remote viewers from the former Stargate program. This decades-long U.S. government program was famously shut down by the CIA in 1995, despite reporting significant results. Its most notable operative was Vietnam veteran Joseph McMoneagle, a Legion of Merit holder, whose experiences with Stargate, and after, are detailed in several books (McMoneagle, 2000, 2002). Can Shermer achieve significant success in, say, ten double-blinded remote viewing exercises conducted according to the stringent protocol employed by McMoneagle? Let me know when he has carried that off; it would be so comforting to know how he did it.

Richard Wiseman's essay seems sound: researchers could avoid the haunting specter of retrospective meta-analysis by pre-registering the key details involved in each of the studies. And finally, Wiseman observed that parapsychologists might agree to stop jumping ship, and instead have the courage to accept the null hypothesis if the selected front-runners do not produce evidence of a significant and replicable effect. Yes, but adamant skeptics like Wiseman, Ray Hyman, James Alcock, and others have an equal responsibility to accept sufficient evidence for psi functioning when it is provided (as I believe it has been). What I see, all too often, is exactly the sort of cherry-picking Wiseman deplores. Does Hyman make a telling point when he claims that any glitch in a body of data can count as evidence for psi, but that nothing can count as evidence for the non-existence of psi? This seems untrue; glitches give rise to *subsequent* hypotheses that can be tested and evaluated, and while some parapsychological papers have been remiss, the general rule, I think, is that experimental probity is maintained. The unsettling way in which apparent psi manifestations seem to skitter about might indeed support the notion that the phenomenon is being actively evasive; comparing this to "intelligent design" is more mischievous than psi itself.

And yet, Hyman also notes that parapsychologists, at various times, have theorized about the nature of psi and these theories have never been developed sufficiently to connect with parapsychological research. Strictly speaking, this is untrue. Observational theories drawn by analogy from quantum mechanics led to unexpected findings, although I would argue that apparent retrocausation was already implicit in the temporal fluidity of precognitive phenomena. Still, it is certainly the case that psi research remains largely empirical and lacks a powerful model fully consilient with other sciences, be it physical, social, neurological, or psychological.

At the other end of the spectrum, I am unpersuaded by Stephan Schwartz's attempt in his chapter to ground psi, creative genius, and mystical ecstasy in some sort of nonlocal apprehension of a larger reality. Indeed, all the evidence he offers about musical and other forms of radiant genius seem consistent with our being embedded in a local rich culture of ideas, urges, received patterns, and other people, while remaining idiosyncratically ourselves. The early twentieth century relativist Sir James Jeans, in 1930 said that the universe begins to look more like a great thought than a great machine. Actually, the more we understand a great thought, the less it looks like a universe and the more it looks like the product of a great machine. Yes, if psi is a reality, we must expect a certain "leakage" of ideas and images and feelings from other people, but we certainly remain adamantly segregated inside our own bodies nearly all the time. I can lift my arm by intending it, but I have no direct influence over yours, no matter how ineffable I feel. (Granted, if you heard my singing, your hands would fly up to cover your ears.)

Schwartz's position reflects an opinion I have found more often than not among psi researchers (although there are significant exceptions); it is captured by Chris Carter's claim, in his chapter, that the worldview defended by modern secular humanists is rightly seen as threatened by the claims of parapsychology. Really? As Dean Radin suggests in his chapter, psi might yet prove to be a consequence of an overarching future theory, perhaps combining quantum theory and relativity. If so, in my view the outcome will be no more (or less) intrinsically *spiritual* than sight, radioactivity, or the cosmological expansion of the universe.

Granted, many counteradvocates do act is if they fear a resacralization or remystification of the cosmos were psi to be validated. Carter claims that he has documented instances where two prominent counteradvocates actually found statistically significant evidence for psi, and both then went to extraordinary lengths to deny it. Meanwhile, hundreds of popular books (e.g., Brown, 2009) preach a New Age doctrine about the failings of scientific "materialism"—that it is an obscurantist doctrine based on fear and denial of our Higher Selves—and cite psi research in support of their perspective. Little wonder that counteradvocates are skeptical about the sort of self-blinding and self-delusion typical of "faith-based" approaches to reality.

Perhaps it is too late in the day to wean parapsychology and other emerging sciences away from this hunger for the transcendental, but I keep hoping that a blend of rigorous evidence and increasingly powerful theory will finally unpack these anomalies and seat them in a new, comprehensive view of how the world works. Then our understanding of psi truly *will* be scientific—and genuinely illuminating, explaining without either unexplaining or "explaining away" parapsychological experiences.

REFERENCES

Brown, D. (2009). *The lost symbol.* New York: Doubleday.

McMoneagle, J. (2000). *Remote viewing secrets: A handbook.* Newburyport, MA: Hampton Roads.

McMoneagle, J. (2002). *The Stargate chronicles.* Newburyport, MA: Hampton Roads.

Williams, R. (1992, Winter). Remembering Asimov. *The Skeptic,* pp. 10–11.

Why Parapsychology Is Not Yet Ready for Prime Time

Elizabeth Loftus

This anthology has a provocative title, *Debating Psychic Experience: Human Potential or Human Illusion?* Looking at the well-written chapters in this admirable book through the lens of my own research, it is apparent that people have a potential for illusion, a potential that has major consequences for the ways in which they construct their worldview and their belief systems. My research, and that of others, has demonstrated that memory is fallible and prone to distortion (Bernstein & Loftus, 2009; Loftus, 1979). One person may swear that the details of a tragic accident were forecast in his dream. Later, after an accident does occur, he checks his dream diary, he may discover that the emotion of the dream was unpleasant but the details only had a vague resemblance to the accident. Another person may return home from a visit to a "psychic," gushing in wonderment to family members about the accuracy of the "reading" she received. Later, when listening to a recording of the session, her enthusiasm might wane as she discovers the plethora of leading questions, generalizations, and second guesses that she had not recalled when sharing the experience with her family.

In these two cases, there were documents (either written or recorded) that could be utilized to determine the accuracy of what had been recalled, a resource generally unavailable when a putative parapsychological experience is narrated. Many parapsychologists, of course, are familiar with the fallibility of memory and other psychological principles. Dean Radin's chapter depicts the progress that has been made in bringing scientific perspectives to the study of what Stephan Schwartz (in his chapter) called "singular people." And James Alcock's chapter contains many psychological principles, such as attribution, that need to be considered when reviewing first person reports of unusual experiences.

Over the years, cognitive neuroscience has produced valuable information about brain areas that might be associated with the production of "true" and "false" memories. For example, neural activity in certain regions is greater for true memories than it is for false memories; regions within the temporal lobe seem to be involved in false memory formation and regions within the prefrontal cortex seems to be involved in memory monitoring processes that reduce the production of false memories (Schacter & Slotnik, 2004). These observations, among others, could find a useful place in the social sciences, even though scientific investigators have yet to develop a neurophysiological procedure that can be used to predict whether a particular memory is true or false (Bernstein & Loftus, 2009). On the other hand, memory reports subjected to content analysis have revealed several criteria that help differentiate between true and false memory reports; for example, the latter contain more sensory detail (Schooler, Gerhard, & Loftus, 1986). These criteria could, when better developed, be used to help police investigators assess the authenticity of witnesses' statements and could assist parapsychologists evaluate eye-witness reports of ostensibly anomalous incidents. In fact, Krippner and his associates (1994) once compared eye-witness accounts of a Brazilian medium's demonstrations, observing several discrepancies in their after-the-fact written reports.

My colleagues and I have had ample success in "planting" false memories through suggestion and imagination. Research participants in false memory work have become convinced that they had been lost in a shopping mall, had spilled punch on a bride's parents during a wedding, had caught their hand in a mouse-trap, or had witnessed a demonic possession (Lindsay, Hagen, Read, Wade, & Garry, 2004; Mazzoni, Loftus, & Kirsch, 2001). Perhaps unscrupulous "psychics" deliberately use similar procedures—but without the debriefing that accompanies ethical psychological studies. Even well-meaning "past-life therapists" may not realize how easily memories of "former incarnations" can be evoked by suggestion and hypnosis.

I do not pretend to be an expert on the parapsychological literature, but in reading Ray Hyman's chapter, I was struck with his deft description of the repeatability issue in parapsychology. Indeed, I have faced this issue in my own work on the production of false memories (see Laney, Bowman-Fowler, Nelson, Bernstein, & Loftus, 2008). There were procedural differences in these experiments that, for me, accounted for the discrepancies, but unsuccessful replications ought to produce a deeper understanding of memory processes (e.g., boundary conditions for a phenomenon) and I would suspect that the same might hold true in parapsychological research.

Let me provide an example. I once hypothesized that just being told about an event can make individuals more likely to think that they actually experienced the event (Loftus, 1993). This hypothesis was criticized by Kathy Pezdek and her associates (Pezdek, Blandon-Gitlin, Lam, Hart, & Schooler, 2006) who maintained that my colleagues and I had not clearly differentiated all of the variables (e.g., Mazzoni, Loftus, & Kirsch, 2001). This criticism helped us clarify our understanding of the role of plausibility and enhanced background knowledge as sources for false memories, along with suggestibility and imagination.

Replicability is more of an issue in mainstream psychology than many of my colleagues would like to admit. But I would propose that there is an important distinction between replicability in parapsychology and replicability in mainstream psychology. Memory research is built upon a foundation of data that is self-correcting in nature. When results are contradictory, differences in procedures may explain the results and modifications can be made in future experiments. Parapsychological data are less than robust; the parapsychologists I have met would like to think that their field of study is self-correcting, but it is difficult to make repairs on a house that has a weak foundation. Further, as Christopher French pointed out in his chapter, the replicability issue is more crucial in parapsychology than in mainstream psychology because the latter data do not have as many implications for science's worldview as do the former data.

Chris Carter's chapter provides a laundry list of unfair, inaccurate criticisms made against parapsychologists. In 2007 I attended a conference at the University of British Columbia, Vancouver, called "The Meeting of the Minds on Anomalous Cognition," and this event attempted to address similar points of contention. About 60 people attended the meeting, including two Nobel Laureates, as well as some of the chapter authors of this book. I found the meetings fascinating and was impressed by the sincerity and dedication of the parapsychologists I met. However, I was not persuaded by the evidence presented for "anomalous cognition" because the results seemed too meager, too weak, and too difficult to replicate. For me, the data were intriguing but not compelling.

At this conference, I detected a tendency for many parapsychologists to make excuses for failed replications, mirroring the examples given by Richard Wiseman in his contribution to this book. Even so, many of the meta-analyses provided by parapsychologists were impressive and I have argued in favor of this statistical technique myself (Bernstein & Loftus, 2009). However, French's chapter dealt with some basic problems with meta-analysis including publication bias (positive results are more likely to be published, especially in mainstream psychological journals) and why this technique is no substitute for replicability.

The study of memory has played a key role in both mainstream psychology (e.g., Danzinger, 2009) and parapsychology (e.g., Palmer, 2006; Roll, 1966), as have other areas of cognition and affect. In her introduction to this anthology, Ruth Richards makes a good case for additional research into exceptional experiences. But if parapsychology is ever to be ready for prime time and enter the mainstream of scientific discourse, its advocates will need to adhere more closely to what has already been established in the behavioral, social, and neurological sciences. Granted, many commonly accepted psychological generalizations do not hold water (see Lilienfeld, Lynn, Ruscio, & Beyerstein, 2010). But vigorous challenges and confrontations, both in psychology and parapsychology, can improve the quality, validity, and reliability of the data. In 2007, at the Vancouver conference, I met many parapsychologists who welcomed constructive criticisms. For this field to gain recognition as a serious area of inquiry, additional "meetings of the mind," both face-to face and virtual, may well accelerate the process.

REFERENCES

Bernstein, D. H., & Loftus, E. F. (2009). How to tell if a particular memory is true or false. *Perspectives on Psychological Science, 4*, 370–374.

Danzinger, K. (2009). *Making the mind: A history of memory*. New York: Cambridge University Press.

Krippner, S., Bergquist, C., Bristow, J., de Carvalho, M., Gold, L., Helgeson, A., et al. (1994). The magenta phenomena, Part I: Lunch and dinner in Brasilia. *Exceptional Human Experience, 12*, 194–206.

Laney, C., Bowman-Fowler, N., Nelson, K. J., Bernstein, D. M., & Loftus, E. F. (2008). The persistence of false beliefs. *Acta Psychologica, 129*, 190–197.

Lindsay, D. S., Hagen, L, Read, J. D., Wade, K. A., & Garry, M. (2004). True photographs and false memories. *Psychological Science, 15*, 149–154.

Lilienfeld, S. O., Lynn, S. J., Ruscio, J., & Beyerstein, B. L. (2010). *50 great myths of popular psychology: Shattering widespread misconceptions about human behavior*. Wiley-Blackwell.

Loftus, E. F. (1979). *Eyewitness testimony*. Cambridge, MA: Harvard University Press.

Loftus, E. F. (1993). The reality of repressed memories. *American Psychologist, 48*, 518–537.

Mazzoni, G. A. L., Loftus, E. F., & Kirsch, I. (2001). Changing beliefs about implausibility of autobiographical events: A little plausibility goes a long way. *Journal of Experimental Psychology: Applied, 7*, 51–59.

Palmer, J. (2006). Memory and ESP - A review of the experimental literature. *European Journal of Parapsychology, 21*, 95–121.

Pezdek, K., Blandon-Gitlin, I., Lam, S., Hart, R. E., & Schooler, J. (2006). Is knowing believing?: The role of event plausibility and background knowledge in planting false beliefs about the personal past. *Memory & Cognition, 34*, 1628–1635.

Roll, W. G. (1966). ESP and memory. *International Journal of Neuropsychiatry, 2*, 505–521.

Schacter, D. L., & Slotnik, S. D. (2004). The cognitive neuroscience of memory distortion. *Neuron, 44*, 149–160.

Schooler, J. W., Gerhard, D., & Loftus, E. F. (1986). Qualities of the unreal. *Journal of Experimental Psychology: Learning, Memory, and Cognition, 12*, 171–181.

Glossary

Compiled and Edited by
Nancy L. Zingrone

Altered State[s] of Consciousness (ASC). An expression introduced by Arnold Ludwig (1966) and popularized by Charles T. Tart (1966) that can refer to virtually any mental state differing from that of the normal, ordinary waking condition; of parapsychological interest as possibly psi-conducive states such as dreaming, hypnosis, ritual or mediumistic trance, meditation of the yoga or Zen tradition, the hypnagogic-like state induced by the ganzfeld, and drug-induced states. Rock and Krippner (2008) have proposed substituting the term "pattern of phenomenological properties," which suggests more fluidity than the word "state" and avoids the use of two words ("state" and "consciousness") that are both defined in terms of content (e.g., perception, cognition, emotion, memory).

Anomalous Cognition. A term adopted by Edwin C. May and his colleagues (May, Spottiswoode, & James, 1994) for "ESP."

Anomaly. A term applied to a phenomenon that implies that such a phenomenon is unexpected according to conventional scientific knowledge, but that does not commit the user to any particular type of explanation.

Autoganzfeld. An implementation of the ganzfeld technique in which many of the key procedural details, such as selection and presentation of the target and the recording of the evaluation of the target-response similarity given by the percipient are fully automated and computerized, the goal being to reduce as far as possible errors and sensory communication on the part of the human participants.

Terms and definitions selected from: Thalbourne, M.A. (2003). Glossary of terms used by parapsychology. Charlottesville, VA: Puente Publications.

Chance. The constellation of undefined causal factors that are considered to be irrelevant to the causal relationship under investigation, often spoken of as if it were a single, independent agency; the expression "pure chance" is sometimes used to describe a state characterized by complete unpredictability, that is, an absence of any cause-effect relationships. The term "chance" is frequently a short-hand expression for "mean chance expectation," as in "deviation from chance."

Clairvoyance. The purported paranormal acquisition of information concerning an object or contemporary physical event; in contrast to telepathy, the information is assumed to derive directly from an external physical source (such as a concealed photograph), and not from the mentation of another person; one particular form of extrasensory perception, it is not to be confused with the vulgar interpretation of "clairvoyance" as meaning "knowledge of the future" (for which see Precognition).

Cold Reading. A set of statements purportedly gained by *paranormal* means but which in fact is wholly based on broadly accurate generalizations and/or on information obtained directly from the person seeking the reading, such as can be gleaned from facial gestures, clues in conversation, and so on.

Decline Effect. The purported tendency for high scores in a test of psi to decrease, either within a run, within a session, or over a longer period of time; the term also may be used in reference to the waning and disappearance of some particular talent of an ostensibly paranormal nature. A decline effect is termed episodic if it is within the run or within the session, or as chronological if the participant's performance gradually falls over time.

Experimenter Effect. An experimental outcome that results not from manipulation of the variable of interest *per se*, but rather from some aspect of the particular experimenter's behavior, such as unconscious communication to the participants, or possibly even a psi-mediated effect working in accord with the experimenter's desire to confirm some hypothesis.

Extrasensory Perception (ESP). The purported acquisition of information about, or response to, an external event, object, or influence (mental or physical; past, present or future) otherwise than through any of the known sensory channels; a term used by J. B. Rhine (1934) to embrace such phenomena as telepathy, clairvoyance, and precognition; there is some difference of opinion as whether the term ought to be attributed to Rhine, or to Gustav Pagenstecher or Rudolph Tischner, who were using the German equivalent *aussersinnliche Wahrehmung* as early as the 1920s.

Ganzfeld. A German term referring to a special type of environment (or the technique for producing it) consisting of homogenous, unpatterned sensory stimulation. Audiovisual ganzfeld may be accomplished by placing translucent hemispheres (for example, halved ping-pong balls) over each eye of the participants, with diffused light (frequently red in hue) projected onto them from an external source, together with the playing of unstructured sounds (such as "white" or "pink" noise) into their ears, and generally with the person in a state of bodily comfort; the consequent deprivation of patterned sensory input is said to be conducive to introspection of inwardly-generated impressions, some of which might be extrasensory in origin.

Meta-analysis. Conducting a meta-analysis involves synthesizing the results of multiple studies of a given phenomenon. Quantitative methods are used to produce a single result. This is done by combining the effect size estimates from each study into a single estimate of the combined effect size (or, at times, into a distribution of effect sizes).

Non-local Consciousness. A term describing an aspect of consciousness not localized to the brain, nor limited by space or time. It has been offered as a more descriptive and accurate replacement for terms such as paranormal, psi, psychic, or extra-sensory perception (i.e., non-local perception) and psychokinesis (i.e., non-local perturbation). The term proposes that while part of consciousness resides in an organism's physiology, part does not, and that this aspect of consciousness has been experimentally demonstrated. Those who use this term assert that experimental evidence further suggests that non-local consciousness is both individual and collective. The term explicitly accepts as experimentally demonstrated that non-local consciousness is not electromagnetic, although it may involve quantum processes.

Null Hypothesis. Stating a "null hypothesis" proposes that an experiment will find no difference between the experimental and control conditions, that is, no relationship between variables. There are a number of statistical tests that can be applied to experimental data in an attempt to confirm or reject the null hypothesis at a predetermined level of statistical significance.

Null Result (also, Null Finding). If an experiment yields a null result (or finding), it indicates that no statistically significant association was found between the variables being studied. In other words, the null hypothesis was confirmed.

Out-of-[the]-Body Experience (OBE). An experience, either spontaneous or induced, in which one's center of consciousness seems to be in a spatial location outside of one's physical body. The term "OBE" is preferred by parapsychologists for the phenomenon also known as "astral projection," "astral travel," or "traveling clairvoyance."

Paranormal. A phenomenon is "paranormal" if it refers to hypothesized processes that in principle are physically impossible and outside the realm of human or animal capabilities as presently conceived by conventional scientists; often used as a synonym for "psychic," "parapsychological," "attributable to psi," or even "miraculous" (though shorn of religious overtones). The term is held in disfavor by those who hold that these hypothesized processes are essential "normal," or will be found to be so by subsequent research.

Parapsychology. A term coined in German by Max Dessoir (1889) and adopted by J. B. Rhine (1934) in English to refer to the scientific study of ostensibly paranormal phenomena, that is, psi; except in Britain, the term has largely superseded the older expression "psychical research." "Parapsychology" is used by some to refer to the experimental approach to the field, while "psychical research" is used to refer to non-experimental approaches such as case studies.

Precognition. A form of putative extrasensory perception in which the target is some future event that cannot be deduced from normally known data in the participant's present. The term can be applied to either spontaneous reports or experimentally-derived data.

Psi. A general blanket term, proposed by B. P. Wiesner and seconded by R. H. Thouless (Thouless & Wiesner, 1947), used either as a noun or adjective to identify ostensible paranormal processes and purported paranormal causation; the two main categories of psi are psi-gamma (paranormal cognition; extrasensory perception; non-local perception) and psi-kappa (paranormal action; psychokinesis; non-local perturbation), although the purpose of the term "psi" is to suggest that they might simply be different aspects of a single process, rather than distinct and essentially different processes. The term psi-theta is often used to refer to ostensible phenomena that suggest post-mortem survival.

Psi-Conducive. A term used to describe a condition thought to be favorable to, or facilitative of, the occurrence of psi, whether it is manifested as psi-hitting or psi-missing.

Psi-Inhibitory. A term used to describe a condition thought to be unfavorable to, or suppressive of, the occurrence of psi, whether it is manifested as psi-hitting or psi-missing.

Psychokinesis. A term probably coined by Henry Holt and adopted by J. B. Rhine (1934) to refer to the direct influence of mentation on a physical system that cannot be entirely accounted for by the mediation of any known physical energy.

Random Number Generator (RNG). An apparatus (typically electronic) incorporating an element (based on such processes as radioactive decay or random "noise") and capable of generating a random sequence of outputs; used in tests of psi for generating target sequences, and in tests of psychokinesis may itself be the target system which the subject is required to influence, that is, by "biasing" the particular number or event output; a binary RNG has two equally-probable outputs; the term "RNG" is often used to refer to any system which produces naturally random outputs, such as bouncing dice, radioactive decay, or even, perhaps, the brain. A near-synonym is "random event generator" (REG), often used when no numerals are involved.

Remote Viewing. A neutral term for general extrasensory perception (i.e., telepathy and clairvoyance) introduced by Russell Targ and Harold Puthoff (1974), especially in the context of an experimental design in which a percipient attempts to describe the surroundings of a geographically distant agent.

Replication. (i) An experiment that is designed to yield the same findings as a previous experiment or a series thereof; some researchers distinguish between "concrete" and "conceptual" replications: an experiment that precisely duplicates the essential conditions of its predecessor is a concrete, or exact, replication, while an experiment that resembles its predecessor only to the extent that it tests the same hypothesis or theoretical construct is a conceptual replication; (ii) the event of conducting a "replication" study; (iii) more strictly, an experiment that does in fact "replicate" the findings of its predecessor(s); in this sense an experiment which attempts to replicate previous findings but fails is termed an "attempted replication."

Retroactive PK. Purported psychokinesis occurring in such a way as to be an instance of retroactive causation; to say that event A was caused by retroactive PK is to say that A would not have happened in the way that it did had it not been for a later PK effort exerted so as to influence it. Sometimes abbreviated to "retro-PK;" also referred to as "backward PK" or "time-displaced PK."

Sheep-Goat Effect (SGE). A term first used by Gertrude Schmeidler (1943) to describe the relationship between acceptance of the possibility of extrasensory perception occurring under the given experimental conditions, and the level of scoring actually achieved on that ESP test: participants who do not reject the possibility ("sheep") are said to generally score above chance, while those rejecting the possibility ("goats") at or below chance; the terms "sheep" and "goat" are nowadays often used in a more extended sense, and "sheep-goat effect" may thus refer to any significant scoring difference between these two groups as defined by the experimenter.

Telepathy. A term coined by Frederic Myers (1903) to refer to the putative paranormal acquisition of information concerning the thoughts, feelings, or activity of another conscious being; the word has superseded such earlier expressions as "thought-transference."

REFERENCES

Dessoir, M. (1889). Die Parapsychologie. *Sphinx, 7*, 341–344.
Ludwig, A. M. (1966). Altered states of consciousness. *Archives of General Psychiatry, 15*, 225–234.

May, E. C., Spottiswoode, S. J. P., & James, C. L. (1994). Managing the target-pool band-
    width: Possible noise reduction for anomalous cognition experiments. *Journal of
    Parapsychology, 58*, 303–313.

Myers, F. W. H. (1903). *Human personality and its survival of bodily death* (2 vols.) London
    & New York: Longman Green.

Rhine, J. B. (1934). *Extra-sensory perception.* Boston: Bruce Humphries.

Rock, A. J., & Krippner, S. (2008). Proposed criteria for the necessary conditions for sha-
    manic journeying imagery. *Journal of Scientific Exploration, 22*(2), 215–226.

Schmeidler, G. R. (1943). Predicting good and bad scores in a clairvoyance experiment:
    A preliminary report. *Journal of the American Society for Psychical Research, 37*,
    103–110.

Targ, R., & Puthoff, H. (1974). Information transmission under conditions of sensory
    shielding. *Nature, 251*, 602–607.

Tart, C. T. (Ed.). (1966). *Altered states of consciousness.* New York: John Wiley & Sons.

Thouless, R. H., & Wiesner, B. P. (1947). The psi processes in normal and "paranormal"
    psychology. *Proceedings of the Society for Psychical Research, 48*, 177–196.

"The Oracle" (© Dierdre Luzwick. Used by permission.)

Index

About the Editors and Contributors

JAMES E. ALCOCK, Ph.D., is Professor of Psychology at York University in Toronto, Canada, where he has specialized in both social psychology and clinical psychology. He is the author of two critical books dealing with psychology and the paranormal, *Parapsychology: Science or Magic?* and *Science and Supernature*, and is co-editor of *Psi Wars*, co-author of *A Textbook of Social Psychology*, and has written 15 book chapters and numerous articles and papers. He is a member of the Editorial Boards of *Skeptical Inquirer*, *The Skeptic* (UK), *The Scientific Review of Alternative Medicine*, the Council for Scientific Clinical Psychology and Psychiatry, and is a Consulting Editor of *The Journal of Near-Death Studies*.

DAMIEN BRODERICK, Ph.D., is Senior Fellow in the School of Culture and Communication at the University of Melbourne. He has written or edited more than 40 books, including *Outside the Gates of Science: Why It's Time for the Paranormal to Come in From the Cold*. He specializes in the interaction of science and the humanities.

CHRIS CARTER, P.P.E., M.A., M.B.A., is the author of *Parapsychology and the Skeptics*, the first book devoted to a critical examination of the arguments of the skeptics and critics of parapsychology. After working in the telecommunications and banking industries in both Canada and the United States, he now teaches internationally.

CHRISTOPHER C. FRENCH, Ph.D., is Professor of Psychology and Head of the Anomalistic Psychology Research Unit in the Psychology Department at Goldsmiths College, University of London. He has published over 100 articles and chapters covering a wide range of topics within psychology. He frequently appears on radio and television casting a skeptical eye on reports of paranormal experiences; he edits *The Skeptic* (UK).

HARRIS L. FRIEDMAN, Ph.D., is Research Professor of Psychology, University of Florida. A clinical psychologist, he studies transpersonal perspectives in psychology and social change, and has written or edited over 100 professional publications. He is Editor of the *International Journal of Transpersonal Studies* and Associate Editor of *The Humanistic Psychologist*.

RAY HYMAN, Ph.D., is Professor Emeritus of Psychology at the University of Oregon. In 2007, Simon Fraser University awarded him the Degree of Doctor of Science for his contributions to psychology as well as his efforts to help the public skeptically evaluate fringe and controversial claims. Hyman's published research has been in such areas as pattern recognition, perception, problem solving, creativity, and related areas of cognition. He has written and published extensively on the psychology of deception and paranormal claims. In 2000, Hyman was cited as one of the ten outstanding skeptics of the twentieth century by *The Skeptical Inquirer*, and in 2003 he received the In Praise of Reason award from the Committee for Skeptical Inquiry.

STANLEY KRIPPNER, Ph.D., is Professor in the Graduate College of Psychology and Humanistic Studies at Saybrook University, San Francisco, where he holds the Chair for the Study of Consciousness. In 2002 he received the American Psychological Association's Award for Distinguished Contributions to the International Advancement of Psychology as well as the Society for Psychological Hypnosis' Award for Distinguished Contributions to Professional Hypnosis. He co-edited *Varieties of Anomalous Experience: Examining the Scientific Evidence* and co-authored *Haunted by Combat: Understanding PTSD in War Veterans*.

ELIZABETH LOFTUS, Ph.D., is Distinguished Professor at the University of California—Irvine where she holds faculty positions in three departments (Psychology and Social Behavior; Criminology, Law, and Society; and Cognitive Sciences), and is also a Fellow of the Center for the Neurobiology of Learning and Memory. She has published 22 books (including the award winning *Eyewitness Testimony*) and over 450 scientific articles, many of them on the malleability of human memory. She has received six honorary doctorates as well as election to the Royal Society of Edinburgh, the American Philosophical Society, the National Academy of Sciences, and the presidencies of the Association for Psychological Science, the Western Psychological Association, and the American Psychology-Law Society.

DEAN RADIN, Ph.D., is Senior Scientist at the Institute of Noetic Sciences in Petaluma, California, and Adjunct Faculty in the Psychology Department at Sonoma State University in Rohnert Park, California. He is author or coauthor of over 200 technical and popular articles, a dozen book chapters, and several books, including *The Conscious Universe* (1997) and *Entangled Minds* (2006). He regularly gives presentations on contemporary parapsychology research at academic, government, and industrial venues, including Stanford University, the U.S. Navy, and Google headquarters.

RUTH RICHARDS, M.D., Ph.D. is Professor in the Graduate College of Psychology and Humanistic Studies at Saybrook University, San Francisco; Research Affiliate in Psychology and Psychiatry at McLean Hospital (Belmont, Massachusetts); and Lecturer in the Department of Psychiatry at Harvard Medical School. She is the editor of *Everyday Creativity* and the author of several articles and chapters in the fields of creative behavior, bipolar disorders, and educational psychology. In 2009 she received the Rudolf Arnheim Award for Outstanding Lifetime Achievement from Division 10 (Psychology and the Arts) of the American Psychological Association. Dr. Richards served on the Executive Advisory Board for the *Encyclopedia of Creativity*.

STEPHAN A. SCHWARTZ is the Senior Fellow for Brain, Mind and Healing of the Samueli Institute, a Research Associate of the Cognitive Sciences Laboratory of the Laboratories for Fundamental Research, and a Fellow of the BIAL Foundation. He is the columnist for the journal *Explore*, and editor of the daily web publication *Schwartzreport.net*, which covers trends that are affecting the future. He is the former Director of Research of both the Mobius Society and the Rhine Research Center, and served as Special Assistant for Research and Analysis to the Chief of U.S. Naval Operations.

MICHAEL SHERMER, Ph.D., is the Founding Publisher of *Skeptic* magazine (USA) and editor of Skeptic.com, is a monthly columnist for *Scientific American*, and is an Adjunct Professor at Claremont Graduate University. Shermer's books include *The Mind of the Market*, on evolutionary economics, as well as *Why Darwin Matters: Evolution and the Case Against Intelligent Design, The Science of Good and Evil*, and *Why People Believe Weird Things*.

RICHARD S. WISEMAN, Ph.D., is the head of a research unit at the University of Hertfordshire and in 2002 was awarded Great Britain's first Professorship in the Public Understanding of Psychology. He is the author of several books and articles on deception, luck, and parapsychology, including one published in the prestigious journal *Nature*. He started his career as a magician and was one of the youngest members of The Magic Circle, a prominent society of professional magicians.

NANCY L. ZINGRONE, Ph.D., is a BIAL Foundation Fellow, Director of Academic Affairs at Atlantic University, Virginia Beach, Virginia, co-director of The Alvarado Zingrone Institute for Research and Education, Director of Publications for the Parapsychology Foundation, the founder of Puente Publications, a two-time past President of the Parapsychological Association, and a member of the American Psychological Association. Her body of research, conducted with her colleague Carlos S. Alvarado and published in a variety of psychological and parapsychological journals, has focused primarily on such personality characteristics of psychic experience claimants as absorption, dissociation, and depersonalization.